Melbourne On Film

MELBOURNE ON FILM — CINEMA THAT DEFINES OUR CITY

Introduction by
Christos Tsiolkas

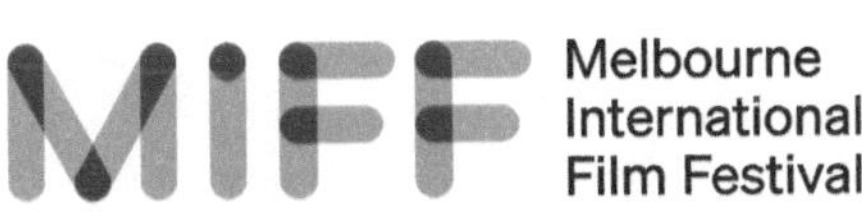

Melbourne
International
Film Festival

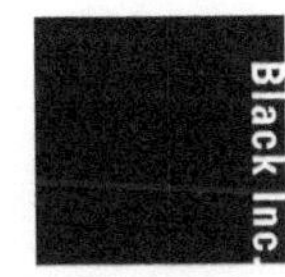

Published by Melbourne International Film Festival
and Black Inc., an imprint of Schwartz Books Pty Ltd
22–24 Northumberland Street
Collingwood VIC 3066, Australia
enquiries@blackincbooks.com
www.blackincbooks.com

9781760643928 (paperback)
9781743822593 (ebook)

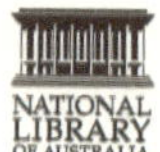

A catalogue record for this
book is available from the
National Library of Australia

Cover design by MAUD
Text design and typesetting by Tristan Main

Contents

●●●

Introduction

Christos Tsiolkas

Many years ago, now, at the turn of the final decade of the twentieth century, I was a youth travelling in Europe. I had spent the spring and summer in Greece, fortified and challenged by being in a place where, though still an outsider, I had connections based on family and language. I then travelled north into an eastern Europe beginning its unshackling from communism. It was an absolutely thrilling time. I couldn't help constantly comparing the blandness of my city, Melbourne, to the dynamism of the crowds I experienced in Athens and Belgrade, in Budapest and Prague. Even though their urban terrains were blighted by the corrosive brutalism of modernism, I loved the layers of history in these cities. How walking down a narrow alley, in the shadow of ugly towering apartment blocks, there were sudden glimpses of the sparkling marble of the Acropolis; the majestic span of a medieval cathedral tower; the glimmering dome of a Byzantine church.

●●●

Nostalgia doesn't excuse ignorance. Looking back, I was woefully uninformed of my nation's own ancient history: mine was a whitefella's view of the city. I couldn't see past the tiny CBD and the endless sprawl of suburbia.

●●●

I caught a train from East Berlin to Paris. Though the French capital is one of the most beautiful cities on earth, I had little money and not enough French language skills, so I found it expensive and forbidding. Fortunately, in the scavenging manner of a young traveller, I contacted a friend of a friend of a friend and found some work tutoring English to a final-year lycée student. He was as passionate a cineaste as I was, and most of our 'lessons' involved seeing films together, then playing pool afterwards in small taverns, arguing about cinema. He was besotted by the films of Scorsese and the Coen brothers. I wanted the world to look like the Nouvelle Vague.

One evening we went to a late-night screening of John

Hillcoat's *Ghosts ... of the Civil Dead* (1988). I had seen it a few years earlier, at the film festival in Melbourne. Memory, as we all know, is not infallible. For years, as an example, I was convinced that the screening was in a tiny cinema off the Rue du Temple. But twenty-three years later, returning to that part of the city, I started questioning my recollections. Maybe we had seen it at a movie house on the Left Bank? What I have never forgotten is the reaction I had when the film ended.

Hillcoat's film is a prison drama of exceptional intellectual force, a film that starkly exposes the institutional savagery embedded in the penal system. The cinema that night was only half-full, mostly with young Parisienne goths who were there to see Nick Cave's performance. The film ends with a long-shot of a released convict, ascending the escalator at Parliament Station in Melbourne. We have seen how he has been brutalised, dehumanised, reduced to that hideous expletive – *cunt* – that is carved into his forehead. We know the violence that he is capable of, and that he will inevitably unleash on the world he is entering.

Yet it wasn't the existential terror of the ending that affected me. Afterwards, in the cinema foyer, my student sensed my distress. 'Christof,' he said (he never managed to forgo adding that Germanic consonant to my name), 'what's wrong?' In between my tears, I spluttered, in Australian English, 'I'm bloody homesick.'

Melbourne is a 'second city', overshadowed internationally by Sydney, by the beauty of that city's harbour and its radiant ocean topography. There isn't a building in Melbourne to equal the iconic authority of the Opera House or the Harbour Bridge. We Melburnians like to claim that our CBD – our 'downtown' – is more vibrant, more cosmopolitan. We also rightly point out that Melbourne has better protected its architectural heritage, that it hasn't experienced the equivalent demolition and destruction of its central heart as has occurred in Sydney. As a city, Melbourne is best appreciated in terms of the close-up, when you are right in the middle of its laneways and its narrow streets. However, in long-shot, looking down at the city and its clump of jutting office towers, it appears conventional, and has the aspect of a North American city. This, of course, is what makes it attractive to Hollywood. Like Canada's Toronto, it can stand in for any number of US cities that achieved their consolidation in the age of the automobile. And as with so many North American cities, what is often outside the frame are the suburbs that ultimately define the city and provide its distinctive character.

Many of the films that are still cited as having best utilised Melbourne as a location set their stories in the inner city. Richard Lowenstein's *Dogs in Space* (1986) begins at the Melbourne Cricket Ground (MCG) and then settles in a grungy terrace in Richmond. Ken Cameron's *Monkey Grip* (1982), based on Helen Garner's novel, famously opens with its main character, Nora (Noni Hazlehurst), swimming at the Fitzroy Pool (though this scene was shot at the Ryde Aquatic Leisure Centre in Sydney). The story then unfolds within share houses and tiny nightclubs. Helen Garner has a dazzling cameo as a speed freak in another epochal Melbourne film, Bert Deling's guerrilla feature *Pure Shit* (1975), which is a virtual tour of a pre-gentrified inner-city Melbourne, following the odyssey of a group of addicts wanting to score some A-grade heroin.

The inner west features even more prominently in the canon of Melbourne-based films, and Footscray, Flemington, Spotswood and Williamstown are central locations in the works of Paul Cox, Ana Kokkinos, Alkinos Tsilimidos, Nadia Tass and Geoffrey Wright. Many factors contribute to the centrality of the inner city in Melbourne films, including the proximity to studios, editing suites, and easier transport and accessibility for the crews. Undoubtedly, the fact that, in the main, filmmakers are part of a cosmopolitan, educated class would also have some bearing on the choice of location. Furthermore, there is a strong realist tradition in Australian cinema, and that too dictated the subject matter and look of the films. All the films cited above take place in a pre-gentrified Melbourne, and many of the filmmakers grew into adulthood understanding the inner city as working-class.

●●●

There is another reason why the west has proven such a constant location for Melbourne films. The city's skyline is best viewed from this aspect. I recall watching a preview screening of Kokkinos's *Head On* (1998), which was based on my first novel, *Loaded*. I realised that the filmmaker had made the story her own, that she had imbued the imagery and mise en scène with her own cultural legacy of growing up in the western suburbs, when there suddenly appeared a striking long-shot of the city viewed atop the Footscray Market. The city looked beautiful. And I realised the story now belonged to Kokkinos – and to the astonishing cast that brought the characters to vivid life – as much as it belonged to me.

It is notable that many of the filmmakers I've mentioned above are migrants to Australia, or children of migrants. Multiculturalism is a key aspect of Melbourne's identity. Part of this is a development of specific government social policy, the story we tell ourselves *now* of what it means to be Australian. The galvanisation of the Australian film industry began with the election of the Whitlam government in 1972, and that watershed election also led to the final dismantling of the noxious White Australia policy. In a sense, then, there is a link to the emerging self-confidence of the national arts cultures – the overcoming of the 'cultural cringe' that saw so many artists, filmmakers and writers leave Australia to pursue careers abroad – and the tentative emergence of an identity that embraced multiculturalism as a defining characteristic of nationhood. Undoubtedly, this identity is still contested: questions of racism and xenophobia *and* parochialism still plague Australia. Nevertheless, multiculturalism is now cemented as intrinsic to our culture, and this is asserted by federal and state governments, by corporations and by cultural institutions. As the pre-eminent industrial Australian city of the twentieth century, with some of the largest migrant communities in the nation, Melbourne prides itself as being the most multicultural city on the continent.

Yet, though a capitalised Multiculturalism is both ideology and social policy, this doesn't mean that it isn't also organic to the reality of how our lives are lived in this city, and, therefore, organic to how our filmmakers have chosen to represent it. One of my favourite Australian films is *The Spag*, directed by Giorgio Mangiamele, an Italian migrant to this country. It was made in 1962 and shot on the streets of inner-city Carlton. The story is ostensibly a tragedy, of a young Italian paperboy who is the victim of racist taunts and violence by a group of 'bodgies' – working-class white youth. The formal naivety of the film still charms, as does Mangiamele's hunger to incorporate so much of the cinema he loves into the half-hour running time. The opening sequence of an unemployed migrant man trying to find work has the dignified simplicity of Italian neorealism. And within the drama, there are beautiful comedic scenes inspired by Mangiamele's love of the classic silent cinema of

Charlie Chaplin and Buster Keaton. The final, touching image of a young mother waiting at the window for her child is a nod to the poetic, experimental cinema of Maya Deren. I watched the film again recently, and I found it remarkable that so much of the Melbourne cinema that was to emerge during the 1970s' 'Australian Renaissance' was already there thematically and stylistically in Mangiamele's work: realism, migration, stories of class and racial conflict. In the private cinematheque in my head, I would love to see *The Spag* paired at a screening with Wright's *Romper Stomper* (1992). Nearly three decades separate the films, yet they speak to one another.

In watching it again, I was also struck by how the distinctiveness of Melbourne as a locale emerges from the intimacy of the child's point of view. The Carlton streets are a pivotal location, for it is there that the boy experiences debilitating jeers and taunts of racism. Yet the most satisfying moments of the film are his interactions with a kind old man who buys a newspaper from him, and his being tutored by a young man who is a boarder in the house where the migrant family lives. Mangiamele was an unapologetically humanist artist, and I think he was suggesting that in these quiet moments of tender empathy there was a possibility for an interaction between immigrant and Australian that was not always to be compromised by racism. Even at the shocking end of the film, where the boy is run over by a van while trying to escape from the bodgies who want to beat him up, the camera settles on the distraught face of one of his pursuers. No-one is irredeemable in Mangiamele's art.

The Spag is a film full of moments of graceful intimacies. It is in the relationships between people, and between communities, that the film feels most 'Melbourne'. I think this is true for many of the films that are identified with the city. In *Dogs in Space*, the world is largely interior, and the shambolic share house in Richmond is as much a character as any other in the film. Our sense of the energy and promise of punk is conveyed by the interaction of the disparate individuals that come in and out of the house. In a pivotal party scene, the camera weaves amidst musos, addicts, suburban disco wogs, uni students, an impassioned Indigenous activist, stone-addled hippies and curious straights. This same sense of a world of myriad communities and identities permeates *Monkey Grip*, which too is a film set largely in domestic interiors. A generation on, in Emma-Kate Croghan's *Love and Other Catastrophes* (1996), the moving in and out of communal student homes builds a sense of a city of shifting, emerging gender and queer selves. These three films form a continuum, a portrait of the changing student milieus, from which each generation of filmmaker came. The Whitlam-era socialists and second-wave feminists of *Monkey Grip* were to be challenged by the abrasive provocations of the punks in *Dogs in Space*. And by the mid-1990s a synthesis would emerge in the young students in Croghan's film, who feel free to borrow their politics and aesthetics, often with a sense of diffident irony, from across the generations. These Melbourne films are *student* films. By that I mean they are about the lives of students or individuals who were recently students, and each of the films features artists of various sorts among their characters. They are self-reflexive works. But I also want to imply something else in this designation of the works as student films, to suggest that Cameron, Lowenstein and Croghan are animated as filmmakers by experimentation, countercultural, political and artistic currents. It's a romance – of course it is – that Melbourne is the city of culture and art. That too is partly a construction of state and corporate sponsorship. Yet within that fabricated narrative there is also truth. I feel it myself, as a writer working in this city. The inevitable compromises you have to make to sell yourself and your art seem a betrayal.

By the time of *Love and Other Catastrophes*, the romance of the inner city, and in particular the sense of the neighbourhoods encircling the CBD grid being spaces of working-class and migrant authenticity, had begun to fade. Those students and artists who had conquered their addictions and had secured jobs in the academy, in the public service and in the arts industries, had started buying up properties in the inner suburbs, and in retrospect we can see that they were integral to that first wave of gentrification.

There are two Melbourne-based films that I think were remarkably prescient in presaging this change to the cultural map of Melbourne; one of them dating to 1973, Nigel Buesst's short film *Come Out Fighting*, and the other being Michael Pattinson's 1983 film, *Moving Out*. The former features a terrific performance by Michael Karpaney as Al Dawson, an Indigenous boxer, struggling to survive in a white-dominated world, where even the most sympathetic of white characters demand the erasure of his heritage as the price of his fitting in. This too is a film of interiors, whether they be the gym, the boxing ring, or the tiny inner-city terraces where the characters live. There's a fearlessness to the film that still shocks today, especially in a shattering scene where Al is accused of being a *gubba* by friends who think his striving to succeed in the ring, and on terms demanded by his white manager, is another form of selling out. The final moments of the film, too, are startling, where we see Al hitchhiking in Melbourne's north, hoping for a lift up the Hume. There is a flash of a vehicle and Al has gone, escaped from the frame. The film has the muscular eloquence of Tony Birch, one of our greatest writers. It has an uncluttered poetic realism that underscores the brutal in-betweenness of what this city can demand of its First Nations citizens.

Pattison's film is also beautiful. It was Vince Colosimo's first film, and it is about the period where the first wave of post-war immigrants started to move away from the inner city and out to the suburbs. That move was part of my own story, and I still remember vividly the kick in the gut I received when I first saw the film on its release. Like the kids in the film, I didn't want to leave the city behind, I didn't want to move away from my friends. And like those kids I was too young and too self-involved to realise what the inner city meant for my parents. It wasn't the site of experimentation and artistic provocation. Instead, it was identified with the harshness of a working life spent in factories. That migrant generational tension is underscored in Jan Sardi's subtle script, where again it is in the gentle observation of characters within the home or in the schoolyard that captures the dynamic of this city and the communities within it. The film arrests a moment in time, when that first wave of immigrants was about to exit the frame of Melbourne's inner city.

Except, of course, that time and movement, and hence representation and film, are not static and do not simply progress in one direction. Migrant communities and Indigenous communities are still part of the inner-city landscape. To imply otherwise is to indulge further erasures. The fact that films such as *The Spag* or *Come Out Fighting* or *Moving Out* still resonate powerfully also affirms that that history is crucial to understanding our urban landscapes.

●●●

During the recent Covid pandemic, I took a walk and ended up at Pentridge. It is no longer a prison; now it is a precinct of high-rise apartments and shops and features a state-of-the-art multiplex cinema. Returning home, I tracked down Tsilimidos's

Everynight ... Everynight (1994), which is set in the prison. The film still speaks powerfully to the damage that the institutionalised violence of the prison system enacts on our body politic. In our very recent memory, when Melbourne is rocked by stories of violent, misogynistic assaults, we can – and I think we must – draw the links to the failures of the correctional system that lead to such outrages. There are ghosts everywhere in Melbourne. Film is one of the mediums through which we can approach and comprehend those spectres.

Yet, there are parts of Melbourne that remain outside the film camera's gaze, and they are the suburbs in which most of us live. The suburbs have not been completely excluded from our filmography, however. One of my favourite films is Brian McKenzie's stunning 1979 documentary, *Winter's Harvest*, which observes an immigrant family creating a season's larder of food from the slaughtering of a pig. Most of the film is shot within the confines of a large shed in suburban Dandenong. Again, by being invited to be guests to the interactions of family and friends, we get a magnificent sense of what this city is. The architecture of place is not only bricks and mortar, steel and concrete. It is embodied in our human relations.

I love the inner city. I was born there, have lived there on many occasions. These days, however, when I think of the parts of my city I love best, I think of Dandenong or Springvale, where diversity isn't just a mollifying bureaucratic rhetoric but something that slams you right in the face with an exhilarating potency. I love the Asian-city-within-the-city that is Box Hill, or the exuberance and vitality of Oakleigh, where cafes, defying the Puritanism of the city's old establishment, feature cheeky stickers in Cyrillic script encouraging you to smoke. And before bloody Covid, I loved walking down Cramer Street in Preston on a Friday evening, checking out the hot guys on their way to mosque. Those parts of my city still feel missing from film.

It may be that it is a new generation of filmmakers that will put the suburbs into the frame. I got a sense of this emergence when viewing Jeffrey Walker's *Ali's Wedding* (2017), where the romantic comedy was played out in the northern suburbs of the city. Co-written by Osamah Sami, the film is alert to how a new generation of migrant youth use and navigate Melbourne, and of how the suburbs are not merely places of ennui, but sites of dynamic interaction. Some of the most delightful moments in that film occur on station platforms all along the Upfield line. And that makes sense, it is where young people hang out in Melbourne. In a car-based city, the train stations and the tram and bus stops are integral to the architecture of the city, which means they are central to the architecture of our lives.

Two other films that have captured a sense of Melbourne's suburbia, and have conveyed the look of the suburbs as integral to their narrative, are Sherine Salama and Amos Cohen's elegiac documentary *Australia Has No Winter* (1999) and David Easteal's stunning short film *Monaco* (2015). The former observes the life of a refugee family from Yugoslavia trying to resettle in Melbourne. It is one of those rare Australian films that allows us to view the city through the outsider's eyes, to glimpse how the same suburban streets and neighbourhoods can be both alienating *and* beautiful at the same time. In *Monaco*, Easteal's portrayal is certainly part of the strong realist tradition in our film culture, but the sensuous, vital framing of the story is unapologetic in conveying the centrality of the car in suburban working-class life. It is often in short films and documentary, where young filmmakers can more freely tell their stories and represent their visions, that we are getting a sense of what Melbourne *now* looks like.

That long-ago night in Paris, it wasn't the memory of the cold, grey metal of the escalators at Parliament Station that elicited the nausea of longing that is homesickness. Or it wasn't *just* that image. It was hearing the Australian accent; it was watching Nick Cave and Dave Mason on screen and being reminded of clubs that stank of sweat and tobacco in which I watched The Reels and The Birthday Party perform. It was remembering first seeing *Ghosts … of the Civil Dead* at the Astor Cinema in St Kilda, and then staying up all night raving and discussing and arguing about that film with friends. It reminded me of the people I love, which is the meaning of home.

I'd like the framing to shift when it comes to representing my city. I don't want to lose the close-up.

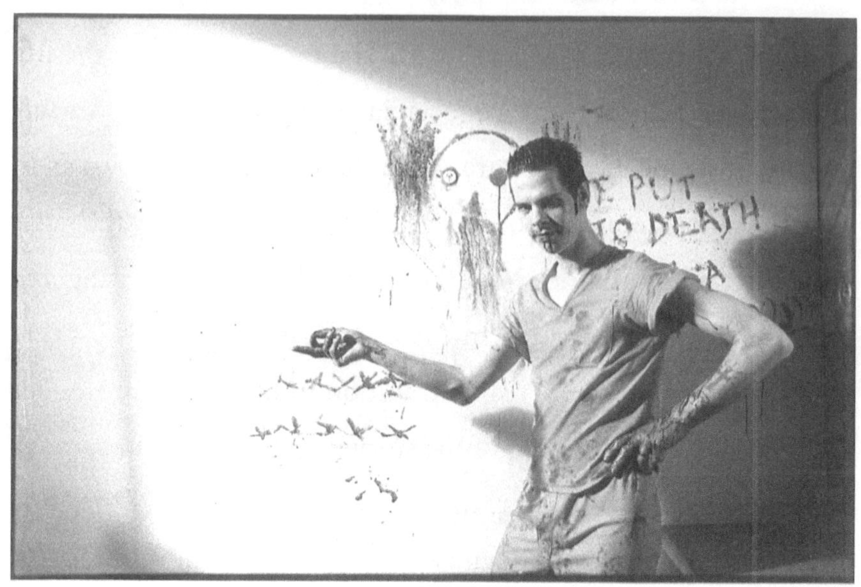

Still from *Ghosts ... of the Civil Dead* courtesy of Evan English.

Ghosts ... of the Civil Dead

Sarah Krasnostein

I am sixteen, seventeen, eighteen and my eyes are opening in the dark. *A Clockwork Orange* at the Carlton Movie House. *The Blues Brothers* at the Valhalla before it became the Westgarth. *2001: A Space Odyssey* at The Astor before we entered the 2000s. The miniscule Erwin Rado Screening Room in Fitzroy where, from the comfort of my seat in that velvety black box, I watch as Timothy Leary's beatific head is separated from Timothy Leary's dead body for his brain to be cryogenically frozen. Other wonders illuminated in the triple dark of Melbourne's cinemas on the dwindling evenings of my adolescence: a new song by someone named Björk in *Tank Girl*; *Angel Baby*'s Jacqueline McKenzie opening her arms in ebullient surrender years before

Kate Winslet in *Titanic*; Judith Vittet's Miette the parentless child, a hero in the old style, striding staunchly into an irredeemable dystopia in *The City of Lost Children*.

After: the still-new feeling of a bookshop at night. Or the smell of nicotine and pizza and the breeze off the bay as I walk from the George towards the Metropolis Bookshop on Acland Street. Or the illicit thrill of simply entering Polyester Books let alone taking a copy of *The Lady of the Sorrows* off its shelves. Or crossing Lygon Street from the Nova, to find a nook in Readings where I can read until closing. Also new to me but instantly familiar: *Meanjin*, *The New Yorker*, *The New York Review of Books*, Borges, Kundera, Kristeva, Calvino, hooks, Whitman, Zinn. The Paradise Motel. The Velvet Underground. Portishead. Tricky. Nina Simone. Tom Waits. Propagandhi. A strange, necessary interleaving. Instead of attending our Year 12 formal, my friend and I read our books by dripping candles in a cafe on Brunswick Street. I am thrilled by this refusal: the women we are becoming, though I haven't met anyone like us yet. Also still new: the loss of the landscape I had been deeply rooted in – a family, a culture, a country. Since moving from America to Australia halfway through Year 9, I am hypervigilant for cues that I cannot read at school, on the street, at home. But the world is full of things that can neither abandon you nor be taken from you. And they are arrayed before me, there in the dark.

●●●

He's been dead nearly fifteen years, but every time I walk through the city I think of Associate Professor David Philips who opened Melbourne like an envelope for me. I assumed, initially, that 'Arts/Law' must be something to do with representing artists. My friend chose that course – at the University of Melbourne because of its green gardens – and I followed her. It's as simple as that. My undergraduate years boiled down to the two classes that taught me how to think: Criminal Law with Peter Rush, and Crime and Punishment in Colonial Victoria with Philips. In both classes, in different ways, the law is of less concern than the relationships it represents. Yes, we learn the order of procedure, the powers of police, the architecture of offences. Why robbery is not burglary, and why manslaughter is not murder. But what I am really learning – in the darkness of those many cases – is how power inscribes itself on a body, a dyad, a family, a nation; how it moves through space and time. And how to judge the judges.

There was Beccaria's *On Crimes and Punishments*, the first critical analysis of capital punishment. There was Michel Foucault's *Discipline and Punish,* which argued that state-sanctioned violence only increased as its assaults on the convict body became less visible. Leon Radzinowicz's magisterial five-volume *A History of English Criminal Law and its Administration from 1750*; his characterisation of the ever-expanding list of capital offences as an 'ideological index' to the society that produced it. And Jeremy Bentham's *The Panopticon Writings*, which revealed how the prisoner internalises the unseen sentry. I am learning how we construct much of what appears self-evident, and what other stories are possible.

Where everyone saw the RMIT buildings banked innocuously up Lonsdale Street, Philips saw the first court. The old Telstra building opposite? The first police barracks; imagine it filled with young men, poorly paid and drunk. Yes, of course, that's the Old Melbourne Gaol, but right behind it is the important thing. That's where they hanged, with brutal lack of expertise, the first men to be 'judicially executed' by the State, in 1842. Think about why they were Aboriginal, look at the flimsy evidence with which they were convicted, and just how many people flocked to watch the hangings and buy the newspapers. In 1880, Ned Kelly became the first person to be hanged inside Melbourne Gaol; in 1967, Ronald Ryan would be the last. Think, Sarah, about the relative terrors of seeing and not seeing. I wrote my honours thesis on it. I've never stopped.

Whenever someone mentions that there's a cinema now in the old Pentridge Prison, I think of Philips – that gruff, generous son of a judge, writing in his solitude about power and its abuses. And how he taught me to look again.

•••

The day before *The New York Times* published a review of his book *In the Belly of the Beast* (1981), Jack Henry Abbott – who had been on parole for six weeks – stabbed a waiter named Richard Adan to death in the East Village for refusing him access to the toilet. For that crime, he would be returned to prison, where he had already spent most of his life and would ultimately kill himself. Abbott's book consists of extracts from his letters to Norman Mailer, who wrote its introduction, about life inside the American prison system.

Born to a soldier and a sex worker at an air-force base in Michigan, Abbott spent swaths of his childhood in foster care, juvenile detention and 'reform' school. At twenty-one, he was serving a sentence for forgery when he stabbed another prisoner to death. He would be diagnosed as a psychopath for a television audience, and Mailer would ultimately express regret for the faith he had placed in him, but threaded through Abbott's life and writing is the golden glimmer of what could have been.

His prose, the *New York Times* critic Anatole Broyard wrote, was capable of a 'tender brutality reminiscent of Jean Genet'. It was also capable of an absurd grandiosity which could be understood as the interior pendulum swinging away from a lifetime of state-sanctioned erasure and brutality. '[T]here are emotions,' Abbott wrote, 'a whole spectrum of them – that I know of only through words, through reading and my immature imagination.' His intelligence did not save him. It may be accurate to say it caused him additional suffering. When the need for basic human dignity is something that needs to be explained – as though its absence were simply a matter of misunderstanding – it will eventually drive you crazy. '[I]n the end,' he wrote, 'I greatly fear we as prisoners will lose – but the loss will be society's loss. We are only a few steps removed from society. After us, comes you.'

To explain the book's grating unevenness, Broyard pointed towards the sustained deprivation to which Abbott had been subjected. How he was a loner long before his years in solitary confinement, talking only to himself. 'Perhaps this explains the two voices,' Broyard speculated. 'When he is eloquent, it is because he is talking to Mr Mailer, making contact with someone. When he rants about justice, politics and philosophy, he is adrift "in the belly of the beast".'

After reoffending, Abbott was swiftly forgotten by his champions in the literary establishment, the whole episode an embarrassing lapse of discernment. But his book would make its mark. And his dangerousness just served to reinforce his message: when a society is free to break a person, no-one is safe. Three years later, his book found its way into the hands of a young director named John Hillcoat, who was living in LA with his mate Nick Cave.

●●●

'Welcome to Central Industrial, part of Correctional Services' rapidly expanding network of new generation facilities, dedicated to the goal of humane containment ...' When *Ghosts ... of the Civil Dead* (1988) opens, the privately run Central Industrial Prison – designed to house the 'most violent, unmanageable, and predatory inmates' – has been in lockdown for thirty-seven months. The prison is geographically and temporally unlocated: in a desert that could be anywhere, a future just over the horizon. But it is inescapably Australian – both in its vernacular and in its central conflict, which plays out in a carceral setting between white men distinguished by factors so flimsy they require constant and brutal policing. As it's gone since the first years of the penal colonial settlement: anything that can be construed as difference or weakness is anathema. 'There was something, once, that set me apart,' one of the men says, by way of introduction, 'and it could have been anything. It marked me out.'

Inspired by Abbott's book, and written by John Hillcoat, Evan English, Gene Conkie, Nick Cave and Hugo Race, the screenplay is a murder ballad – less in its narrative neatness and more in its drive to tell. Through flashbacks, the events leading to the lockdown are revealed and we learn that the unseen but all-seeing administration has provoked both the inmates and officers to foment the violence that is ultimately more profitable to its enterprise than good order. And while that thesis is perhaps to be expected from a film with its own 'Foucault

'Authority', when viewed in its historical context – researched and written a few years after the English translation of *Discipline and Punish*, when supermax prisons were not yet the norm – we can understand just how radical it was for its time.

One of the interesting things about *Ghosts* is that it both is and is not an Australian story. Cave and Hillcoat have lived outside of the country for longer than they lived in it, and both were living in California when their imaginations were seized by Abbott's book. Their interest in the prison industrial complex grew in an American context: they visited the world's first supermax prison in Illinois, which had been in lockdown for about four years by the time they began making the movie in 1987. Their engagement with critical theories about the carceral system was informed by the French Foucault and the English Bentham. And yet, all this would prove perfectly suited towards understanding the carceral enterprise in the Australian context – where it had come from and where it was going.

●●●

The story itself is fragmented, pieced together across flashes of dialogue, monologue and fly-on-the-wall-style glimpses inside cells and offices. That medium is the message: hypervigilance won't save you from the hyper-surveillance of the all-powerful state. 'I'm always seeing blood,' a prisoner says. 'Even before

I can see the cut, I can see the blood … That's all I know. That's all any of us ever know. We were united once, even if only in our misery. And then we were divided. And then there was nothing. Nothing except fear. Fear of each other. Always watching our back …' Positioning the film as Australian Gothic, academic Rebecca Johinke wrote that unlike the highly romanticised interpretations of prison life that appear in many fictionalised prison narratives, *Ghosts* is better placed 'in a more recent subgenre of prison films with a harder political edge that attempt to give viewers a more realistic insight into the brutality of prison life and the broader political and economic conditions that perpetuate a system of locking up those who are already marginalised by race or socio-economic position'.[1] She continued: 'Often based on true stories and filmed in a documentary style (part of a rhetoric of authenticity), these reformist films provide a more challenging and elastic version of masculinity and there are few heroes or innocents on either side of the bars.' This perhaps accounts for the fact that the film was not a commercial success in the Australia of 1988. But Johinke argues that – despite often being ignored in discussions about Cave's oeuvre as well as Australian cinema more generally – it is a film that deserves a larger audience.[2]

Speaking on an episode of *The Movie Show* that aired in May 1989, producer Evan English explained that *Ghosts* is about the way in which human society generally, and criminalisation specifically, can be manipulated to achieve certain ends. He continued,

'It illustrates, I hope, modern methods of social control in the prison. We're talking about environmental methods – architecture and colour. We're talking about group dynamics ... We're talking about drugs and controlled supply ... Fear as a method of social control, that it divides and rules the masses ...'

The story of Wenzil (David Field) acts as a loose narrative spine. The film traces his interpellation from clean-skinned 'new boy', in English's words, into a hardened prisoner; a change marked – as in the original sense of stigma – by visual warnings on his body about his polluted status. Others have far less detailed trajectories but, like a Russian novel, they all haunt us even when sketched in outline. Ruben (Vincent Gil) in his book-lined cell. Grezner the guard killer (Chris DeRose), cocky under 24-hour police protection from retaliation by correctional officers. Maynard (Cave), jolting into the film as one of the high-risk prisoners strategically introduced into the general population, radiantly psychotic and racist, drawing on the walls with his own blood. The unnamed Aboriginal prisoner who is his target. Lilly (Dave Mason), showing more bravery than anyone in the entire film by simply walking down a corridor, past the bathroom where she will later be murdered while the televisions drone on.

English noted that there were 'only three instances of violence in the film, as opposed to 483 in *Rambo*'. For me, at least, whether that violence was alluded to or shown directly, it was nearly unbearable. English explained this is because the actors 'look real' – many were non-professional, formerly incarcerated – and Hillcoat discussed the ways in which the use of documentary devices heightened verisimilitude. Ultimately, however, it is more accurate to say that because the threat of violence is always present, each of the film's passages are violent.

The fact that the targets of that violence include the film's single trans character and single Aboriginal character is notable. It speaks, from one angle, to the historic and continuing egregiously disproportionate violence faced by members of those communities. But while the screenplay gestures towards Lilly's interior life, the solitary Aboriginal man appears only as the encaged target of Maynard's murderous rage. It was not possible in 1988 and it is not possible today to construct an authentic prison narrative – Australian or American, Foucauldian or otherwise – that erases the fact of structural racism as it manifests in the over-representation of Black people in prison. In this way, the film bears out an observation made by Johinke about Australian prison narratives generally: Aboriginal Australians are noticeably absent or marginal, when in reality they form a disproportionately large percentage of the prison population. The reason for that over-representation – the ongoing, brutal impacts of colonisation – would have sat squarely with the film's animating concerns and documentary impulses.[3] There is no group in Australia – or, proportionally speaking, the world – who has known longer or better about the ways in which Western society can be manipulated to achieve unjust ends. *Ghosts* was filmed in 1987, the year the Royal Commission into Aboriginal Deaths in Custody was launched, and Abbott writes directly about race in his book. For this reason, the handling of race is jarring in a film otherwise sensitive to the business of seeing and not seeing.

Cinematic – or any artistic – representation of prison life by those who stand outside of it opens a range of ethical issues. 'One of the great mysteries of aesthetics is where to draw the line between exploitation and art,' wrote critic Ina Bertrand in her review of the film on its release to video in 2002, the same year Abbott killed himself in his cell.[4]

> This problem was addressed by many of those who reviewed *Ghosts ... of the Civil Dead* at the time of its first release ... Here was strong meat – tasteless and confronting! For those of us without direct experience of the prison system, it made us afraid both of the people who are 'contained' within prisons, and of what is being done to these people in our name. So was it art? In 2002 ... *Ghosts'* aesthetic status seems more assured, less controversial, but it is not more comfortable to watch than on its first release.

The way in which the camera goes inside the cell of a prisoner in solitary confinement and lingers on his covered head, his exposed flesh, brings to mind Susan Sontag's argument that images displaying the violation of an attractive body are pornographic, to some degree. Also, Susie Linfield's response to the categorisation of war photographs as 'war porn' and photographs of the poor as 'development porn': 'You can make the argument that sex should remain private,' she wrote, 'but when it comes to torture or hunger or genocide, privacy is an integral part of the problem. It is the opposite of privacy that is demanded. It is visibility. It is light.' To the degree that this is true, it relies – as a matter of first principles – on accuracy. And while that can sit uncomfortably with both art-making and journalism, both of which are inescapably partial, selective and subjective, it must function as a categorical imperative for anyone concerned with documenting and critiquing social realities. Close research went into the making of this film, but its treatment of race means that twenty years after Bertrand posed her question, its status is still not assured.

●●●

What is not shown in *Ghosts* – the decision-makers, the attack on Wenzil, the riots – is almost as disturbing as what is shown, not least because those acts of primal violence take place behind the sleek surfaces of the modern world. 'The fact of using a square ratio – the boxed-in 35 mm frame with optimum film quality – is that instead of the grainy newsreel effect, you get the sterile, clean, clinical look of these prisons,' Hillcoat explained on *The Movie Show*. He was aided by the magic conjured up by the superb production designer, Chris Kennedy, in an old aeroplane factory in Port Melbourne where the interiors were shot (for which Kennedy won an Australian Film Institute Award). Like Bentham's panopticon plans, those spaces afford maximal surveillance at minimal cost while bearing out the banality of evil in their pastel colour schemes, piped-in muzak and incessant clatter of daytime telly.

Hillcoat's framing of forms that eloquently articulate the deliberate design of dehumanisation invites painterly comparisons. That hooded figure sweating in the dark of solitary has the unlikely autoluminescence of a Zurbarán. The straight planes of the prison's wall against the rugged vastness of the sky and landscape evoke the numinous emptiness of a Jeffrey Smart. But despite the bright palette, my mind kept returning to the monochromatic minimalism of Robert Morris's 1978 ink-drawn series, *In the Realm of the Carceral*. Across Morris's line drawings, prison architecture – that crucible in which autonomy is melted into subjugation – is dispassionately rendered in all its bureaucratic brutality. His drawings have the same quality as the spaces depicted in the film: a chilly exactitude unconcerned with human scale or needs, which – as English has pointed out – has been replicated in the fast-food outlets and shopping malls of every city. This is one of the many ways that the ideologies supporting institutionalisation 'filter down into our everyday life', as Hillcoat observed.

It was English's wish that the film would provoke its audience into thinking not just about prisons, but the way society is organised. That society, like the entity referred to as 'the prison system' and all our public institutions, comprises billions of human interactions occurring within the ad hoc conceptual container of successive legislative measures, policy frameworks, economic choices, political choices, and interpersonal influences ranging from moral imperatives to projected panic. As such, its complexity is greater than Foucault first conceived, but the inescapably relational context means that the possibilities for resistance and reform are also greater. And yet, that optimism might be misplaced, considering where we find ourselves more than three decades after the film's release.

Both in what it gets wrong and what it gets right, the truly startling thing about *Ghosts* is its continuing relevance. There is a freshness in it that speaks to the fact that the civil dead are not ghosts, they're not even dead. 'As long as I am nothing but a ghost of the civil dead, I can do nothing ...' wrote Abbott, on behalf of those whose ability to participate in society was deliberately destroyed by the machinery of the state. The Howard Government banned all prisoners from voting in 2006. While the High Court rolled that back somewhat the following year, it remains true that people serving a sentence of three years or longer in Australia cannot vote in any federal election; they've been rendered dead, so far as those rights are concerned. But they remain of other benefit to the nation. 'Proportionally speaking,' Dan Butler wrote for NITV, 'Australia has the most inmates in for-profit prisons in the world.'[5]

Discussing the film in 2015, critic Luke Buckmaster wrote that the fact that Central Industrial is less concerned with rehabilitation than it is with its business model remained, '[i]n the era of Serco and its $3b government contract to run Christmas Island and seven other onshore Australian detention centres ... a particularly salient message'. Six years later, the fact that lockdown is business as usual for Central Industrial is part of that continuing relevance. I am not referring to the fact that, thanks to a pandemic, we all now have direct experience of the mind-breaking impacts of social isolation, although that too is relevant. I am referring to the refugees detained indefinitely in the centre of Melbourne as I write this. And the fact that, in the same year during which the prime minister refused to use taxpayer funds for Rapid Antigen Testing, there was an $811.8 million federal budget allocation to offshore management of asylum seekers. I am referring to the fact that 500 Indigenous people have died in custody since the 1991 royal commission, and that First Nations young people comprise 6 per cent of the Australian population but 48 per cent of the youth prison population. Also: one of the country's newest prisons, the $700 million Clarence Correctional Centre, is run by Serco and located near a large regional Aboriginal community.[6] 'What we are seeing,' Debbie Kilroy OAM, the CEO of the female prisoner advocacy organisation Sisters Inside, told SBS *Insight* at the end of 2021, 'is the rates of crime are down, but the rates of imprisonment are increasing and … it means that the prison industrial complex is getting bigger.'[7]

The ability to create fear and then convert it into clicks and profits and political donations and votes has grown exponentially since Foucault wrote his books and since *Ghosts … of the Civil Dead* was released. And it remains, for the most part, wilfully unseen; invisibly normative to those lucky enough – for now – to remain unscathed by the destruction left in its wake.

Notes

1 Rebecca Johinke, 'Welcome to Hell: Nick Cave and *Ghosts … of the Civil Dead*' in *The Art of Nick Cave: New Critical Essays*, ed. John H. Baker, Intellect Books, 2013.
2 Ibid.
3 Ibid.
4 Ina Bertrand, 'Bordering Fiction and Documentary: *Ghosts … of the Civil Dead*' in *Senses of Cinema*, vol. 19, March 2002.
5 Dan Butler, 'Prisons for Profit: The Business of Incarceration', NITV, 27 August 2021.
6 Ibid.
7 Ross Turner, 'We Need to Have an Honest Conversation about Incarceration', *Insight*, SBS, 8 November 2021.

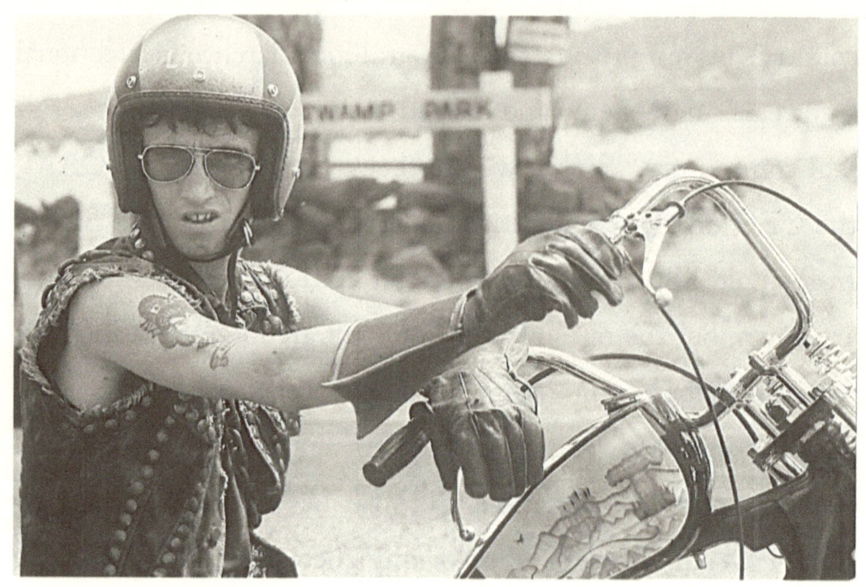

Still from *Oz* courtesy of Smart St Films Pty Ltd.

Oz: A Rock 'n' Roll Road Movie

John Safran

Before the ABC ran commercials for *Q&A* and *Bananas in Pyjamas* between shows, they ran meditative interludes – waves crashing against rocks, hot air balloons drifting through the clouds, that sort of thing. This is how the director of *Oz: A Rock 'n' Roll Road Movie*, Chris Löfvén, got his start. At fourteen years old, he darted around Melbourne with his 16 mm camera, licked a stamp and posted the footage to the television station. They liked it and ran it.

Löfvén's first job out of high school was working for director Fred Schepisi (who'd go on to make *The Devil's Playground* and *The Chant of Jimmie Blacksmith*). 'I trained as an assistant cameraman,' he recalls. 'Fred, he was very good about lending out equipment on the weekends.'

One such weekend, in 1971, he jumped on a bus with Melbourne band Daddy Cool, travelling to Myponga, South Australia for a rock festival. 'So, I was shooting little bits and pieces of that trip. And we ended up using it for Daddy Cool's "Eagle Rock" film clip.'

Chris helped pioneer a whole genre. 'And what is a film clip? They didn't really exist back then,' he says. There were few television shows that played rock music and those that did wanted the bands performing in the studio. With nowhere to play video clips, no-one thought about filming them. 'I didn't shoot very much because I was on a really tight budget. I would've only shot about a hundred feet on the whole trip.' A hundred feet is two and a half minutes. So scarce, so precious. How times have changed. You can't even get murdered these days without it being caught on seventeen iPhones.

'Eagle Rock' became the bestselling single in Australia that year, the film clip an important part in its success. So, 23-year-old Chris and his co-producer Lyne Helms headed to London (they were also boyfriend and girlfriend). He found work as assistant editor on Bruce Beresford's *The Adventures of Barry McKenzie*, the tale of an Aussie yobbo lost in the United Kingdom.

Around this time, Chris caught the US film *Easy Rider*, directed by and starring Dennis Hopper. 'That was a really loose road film with lots of great music. And the plot came into it about three-quarters of the way through. I thought, oh, what did they have to do that for? It was just so nice cruising along the highway and nothing happened.'

Chris originally conceived *Oz* to be like *Easy Rider* before the pesky plot barged in. 'It was never meant to be a narrative feature. It was originally going to evolve around the idea of a loose doco-style film, covering all the things that I thought were oz youth, like panel vans and Holden cars and motorcycles and music.' Chris decided that even a loose film needed something to hold it together. 'So, I thought maybe you could have a wizard character and one thing led to another. Why don't we make it an allegorical story, of *The Wizard of Oz*, which I'd seen when I was a kid.'

That 'Oz' means 'Australia' seemed a sign from the slang Gods that there was something here. Chris and Lyne flew back to Australia.

The pitch went like this:

Dorothy is a sixteen-year-old groupie riding with a rock band in country Victoria (Kansas) when their shaggin' wagon crashes, knocking her out. She wakes up in a fantasy world and learns they ran over a local thug (The Wicked Witch of The East). As a reward for killing the unpopular thug, a gay shop attendant (The Good Fairy) at a nearby boutique gives her a pair of red shoes, to help her see the last concert of The Wizard, an androgynous rock singer, who will be hitting the stage in the Emerald City (Melbourne). She is pursued by the thug's brother (The Wicked Witch of The West) who attempts to rape her on several occasions. Along the way she meets a dumb surfer (The Scarecrow), a heartless mechanic (The Tinman), and a cowardly biker (The Lion).

The Australian Film Commission kicked in $90,000 of the $150,000 budget. They needed to find a distributor who would cough up the rest. 'There were only about three distribution companies in the whole country. Village Roadshow knocked it on the head. They said, "Oh no, it's all too gay and we don't want to know about it."'

The Good Fairy was played by Robin Ramsay, mincing about rural Victoria like Mr Humphries in *Are You Being Served?*. The Wizard is based on David Bowie during his gender-bending Ziggy Stardust incarnation. Graham Matters, who sadly died in 2021, was primed for this role, having appeared in local productions of *The Rocky Horror Picture Show* and *Hair*. Joy Dunstan played Dorothy, and Bruce Spence, Michael Carman and Gary Waddell rounded up the cast as The Scarecrow, The Tinman and The Lion.

Chris and Lyne flew to Sydney to pitch to Greater Union's board of directors. 'We had to go through an exercise of saying what an innovative thing this was, how it was dealing with the youth market, which they had never touched on before. We had no idea whether we were talking bullshit or not.'

The film version of The Who's rock opera *Tommy* was a huge hit at the time, so bullshit or not, it sounded true that the rock-fuelled *Oz* could work. Greater Union committed to the film, but wouldn't throw in all the money needed. 'The only money *we* could put into it was our deferred wages, which meant we were really struggling with the backsides out of our pants to get the thing made.'

The Australian Film Commission eventually agreed to provide the final $25,000 required but this was in the form of a personal loan. 'It's stressing me just remembering,' Chris says.

The shoot took five weeks, over January and February 1976. They couldn't afford hotel accommodation for the cast and crew. 'We had to keep locations close to Melbourne and still make them look like they were out in the middle of nowhere.' Little River in Greater Geelong was chosen. A few years later *Mad Max* filmed there.

'We shot in the middle of summer to get all the exteriors really hot and steamy.' Chris was too successful in this regard, hit with sunstroke on day one, so he couldn't make it to the first day of rushes. (Chris didn't learn his lesson. He now wears a pirate's bandana, having lost an ear to skin cancer.) But, Chris says, it wasn't the weather that taxed him most. He found himself at odds with the most accomplished actor on set, Bruce Spence. He had won Best Actor in the Australian Film Institute Awards 1972, for *Stork*. He was now playing the surfie, a stand-in for The Scarecrow.

'I don't think he enjoyed the experience at all,' Chris says. 'He wanted a lot more input. And he didn't like the casual way I was directing. He kept wanting motivation for things that were just not requiring it.' The hitherto laid-back Chris becomes animated recounting this. 'I kept saying to him, look, this character's based pretty much on me. So just watch me and the way I behave. It's very simple. Don't try and read too much into it.' Chris huffs. 'It's up to you whether you contact Bruce, but he won't say anything nice about it.'

I contact Bruce.

'It was a strange, strange film to shoot,' Bruce says. He doesn't think Chris directed in a casual way, rather the opposite. Bruce explains *Easy Rider*, Chris's influence, was part of the New Hollywood movement, which itself was inspired by French New Wave cinema. 'What they were trying to do was refer to the world in a more contemporary light,' Bruce says, compared to the films coming out of American studios. They were rejecting the filmmaking conventions around pacing, editing and plot. 'The style of their films was much more personal.' Furthermore, these directors did not see themselves as a cog in the creative process, like in traditional Hollywood. They were auteurs, holding control (or trying to) over everything from writing to filming to editing. 'We started to see a lot of auteurs in Australia. And that's the way Chris saw himself,' Bruce says. 'Chris was very protective of what he was doing, and almost obsessively.'

They rehearsed *Oz* in Chris's backyard. 'He and I had a difference of opinion because he didn't want a syllable altered in his script.' Bruce feels Chris was too auteur-y even for an auteur. Bruce worked with German director Werner Herzog on *Where the Green Ants Dream* in 1984. 'Herzog could get relatively obsessive with his script but would acknowledge that a scene might need some massaging.'

Things didn't ease up, moving from rehearsals in Chris's backyard to the shoot. Chris became worried Bruce was lobbying the other actors to turn against him. 'They used to have all these little sessions in the caravan,' Chris says. 'Where I suspected they were going on about this, that, and the other.' Now, Bruce wonders if Chris was so controlling of the syllables because it was hard to control much else when shooting a film like *Oz*. Chris couldn't shout at the sun to come out from behind the clouds in Little River and he didn't have the budget to sit around and wait.

Bruce remembers one hectic night of filming. The script called for The Wizard to perform with his band in the Emerald City with Dorothy watching on in awe. Chris had convinced music mogul Michael Gudinski to let the fictitious band insert themselves into the line-up at a concert at the Sidney Myer Music Bowl.

'AC/DC were the headliners, and we were to go on just before them,' Bruce recalls. *Countdown*'s Molly Meldrum served as MC. 'The audience were chanting *"AC/DC! AC/DC!"* And Molly said, "Just before AC/DC, I'd like to introduce you to a new band." And as soon as we go on and they can see all this camp get-up we wore, you can hear chants of *"poofters! poofters!"* We hadn't even started playing.'

Bruce, on bass, feared for his safety. 'Music starts, and away we go, and the audience sort of calms down. And I think, we're cruising now.' Unbeknownst to the audience, they were miming. 'About two-thirds through the song, somehow, somebody, somewhere pulls the plug. We lost the sound. And immediately the audience knew this wasn't real, this was bullshit, and they got even *more* aggressive with us. The invective from audience, they wanted to tear us apart. The Music Bowl has a moat between you and the audience and if it hadn't been for that moat we would have been dead.'

The music was plugged back in, they finished the number and fled the stage. 'And Chris, I remember came in backstage and said, "Look, we might have to go back on again later." And we said, "*Like fuck we are.* You've got your footage."'

The insanity of the shoot pulsates through *Oz*, in an appealing way.

Chris couldn't control the sun in Little River or the tech at the Music Bowl. And ultimately, he couldn't control all the syllables either. There was the matter of the soundtrack and its lyrics.

Ross Wilson, from Daddy Cool, agreed to put together the soundtrack. This was quite the get for Chris.

Chris couldn't believe his luck. Coincidentally, Ross had already written, but was yet to release, a song called 'Living in the Land of Oz', with the perfect chorus to cut into any wacky chase sequence in the film: *'We're living in the land of Oz, We gotta shake it up now.'* The verses, however, didn't immediately match the vibe or storyline of the film. They were something else altogether.

> One hundred and fifty years ago
> The black man lived in peace and the land was still
> Now a city of millions covers the soil
> And the blacks have all been killed
> I don't know how it happened
> But it happened just the same
> Now the whites are rich and the blacks are dead
> And nobody seems ashamed
> And we're still living in the land of Oz
> We gotta shake it up and change it.

'It was more about the politics of white invasion,' Chris says. 'That wasn't the point of what the movie was about.'

'I recall exactly how it came about,' Ross Wilson says of his song. He had gone to visit his parents in Hampton, Melbourne. 'I was sitting in the backyard of the house I grew up in, with the guitar and thinking, how did I end up here? What happened? And it prompted this whole thought about how my folks came from far away and someone else was living here first. What are the implications of that?' Ross says the song *did* fit perfectly with Chris's movie – its dreamy, off-kilter quality, where you don't immediately know the mechanic is The Tinman or the biker is The Lion. Australia isn't quite what it seems at first.

Ross was booked to perform the song on a Channel Nine pop show. During rehearsal, the set designer projected photos of Aboriginal people onto the backdrop. 'And the fucking producer came out, going "You can't use that! We can't have anything like that!" So, they took that out.' (The Australian media landscape was such back then, that Greater Union's distribution arm was named British Empire Films). Ross says that a white guy singing about dispossession wasn't a thing back then. Indeed, 'Living in the Land of Oz' pipped to the post Midnight Oil's 'Beds Are Burning' by about a decade. One more thing that makes *Oz* compellingly strange.

Greater Union rushed editing and post-production, wanting *Oz* out by school holidays, for the teenagers who supposedly were going to storm the cinemas like they had for *Tommy*. *Oz* premiered on 29 July 1976, only six months after the final day of the shoot.

'We found out the marketing budget for *Tommy* in Australia was 300 grand,' Chris says. 'And they were only prepared to spend thirty grand on ours, and they thought it was going to do the same kind of business.' According to Chris, Greater Union engaged in 'magical thinking', booking *Oz* in enormous cinemas, bigger than the ones that screened Hollywood blockbusters of the time, like *Jaws*. 'It was mental. They just put it into all these barns because they owned all this real estate and they had to put something in there and didn't seem to care that our movie was going to only last a few weeks and die.'

The premiere took place at the Chelsea Theatre on Flinders Street, Melbourne. Michael Carman (The Tinman) has kept a black-and-white photo of the night. Journalist Kerry O'Brien, of *7.30 Report* and *Four Corners* fame, holding up a light for his cameraman, as Chris and the cast make their way into the theatre. Well, the cast minus one. 'Bruce was so peed off he refused to be involved in the marketing and promotion,' Chris says. 'He didn't even come to the premiere. An a-hole from start to finish.'

Bruce says he had something else on that night.

Oz was struck by a tornado of poor reviews. *The Age* declared, '*Oz* can claim neither the charm nor magic, moving fantasy of the original [as it] lacks cohesion, suffers an inconsequential script and self-indulgent acting.'

Impossibly quaint, looking back on it now, *Oz* caused a stir because it featured the f-word. Dorothy, in the beloved 1939 original film, discovers the Wizard is a phoney. Her realisation – 'There is no place like home' – breaks the spell, and she wakes up at home in Kansas. In *Oz*, Dorothy's exposure to rock star Wizard's hedonism and smallness makes her realise 'fame really fucks you up', snapping her out of her dream. Brisbane's *The Courier-Mail* sneered, 'The Australian Film Commission helped provide a big slice of the $150,000 budget. Some of the money should be used to buy Mr Löfvén some soap – for his mouth.' They warned parents not to confuse it with the Judy Garland classic.

Chris's sister piled on, after she invited her friends and their kids to a screening. 'She had no idea what it was about or anything. And she was horrified. She wouldn't speak to me afterwards. Really embarrassed her in front of all her friends because of the language.'

The Melbourne Times was no kinder than Chris's sister. 'With the release last week at the Chelsea, and one suspects the imminent commercial failure, of Chris Löfvén's *Oz*, the final nail may have been driven in the coffin of low-budget Australian features.'

People will disagree with the *Times'* assault on the film's creativity, but its financial prediction came true. Unfortunately, *Oz* was a flop.

Not all hope was lost, though – there was still the rest of the world. However, pitching to foreign distributors would require travel, that would require money, that would put the film further in the red.

'The tricky thing we didn't realise, working on such a tight budget, that only went up to the point where the thing was edited and ready to hand over to the distributor. We had no idea that you had to go to festivals. So, we had to go back to the Film Commission and get more money.'

Lyne flew to the Cannes Film Market. Only one of them could afford to go and she convinced Chris she was a better talker. It worked. She secured a US release with a company called Inter Planetary Pictures. Other films they put out around this time were a horror, *Summer of Fear*, directed by Wes Craven and starring Linda Blair, and a comedy, *Goin' Coconuts*, starring Donny and Marie Osmond.

'We were getting all these congratulatory telegrams,' Chris says. Inter Planetary saw *Oz* as a potential blockbuster. They changed the title to *20th Century Oz* and redid the poster so it hints the film is more futuristic than it is, and might possibly have something to do with outer space. 'They planned a really huge release, all through New York and everywhere. They had all the cinemas booked. I think they had about a hundred prints.

We only had like six prints for the whole of Australia.'

Dorothy got her tornado: the weather conspired against Chris in another way. The weekend of *20th Century Oz*'s release, New York was hit with a horrific blizzard, killing twenty-three people, snowfall over 2.5 metres, thousands abandoning their cars in the streets. 'Everyone stayed home. No-one could get out of their home to go to the cinema or anywhere,' Chris says. 'They lost a fortune on the cinemas they booked. And they didn't have the funding to rebook it after that.'

That was that. The silver lining in the storm cloud, Chris had already cashed the check from Inter Planetary Pictures. 'They put up a pretty substantial advance. So, we were able to get some money back. We didn't get our whole lot back because all the other investors had to get the best pickings. We only got a very small amount, but we got something, at least.'

Revered film critic David Stratton was ticked off by the short shrift *Oz* received. In 1980 he wrote in *The Last New Wave*, '*Oz* is one of the most inventive and enjoyable of Australian films – clever, brash, noisy, gutsy and uninhibited.' He took a stab at the harsh reviews. 'Why, oh why, will critics not review the film for what it is, not for what they think it ought to be?'

Oz has been Chris's only feature film. 'I said to Bruce Beresford, "Why would you even want to be in this bloody business?" It's just such a pain in the arse,' Chris says. Inter Planetary

Pictures was still interested in another project. 'Lyne and me were trying to work on the idea of doing another movie, but our relationship disintegrated before we could get to that point.' Lyne passed away in 2003, only fifty-two.

The Sidney Myer Music Bowl shoot may have gone haywire, but it hooked Chris up with Michael Gudinski. 'He kept me in work for the next ten years making music videos for *Countdown*.' Chris now hosts a music show on Noosa FM.

A black-and-white photo published by the *The Herald and Weekly Times* in 1964 shows sixteen-year-old Chris on the streets of Carlton, shooting a six-minute film, *The House of Secrets*. Like Dorothy, he was whirled into a full-colour adventure that most don't get to have, and then returned home.

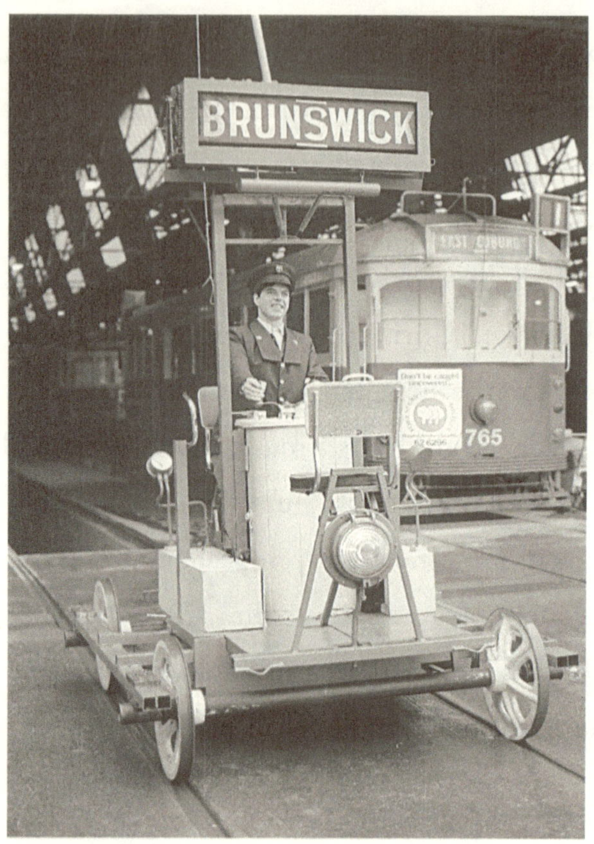

Still from *Malcolm* courtesy of Umbrella Entertainment. Photographed by Greg Noakes.

Malcolm

Judith Lucy

I didn't see the film *Malcolm* when it came out in 1986 because I was far too busy being an adulteress. My name was Millie Crocker-Harris and I was the wife of a headmaster in the Terence Rattigan play *The Browning Version* at Curtin University in Perth, where I was studying a BA and majoring in theatre arts. That's a very long way of saying, I was a wanker. They were a couple of the most enjoyable years of my life, full of trust exercises, massages, plays and goon sacks, but I still spent a lot of that time dreaming of moving to Melbourne. That was where I would study drama at the VCA and become famous. I had some vague idea that if that didn't pan out, I might try comedy. I knew virtually nothing about the city, but I'd always known that I was going to leave WA, and somewhere along the way I'd decided that my adult life would all fall into place in Melbourne. And that did happen. Eventually.

I didn't see *Malcolm* at the cinema, so I must have watched it on a VCR in some gloomy share house in inner-city Melbourne sometime around 1988, when I moved here. Possibly, my friend Audrey, the only person I knew in this city at the time, insisted that I watch it, in the same way that she had made me read Helen Garner's *Monkey Grip* so that I could get some idea of what this new town was all about. I don't think that she wanted to give me the impression that Melbourne was all heroin addicts, criminals and getaway cars that split in two, but maybe she did want me to know that I was a long way from my childhood and the sunny streets of Western Australia. I didn't need any cultural touchstones to point that out to me, though; I struggled for years when I first moved to Victoria. I hated the cold, I missed the outdoor life of Perth and I found the people cliquey and unwelcoming. Oddly, possibly because I'm not very bright, I never considered returning to my home state, but for a long time I did wonder what the hell I was doing here.

I remember being surprised by how much I loved *Malcolm* when I first saw it, for no other reason than that it was Australian. I'd not long left my parents' home, where if a local movie came on my father would always announce during the opening credits, 'Is this Australian? We're not watching this shit.' He was quite the film critic. We still haven't left that cringe behind altogether, but back then it was more of a moan that ended in a chunder.

It's a hard heart that could not be charmed by *Malcolm*, though – the little film that could, that came out the same year as the mega-hit *Crocodile Dundee*. The simple story of *Malcolm* revolves around the titular character (played by a perfectly cast Colin Friels), an innocent man-child, devastatingly shy, who's 'never been with a sheila' but rather pours his energy into making ingenious gadgets. Some of them make his life easier by bringing him his mail or his milk, but mainly they give him immense joy, particularly the miniature tram he builds while working for the Metropolitan Transit Authority (operator of Melbourne trams). Unfortunately that results in his sacking, as his boss – played by an uncharacteristically heartless Charles 'Bud' Tingwell – mistakes him for a fool. This paves the way for Malcolm, now without an income, to take in the boarder, Frank (a gnarly but handsome John Hargreaves), and his girlfriend, Judith (the wonderful Lindy Davies). Frank is recently paroled and not the sharpest tool in the box. Judith loses her cafe job, and so the three of them soon have a cash-flow problem. One of the delights of the movie is our slow realisation that there is a lot more to Malcolm than we might think. Rather than being intimidated by Frank's line of work, he is fascinated by it and builds the famous yellow Honda getaway car for his housemate.

In the most iconic scene of the movie, we learn that the car can split in two, allowing the drivers to bamboozle and then escape the police.

It doesn't take Malcolm long before he is trying to rob a bank from the safety of his home by remote-control gadget. Even with the last-minute help of Frank, the attempt fails and it becomes clear that the trio's best bet is to join forces, pool their limited resources and start committing crimes in earnest. Malcolm builds mechanised bins that enable them to case and then rob a bank in the film's climax, and they ultimately escape in the miniature tram that got Malcolm fired. The closing scene sees the three of them about to conduct a similar operation in another tram-loving country, Portugal, and it is implied that this is now their life. And it looks like a pretty good one. It has echoes of an Aussie *Butch Cassidy and the Sundance Kid*, except no-one gets hurt.

Directed by Nadia Tass and co-written with her husband, David Parker (who is also Director of Photography), the film was warmly received by audiences and critics, here and over-seas, with one of the few negative reviews appearing in Rupert Murdoch's *New York Post*, where, hilariously, the reviewer had issues with the morals of the story. The movie won eight AFI Awards, including Best Film. The performances were lauded, as were the machines designed by Parker.

Watching the movie again, I was surprised by what I did and didn't remember. I recalled the wonderful opening scene of

Malcolm driving his tram past the MCG and through the city, and much of the humour that was produced by the Dalek-like bank-robbing bins along with the iconic banana-split getaway car. But I didn't really remember what makes the film: the love, largely thanks to Judith, that develops between her, Frank and Malcolm. Separately, they might not be seen as life's winners, but together they are the three musketeers of feel-good robberies.

I'm happy to say that I enjoyed rewatching *Malcolm* almost as much as I did thirty years ago. Sure, it's dated. Malcolm's character is based on Tass's late brother, John Tassopoulos, who died while having an epileptic seizure after being hit by a car in 1983. It certainly seems that Malcolm's traits could be the result of high-functioning autism, but his neurodiversity is never really addressed and I doubt that would happen now. The technology that impressed back then now looks like something that a drunk monkey could knock up in an afternoon, and the famous getaway car is so obviously driven by a couple of blokes other than Friels and Hargreaves that it made me wonder how many bongs I'd had the first time I watched it. The language seems quaint by our standards, with lines like 'You dirty mole!', 'Up yours' and 'Dickhead', and we're meant to be impressed by them robbing a bank of $250,000. That wouldn't keep them in pots and Chiko Rolls for long, these days. And of course, in the movie, EVERYBODY SMOKES.

None of this detracted from my enjoyment, as friendship doesn't have a use-by date and neither does the film's affection for Melbourne. It was one of the first ever productions to truly embrace the city, with much of it being shot in and around the CBD, Collingwood and Carlton. There is only one scene that features sunshine, with the crew deliberately filming inside when the sun was out. (How I struggled with the grey skies when I moved here. I remember, not long after I'd relocated to Melbourne, talking to some dude in a bar about his recent trip to Sydney. He mentioned that he'd had fun but that the Emerald City was just 'too fucking sunny'. My Perth brain went, 'How is that possible?'). Melbourne's quirks were celebrated rather than hidden and this was unusual even up until the '90s, when the people making *Halifax f.p.*, produced by Channel 9, were told to film around trams so as not to alienate the Sydney audience. Can you imagine a similar conversation about the Opera House?

I know and love the Melbourne of *Malcolm*. I drank beer, played pool and smoked in those dark pubs. I lived in share houses around Fitzroy that were freezing and damp and had kitchens constructed in the '60s. One such place had nothing but a tiny gas heater which was meant to warm the living room, kitchen and back room. One night I was standing in front of it wearing nothing but a bathrobe, thinking, 'I've really been wrong about this heater, I am toasty warm.' It was then that I glanced behind me and realised that I was actually on fire.

Thankfully I kept my cool and screamed, 'I'M ON FIRE!' while running through the house, turning myself into a human torch. That same place was one of many leased out by the owner of a smash-repair business, who parked his cars in the alleyway next to our home. The owner had quite a knack for appearing in that alley whenever we were getting changed. Maybe he was looking for additions to the enormous wall of pornography that covered his garage wall, which we always had to encounter when we went to pay rent. We certainly let things slide in that place, going so many weeks without taking out the rubbish that when we happily pointed out to a friend how unusual it was to have seagulls in our back garden, so far from the beach, he replied, 'That's because your yard is a tip.' We packed up in the middle of the night, figuring the rent we owed would just about be covered by the bond that we would never have gotten back.

But while I remembered that inner-city Melbourne well, it was Malcolm's innocence that I really related to. Like Malcolm, I was a virgin when I moved here and, having not been accepted by the VCA, embarked on my Plan B of trying stand-up comedy. That didn't happen for a good year, though, and as I worked at my sandwich-hand job and hung out with my one friend, I struggled to get the hang of my new home. A guy in my first share house had warned me that I wouldn't meet Melbourne people for a while as I'd arrived in winter, but the hibernation he referred to lasted for several years and I seemed to meet more people from Perth and other states than I did locals. Of course, I now know that Melbourne people often have friends from childhood and that they are born, grow up and die here because why would you ever want to move? And who has time for new friends when you have so many old ones?

But how could I return to the country town of Perth now that I'd encountered the big smoke? I'll always remember the first time I saw the 'Entertainment Guide' (EG) from *The Age* and was astounded by how much there was to do. It dwarfed the entire Festival of Perth program that lit up our city for only a couple of weeks. I remember going to the wonderful art-deco cinema The Astor and seeing Mark Seymour from Hunters and Collectors just sitting in the audience. What was this magical place with celebrities everywhere? I came from a town where you lost your mind if the Channel 7 weatherman passed you in the mall.

But maybe the place that blew my mind the most was The Last Laugh in Smith Street, where I wound up doing my first ever gig. The theatre restaurant was full of wacky wait staff, dumb props like ceiling fans with severed heads stuck to them, and every form of comedy imaginable. There was straight stand-up but you could also see magicians and jugglers along with sketch- and song-performing troupes. I saw Liz Sadler play the saw, I fell for most of the members of the Cabbage Brothers and could not have loved the female four-piece who dressed up as sleazy male singers The Natural Normans more. I adored the physical comedy of The Found Objects (who went on to become Lano and Woodley) who I'd seen on *Hey Hey It's Saturday*, and split my sides to the hilarious patter and music of Bob Downe (Mark Trevorrow) and Coralee Hollow (Gina Riley). There was nothing like this in Perth. What I can't quite believe is that, somehow, I saw these acts and thought that I could do what they did.

I don't even know how comedy became my backup plan. I seemed to be aware of the fact that comedy was coming out of Melbourne, probably because I was obsessed with the television show *Australia You're Standing In It* and anything *The D-Generation* did. When it came to drama classes at both school and university, my self-devised stuff was always humorous so I must have put those two things together. My audition for the VCA and the bit of acting that I'd managed to scrounge up in that first year here made me realise that I was actually a bit shit, but I was still enough of a tosser to want to keep performing and I'd always been attracted to the idea of – a line from the VCA brochure – 'making your own work'. I wasn't just hanging out at the Laugh either, it felt like every other pub was running a comedy night, and seeing all those funny people just get up and perform, often with only the help of a microphone, really appealed to me.

Fuck I was bad. For years I struggled. I struggled with being funny, with often being the only woman on a bill and with simply being accepted in this new city that I so desperately wanted to call home. My first gig was totally mystifying for the audience. I wrapped them in toilet paper, made them shoot water pistols at each other and ultimately tried to re-enact a documentary about fundamentalist Christians in the deep South of America, who danced with and were often bitten by rattle snakes. I did this with the help of nothing but a metre-long dried sausage that I'd picked up at a gourmet deli, and it disintegrated as soon as I attempted to twirl it above my head. With the wisdom of hindsight, I really should have explored a career in performance art because whatever I was doing, it certainly wasn't comedy. I did about seven more spots before the manager of the small upstairs theatre at the Laugh, Le Joke, finally offered me a paid gig. It was months away, and in the interim I died every time I got up on stage in various pubs, often between bands, sometimes wearing nothing but a green garbage bag and pointy rubber ears. I'd say that you had to be there but thank Christ you weren't. I didn't know what I was doing. I was still learning the craft, but more than that I was still learning to be an adult in a job that often put me in bars at night with a bunch of male comics who wanted very little to do with me. I was in a permanent state of anxiety, which I dealt with by taking full advantage of the available cheap or even free booze. The few women comics I met were always lovely to me but those rare encounters never seemed to turn into friendship. I felt stuck;

I was barely surviving financially and I was lonely. Was I just not cool enough for Melbourne? Would I ever work out that I needed to stop wearing summer dresses with cardigans in winter and buy a fucking coat, along with finding a house that had decent heating? Would I ever find my people? Would I ever stop pronouncing the suburb Prahran like I was an English butler? Would this city ever make me feel truly welcome?

And then it happened. I was at a party in a theatre in Fitzroy, and the partner of a beloved and respected comedian approached me and said that they were backstage and wanted me to have a line of coke with them. I couldn't believe it. I'm pretty sure that I'd never had cocaine in my life before then, but this was an invitation I couldn't pass up. Thank God he hadn't suggested injecting some horse tranquilliser into my eyeball because I probably would have given that a crack as well ... but all I knew was that I HAD ARRIVED! Melbourne was like Frank to my Malcolm. I had to earn its trust and prove that I was never going to dob to the cops. I had to show my loyalty and perseverance, but once that door opened I'm thrilled to say that it has never closed. Most of my closest and oldest friends are now from this great city.

I've lived in Sydney a couple of times over the years but those stays only make me fall for Melbourne more. I was up there once during a heatwave back in Victoria, and an old friend said, 'You should see the footage of Melburnians going to the beach. It's like a Russian documentary.' I remember thinking, 'Yeah, these are my people.' I would look much more at home in the series *Chernobyl* than I ever did at Bondi Beach.

One of those close, old friends is a little lady who had a tiny part in *Malcolm*. She is simply billed as 'Willy's wife', and all she does is walk into a pub and give Willy (Chris Haywood) a withering look before he follows her out. I know that look well because the woman is the fantastic comedian, who I saw in The Natural Normans all those years ago, Denise Scott. Apparently, she went to teachers' college with Nadia Tass (of course she did, it's Melbourne). Scotty and I have been friends and worked together for well over twenty years. We did two shows with the late, great Lynda Gibson and we are about to do our third show together, the aptly named *Still Here*. I asked Scotty what the experience was like, and her main memory was of having to leave a hospital appointment to film the scene, as she was pregnant with her first son, the much-loved singer-songwriter Jordie Lane.

If it's not already obvious, what I love about *Malcolm* is what I love about Melbourne: friendship and heart. I loved the movie immediately and I have come to love this city in such a way that a part of me still lights up whenever I'm flying into Tullamarine Airport, even though the weather I'm arriving into is often a bit crap compared to wherever it is that I've come from. I still get excited when I cross the Bolte Bridge and see the port on one side and the city on the other. It always feels like home.

I will never forget flying back from Perth a couple of years ago, and as the plane was about to land my travelling companion suddenly struck up a conversation with me. He was a FIFO worker who was based in Melbourne and when I mentioned that I'd been in my home state visiting family he paid me the biggest compliment he could have when he said, 'Really? I always thought that you were Melbourne born and bred.' Just then the plane touched down and he turned to me and said, 'I fucking love this city.' I turned and replied, 'I fucking love it too.' We didn't need to say another word. Our faces were lit up like Malcolm's when he drove his miniature No 8 tram past the MCG.

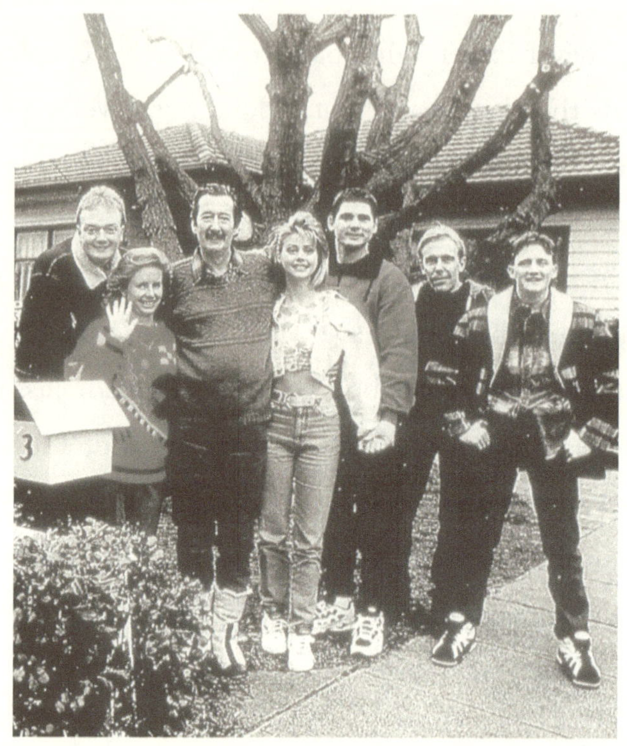

Still from *The Castle* courtesy of WORKING DOG / Ronald Grant Archive / Alamy.

The Castle

Osman Faruqi

The Castle is an unusual favourite film for a Pakistani-Australian engineer and part-time taxi driver.

At least that's what I thought growing up, when my dad would quote it endlessly, and force us to sit down and watch it whenever it was being aired on TV. At times I couldn't figure out if he was shaping his personality around the main character, Michael Caton's Darryl Kerrigan, or if he was drawn to him because they already had so much in common.

A love of cars and home renovations, an addiction to finding the best bargains in the *Trading Post*, and, most significantly, a deep belief in the importance of family and unconditional love. These are traits my dad shared with Darryl Kerrigan.

There's a story from my childhood that feels like it could have been lifted out straight from the film. Actually, there's plenty, but this one *really* feels like a deleted scene. When my parents moved to Australia in 1992, they couldn't afford a working car – new or second-hand. The best they could do was buy two beaten-up and non-functional Datsun 120Ys for $400.

Why two? Because even though neither of the cars ran, their problems were complementary. One had a working engine but a rusted and broken chassis. The other had a solid chassis but a busted engine. They were basically being offered up as scrap metal, but Dad – in a very Kerrigan-esque manner – figured he could buy both, convince the neighbours in our apartment block to lend us their garage space, hit up a mechanic mate for the right equipment and conduct his own engine transplant. Which he did. And that's how our family got our first car.

Thinking about these kinds of stories and the animated way my dad would tell them time and time again, as though we couldn't already recite every detail, helped me realise why it wasn't really that unusual for a man like him to love *The Castle*. Over time, I came to understand why people like my dad would relate to a story of a multiracial, multi-gender, multi-generational alliance of working-class Australians taking on elites, even if on the surface the central Kerrigan family had little in common with us.

But what's fascinated me the most about *The Castle* over the years is how universally praised it is by Australians across class, social and political lines. It isn't just people whose material interests align with the Kerrigans' who love the film. Intriguingly, the kind of people who are cast as villains in the film claim it as one of their favourites. Even Australia's conservative former deputy prime minister Mark Vaile heaped praise upon the film, saying, 'There is nothing more important than family, and sticking together through the tough times is what will get you through.' When I first saw that quote, I was floored. To me, and to most people (so I assumed), this film was a rejection of Howardism and the kind of Australia that Vaile's government had created over their decade in power.

The Castle was released in 1997, just a year after John Howard's Coalition rose to power. As a result, the film's political themes aren't explicitly about Howard-era policies; instead they evoke the political debates of the early 1990s: privatisation, globalisation and social reform. Nevertheless, the kind of ruthless neoliberal pragmatism the film rejects, ushered in by Hawke and Keating, was turbocharged under Howard's reign.

Unusual for any kind of Australian comedy, let alone a mainstream blockbuster, the film has a blunt critique of the economic ideology that swept the West, including Australia, in the 1980s and 1990s. What drives *The Castle*'s narrative is the battle of the Kerrigans and their neighbours against a government corporation called AirLink, who are seeking to expand the airport in order to boost their profits. It's revealed that

AirLink is backed by a shadowy group of investors known as the Barlow Group.

Already you have a pretty clear and morally unambiguous frame for the film: a ragtag group of working-class Australians pitted against an amorphous collection of investors and industrialists, represented by slick corporate lawyers. It's David v. Goliath, it's the everyman v. the Big Corporations, it's one family v. a rigged legal system. The stakes are set.

But *The Castle* takes things a step further. When Darryl expresses confusion at the apparent collusion between what appears to be a government organisation in AirLink, and the private investors the Barlow Group, his suburban lawyer, Dennis Denuto, explains: 'The Barlow Group *is* AirLink. It's government authority, but the money's coming from the Barlow Group … It's a way of privatising without privatising … They wrote the rules. They own the game.'

Now, at this point, the tension in the film has already been clearly established. We already know who the heroes and the villains are. But at this moment, we get a new bad guy. It's not *just* the government. It's not *just* the Barlow Group. It's pure capitalism. It's neoliberalism. It's a doctrine about the state's steady withdrawal from society, with its functions replaced by the private market.

It's an incredible shift. It doesn't change the narrative arc of the film, but it does elevate the stakes. Now the Kerrigans are fighting ideology itself. Not just any ideology, but the most powerful ideology in human history. It's also a battle that makes sense in the context of the film, and the experiences of Australian audiences. Waves of privatisation had become commonplace across the developed world as right-wing economic orthodoxy took hold even within social democratic political parties, including in Australia.

The two highest-profile privatisations of the Keating era involved the Commonwealth Bank and Qantas, which both took place in the early 1990s. A few years later, the federal government announced the privatisation of the nation's airports. In Melbourne, the airport was taken over by a private corporation owned by several fund managers. Soon after its privatisation was complete (ultimately signed off by the Howard government), the airport began a massive expansion program. Sound familiar?

Of course, in Melbourne, where *The Castle* takes place, privatisation was an even more familiar – and reviled – experience. The election of the Kennett Coalition state government in 1992 led to hundreds of school closures, the sacking of thousands of public sector workers and the privatisation of electricity, gas and rail networks. Nearly 30 billion dollars' worth of assets were transferred out of public hands and into the private sector. The consequences were devastating. They further deteriorated the link between the public and government, service quality declined, unemployment went up and the largest street mobilisations since the Vietnam War took place.

These privatisations, celebrated by politicians, bankers, fund managers and think tanks, proved deeply unpopular among the general public. Even at the time, working-class Australians, including my dad who continues to rail against them to this day, could tell they would lead to higher costs and cuts to services. That's why *The Castle* doesn't even need to explain why the privatisation by stealth of Melbourne Airport by the Barlow Group is a bad thing. It's simply a given.

It also helps explain, I think, *The Castle*'s broad appeal to Australians. Despite the economic policies foisted on us by the elite alliance of policymakers and big business, most Australians remain sceptical of privatisation. In 2014, the research company Essential asked Australians: 'Generally, do you think that privatisation – that is, having public services owned or run by private companies – is a good or bad idea?' Across the political spectrum there was a resounding response that privatisation was a bad idea. Fifty-nine per cent thought that, generally, privatisation was a bad idea and 21 per cent thought that it was generally a good idea.

Another survey, this time in 2010, found that *The Castle* was the film most Australians identified as best representing the country. These figures speak to a cultural and political paradox that I believe *The Castle* exemplifies.

Australians despise privatisation, and they love *The Castle* partly because it's one man's battle against the odds to take on the combined interests of neoliberal government and big business.

But Australians repeatedly voted in one of the most right-wing governments the country has seen, which accelerated privatisation, among a raft of other economically devastating policies that would have squarely targeted people like the Kerrigans. Then, after ensuring John Howard reigned for eleven years – including a final term with total control over both houses of parliament, which he used to further implement his neoliberal agenda – Australians say the film that best represents them is one explicitly about active resistance to the kind of policies Howard foisted on the country. In fact, the cognitive dissonance is so extreme that the second-most powerful man in the Howard administration, Deputy Prime Minister Mark Vaile, can say with a straight face that he is a fan of the movie because of how the Kerrigans mobilised as a family against the kind of policies he implemented over a decade.

So how do you explain the universal adoration for a film that expresses a vision of society that Australian voters seem unwilling to actually embrace? I think there's a couple of different factors at play.

The first is what I refer to as 'The Great Australian Denial'. It's a foundational teaching in this country that post-invasion, white Australian culture is defined by its larrikinism and distrust of authority. Characters like Darryl Kerrigan, and Paul Hogan's Mick Dundee, supposedly embody those generic traits.

The problem is the idea of Australians as relaxed and distrustful of authority is entirely confected. This is a country founded on the colonial subjugation and genocide of an entire race. When British rule was established, the convicts, who are themselves widely considered the origin of the myth of the subversive Australian, were incorporated into Royal Police units that hunted down and massacred Indigenous people. The first laws passed in our federal parliament involved the forced expulsion of immigrants because of the colour of their skin.

A country founded on these beliefs, that continues to persecute refugees in such a way that led former US president Donald Trump to declare, 'You're even worse than I am', and continues to incarcerate First Nations people at a rate that makes them the most imprisoned people on the planet, cannot claim the title of 'larrikin' or 'anti-authority'. But the myth persists, because it's easier to deny than to reckon with reality.

So, the professed love for cultural objects like *The Castle* and what they embody, as well as the idea that it 'best represents' Australia, is less a statement about the values Australians *actually* possess, but the values they *wish* they possessed.

By defining themselves through characters like those on *The Castle* (or really any kind of Anglo suburban drama – think *Kingswood Country, Always Greener, Packed to the Rafters*) Australians can reassure themselves that this really is a country where the stakes are low, where they are isolated from any kind of serious hardship, and where the only thing that matters is ensuring your nuclear family is relaxed and comfortable. It's much more convenient than being forced to confront the reality of what Australia looks like outside of specific pockets of white suburbia: a country with deepening inequality, institutionalised racism and a political leadership entirely captured by mining oligarchs. We'd rather be coddled.

To be clear, this isn't any kind of indictment on the filmmakers. They are perfectly entitled to tell this story and portray the Kerrigans as they have. But the way that Australians across class and political divides have latched onto it as a kind of modern origin story for an Australia that doesn't actually exist is what's notable.

The other factor that I think helps explain this disconnect is slightly more forgiving of Australia. I don't think that everyone who says they love *The Castle* is some kind of secret class traitor, pretending to support the working class while doing everything they can to enrich themselves. I think that *a lot* of them are, but there's another category.

Politicians excel at making people vote against their own interests. It's the precondition for how right-wing economic ideology has become so embedded across modern democracies. It doesn't make any sense for ordinary working people to vote for politicians who promise to slash tax on big business, and cut back on social services, health and education spending. But they do it, time and again.

Older Australians will bemoan how hard it is for their children to break into the housing market while rewarding politicians for retaining lucrative tax breaks on investment properties. The exact reasons why are complicated and for another essay, but parts of the problem are the lack of genuine policy disagreement between our major parties on these issues, a narrow and insular media that limits debate, and the insidious way that Australians have been convinced that their wellbeing is tied to that of private industry following the financialisation and privatisation of basically everything.

What all of this means is that people can genuinely relate to the story of the Kerrigans, see Darryl's plight as an avatar of their own problems, but still be convinced that the solution is to vote for John Howard, Tony Abbott or Scott Morrison.

Which brings us to the most important question of *The Castle*: who would Darryl Kerrigan vote for today? The answer is both obvious and depressing.

There's one party that has been the biggest beneficiary of broad disenchantment with the political consensus of the past few decades. This party, to be clear, isn't actually coherent about what it would change, and in fact has supported some of the worst attacks on working people in recent times. But its rhetoric is aimed squarely at people like the Kerrigans. People who played by the rules but feel like they've been betrayed by the people in the charge and the system they operate.

That party is One Nation.

Demographically, Darryl Kerrigan is almost a perfect match for the cohort most likely to vote for One Nation: an outer-suburban blue-collar man who views himself as self-sufficient rather than someone reliant on government support. But One Nation voters aren't just identifiable by their economic status; it's also a question of values, particularly on race and immigration.

The Castle's portrayal of race issues is … messy, to say the least. The only non-European character in the film is Darryl's neighbour Farouk, a Lebanese-Australian with an apparent background in explosives. It's not exactly a subtle or complex portrayal. The character is played by Costas Kilias, a Greek-Australian, further complicating things. On top of that, there's the use of an explicit racial slur by Darryl.

The moments where is race is explicitly discussed in the film and few and far between. They're certainly not frequent enough to make a judgement about whether Darryl Kerrigan is a racist or not, but in some ways that isn't really the point. One Nation voters, and even their politicians, regularly deny charges of racism. And many of them claim to have immigrant friends; in fact, many are immigrants themselves. It's entirely believable to think of Darryl as someone who has a Lebanese-Australian neighbour he's mates with, but still feels wary of rising immigration threatening the livelihoods of his family.

Intriguingly, where the film gets more explicit about race is on the issue of First Nations sovereignty and land rights. *The Castle* was written and produced in the aftermath of the Mabo High Court case, and the film doesn't hide the fact that it sees Darryl's attempt to rebuff the government as a direct parallel to the fight-back against terra nullius. At one point Darryl even says, pointedly, 'This country has got to stop stealing other people's land!'

There are two ways to interpret this. The more generous reading is that *The Castle* is using the airport dispute as a kind of Trojan horse to get middle Australia to feel more sympathetically towards First Nations people. The other is that it's a shameless exploitation of invasion, land theft and genocide to make a few gags. Either way, Darryl's apparent sympathy for Mabo is probably the strongest character trait of his that points against an embrace of One Nation. But that's a reflection of Darryl frozen in time, in the Australia of the film's release in 1997.

How would he respond to contemporary political questions after twenty-five years of dog-whistling and race-baiting by politicians across the political spectrum?

The sad thing is we actually don't need to guess, we know. Darryl Kerrigan isn't real, but voters like him are. And sure, there are exceptions, but by and large Australian politics has shifted dramatically to the right – especially on issues of race and immigration. And the vanguard of that shift has been voters who look exactly like Darryl Kerrigan.

A decade of John Howard's prime ministership – including the Tampa affair, the Pacific Solution, the indefinite detention of children, the War on Terror – leading into Tony Abbott's 'Stop the Boats' rhetoric. All of these things occurred after the events of *The Castle*, and they were explicitly about radicalising people like Darryl Kerrigan into voting for right-wing parties. Since then? We've seen the resurgence of Pauline Hanson, the election of overt neo-Nazis like Fraser Anning and the rise of another right-wing populist in Clive Palmer.

This realisation doesn't bring me any joy. In fact, it's the total opposite. When I reflect on the kind of Australia that existed just prior to *The Castle* being released, I think of a country where someone like my dad and someone like Darryl Kerrigan were on the same side, and thought of each other as such. Obviously, things were very far from perfect, but the calculated attempts to further wedge, divide and atomise Australians by the likes of John Howard hadn't yet shaped the country into the insular and terrified country it has become.

This doesn't make me like or appreciate *The Castle* any less. But it does make me wish that when Australians watch it now, they think harder about what kind of country is being portrayed and how that stacks up against the kind of country we actually are. Yes, there's an enormous disconnect and there probably always will be. And the answer isn't simply to rewind the tape back to 1997.

But the moments of the film that made people like my dad fall in love with it – the solidarity across individuals and communities of so many different backgrounds – are genuine. And they provide a glimpse into the kind of Australia this place could be, if we wanted it.

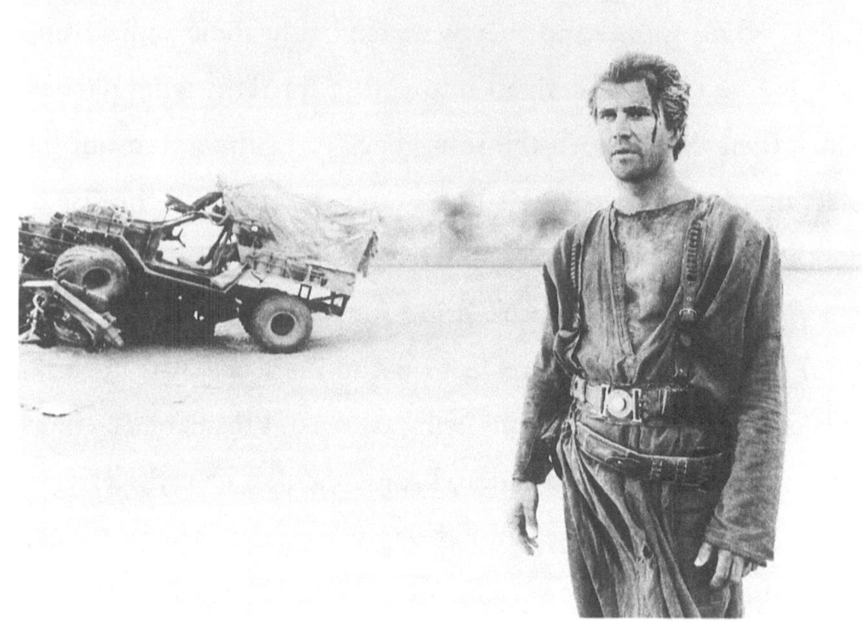

Still from *Mad Max* courtesy of AIP Filmways / Album / Alamy.

Mad Max

Tristen Harwood

I

False memory

what is the chaos of fire to memory?

—Susan Howe

When I was first asked to write an essay on George Miller's landmark movie *Mad Max* (1979), co-created with producer Byron Kennedy, I imagined framing the film's post-apocalyptic vision of merciless barren landscapes in the context of settler-colonial violence. The frontier violence inherent in the foundations of this country, the undoing and wearing down of Indigenous culture. I felt – in an intergenerational, corporeal and intellectual sense – that this was a debasement graver than any apocalyptic vision that could be shown on a movie screen. The massacres, dispossession and child removal. This was how Australia was made. Hadn't we already been living in a dystopia? My question was, did *Mad Max* romanticise or undermine the colonial mythscape, was it a modern frontier fantasy or a nightmare showing colonialism's logical consequences?

With this in mind, I began watching the film. I was struck by the simultaneous familiarity and strangeness of its landscape. Early in the movie, an establishing shot shows the misty silhouette of Melbourne city from afar. Other scenes take place in the University of Melbourne's South Lawn car park, with its distinctive parabolic concrete shells, supported by short columns that look like inverted concrete tree trunks sinking underground. The film's roads, buildings, sunlight and plant life are all reminiscent of Melbourne and its suburbs, not the desert wasteland I remembered.

Was this memory false? The most successful domestic exploitation film ever, *Mad Max* is a straight revenge narrative that visualises disaster. With elements of heavy-metal action, revisionist Western, suburban horror and awe for fast cars, the movie tells the story of Max (Mel Gibson) and what drove him 'mad'. Max is a Main Force Patrol (MFP) Pursuit Officer caught in a V8-powered suburban road war with Toecutter (Hugh Keays-Byrne) and his motorcycle gang. It's eye for eye and, driving 1970s muscle cars, Max and the MFP leave a trail of fire and carnage that parallels the damage wrought by the villainous gang.

I had misremembered the movie or mashed it up with the mythology of Max and the film's sequels, *Mad Max 2* (1981), *Beyond Thunderdome* (1985) and *Fury Road* (2015). Now, I wondered if I had even seen the original *Mad Max* before. I'd thought of Max as a wasteland vigilante who battled it out against other deranged characters, trying to keep their vehicles moving in the aftermath of a global oil crisis. When I spoke to friends about the movie, around half of them similarly (mis)remembered.

Mad Max is a cultural object. There seemed to be a kind of collective false memory that had coalesced around this mythologised artefact of Australian cinema. Adrian Martin, in his study of *Mad Max*, writes of how it conjures phantasm: 'In the case of *Mad Max*, many have testified that its violence is completed in the mind and expanded in the memory, to the extent that they swear they saw things on screen that, literally, they never did.' This, I think, has to do with Miller's use of montage in his action sequences. The fast cuts that create perpetual ruptures leave gaps in the action that the viewer's mind (consciously or not) must fill, setting fantasy in motion. False memory is forgetting. There is a psychic tension between the absence of the past and the impossible presence that narrative – making sense of things – demands. *Mad Max* grinds at this tension.

The movie takes place 'A Few Years From Now …' as the intertitles say. Not the fantastic dystopian vision that I'd remembered, *Mad Max* is a subdued, long emergency, ecology after the world is over, apocalypse without disclosure or revelation. The condensed, conflated, confluent visions and memories of machine violence are part of the movie's alchemy, its vertiginous effect – speed and slowness experienced at the same time. This all-too-familiar environment conceives what ecological and societal collapse feels like, in its 'unremitting banality and inconceivable terror'.[1]

Hell changed its plans
And came in the middle
Instead of the end.[2]

Apocalypse isn't dramatic, spectacular or readily perceivable as most dystopian fictions or our imaginations make us believe, but it's here – as we live with the consequences of imperialism, colonialism and extractive capitalism: climate change, species extinction, dispossession, eternal ambiguous loss. The present is the end of the world.

In *Hyperobjects* (2013), Timothy Morton suggests the end of the world has already happened – most humans are just living with it without consciously knowing. 'Hyperobjects', of which global warming is one example, surround us, stick to us, get inside our bodies and our psyches. This might be that impending sense of doom, which even in what seems like its stalled approach lurks closer with each day, but never *appears*. The implied or symbolic violence that isn't necessarily seen but is completed in our psyches, mixed up like a memory of the future, so that we know it exists even when we haven't located it.

II

Personal narrative

you are more interested in the shadows of objects than objects themselves

—Mary Ruefle

Some of my earliest recollections are cinema memories confused with facts, imprinted by signal repetitions, echoes, distortions, recollections of losses. Cinema is the diaphanous form of the facts of time and space condensed, of dreams that cross the threshold of the screen. What the camera recalls are wondering and weaving pictured events, movement, word stamps, the visible world dissolving. The viewer's memory simultaneously inhabits each side of the screen, meeting and cutting its threshold. The screen simply mediates the relation between two hoarders of reminiscences: the camera and the viewer.

Ambiguous loss, homesickness and dispossession incise my family culture.[3] It was in cars that we sometimes lived out the constant desire for departure and return. The road meant separation: 'nothing but straight ahead', driving towards and away from a world without ancestral haunting, spirit guiding – haunting.[4] But in the end the road's dizzying space between 'here' and 'home' became the locus of knowledge, however scarred or bleached in its tapestry.

The road itself was not the symbol of hope or 'discovery' that it is in frontier mythology. It was something like what poet Ali Cobby Eckermann, I think, has in mind, when she says she loves driving around Country – she takes a voice recorder and records her thoughts as she drives, making poems about kin and Country. Here, the collective 'self' is set forth in movement across the site of erasure, not finding but searching for it on an obstinate journey of (impossible) return to the home. Roads are directives, they lead *somewhere*, but they are also tracts of erasure, scars across Country and bodies.

When my grandmother (Nana) was six years old, she and other Aboriginal children – Stolen Generation children – were loaded onto a truck. Taken from their families and what they knew as their homelands in the Northern Territory and placed into state 'care' in Western Australia.

We would go driving, me and her, woman who grew me up. Memories formed inside and with the car. The road, which had put so much distance between Nana and her home, became something other than wound or rupture when we drove. She reconfigured the road as a space of joy, care, education, family history transmission. We ate bush foods, honey; she told me about Roper River, her sisters Helen and Penny. Once, we rescued a talking pink-and-grey galah, another time a joey, an echidna – injured animals were always rescued, if only so that they didn't die alone at the side of the road.

III

Emptiness

all materials are innocent but how we use them is not

—Jimmie Durham

In her book on gravel-pit mining in the United States, Lucy Lippard observes that 'travel is fundamental to traditional frontier iconography; from the horse, to the rail, to the telegraph, to the truck, expansion and connection are symbolic'. Miller replaces the horse with the muscle car, personalising the frontier in the context of what British anarchist Colin Ward labelled 'the ongoing crisis of the combustion engine'. Emblematised in the film by the 'V8 Interceptor', a highly modified (personalised) Ford Falcon XB GT Coupe 1973 – which stuttering mechanic

Barry (David Cameron) says was put together with 'a piece from here and a piece from there' – the muscle car is the 'ultimate decentralisation of transport and its final absurdity'.[5]

Although it's not set in the mythologised 'outback', *Mad Max*'s action takes place at the edges of suburbs and the city, a seemingly 'empty' liminal space between 'civility' and 'wild' lawlessness akin to what the outback represents.[6] Essential to frontier mythology is the coloniser's constant, usually violent and masculinist expansion into the so-called 'unoccupied' space in which identity is always being made through *occupying* – it depends on the creation and maintenance of 'emptiness', which in turn is underscored by the erasure of Indigenous inhabitants.[7]

In *Mad Max*, absence is figured by what the camera does and doesn't show us. On one hand, wide-angle shots show open fields, the endless sky and never-ending road; on the other, Indigenous people and traces of Indigenous iconography are completely absent from the film. This is all typical of frontier mythology.[8] This absence fulfills a nightmare vision of the senseless violent motion across the land and complete disregard for human life that underpin the possessive logic of colonialism.[9]

In *Mad Max*, wherever the road goes is the frontier. Rather than bringing 'civilisation' to 'uninhabited' space, the MFP is at war with Toecutter's gang over whose behaviour – that is, whose identity – gets to define and control the empty space of the road.

The MFP and the motorbike gang are equally destructive and murderous. At one point, Max says to the MFP Chief, Fifi (Roger Ward), 'Any longer out on that road, and I'm one of them.' And after Toecutter's crew kill Max's wife, Jessie (Joanne Samuel), and his baby, Sprog (Brendan Heath), he repeats their vengeful brutality in his own way.

IV

Turbulence

...the aesthetics of destruction ... the peculiar beauties to be found in wreaking havoc, making a mess.

—Susan Sontag

Mad Max is a protracted vision of catastrophe, with its scorched landscapes, decaying infrastructure, and powerlines that stretch forever into the distance, supported by endless utility poles – the sentinels of fossil capitalism. The muscle car and fossil capitalism, which it stands in for, are avatars of what Walter Benjamin called the 'storm of progress', propelling the film's characters and everything in their path into the growing pile of debris. Partly why the film, which only ever partially depicts corporeal violence, evokes a frisson among viewers is because Miller viscerally forces all this carnage on the viewer in both its subjective and systemic sense.

Take the first action sequence in the film, for example. Seen from a distance, a naked couple is out in the open, exposed against the stark light of day. Their bodies are entwined, fucking, amidst the parched grass. We're looking at them through the sight of a rifle: they are prey. The rifle belongs to Roop (Steve Millichamp), an MFP Pursuit Officer. The gunsight is trained on the couple, at whom he's looking – or is it *Mad Max*'s cinematographer, David Eggby, who is looking? Is it that the movie camera is a gun? Each optical device predicts and captures carnage, essential to and always at the threshold of the decisive moment.

There's a wasp-yellow Ford Falcon XB Sedan 1974 'Big Bopper' parked on the side of the road. Pursuit Officer Charlie (John Ley), Roop's partner, is casually sitting at the wheel, waiting for some action. A voice comes over the police radio. There's a cop killer on the loose, 'March Hare', another MFP unit tells Charlie. The outlaw is Nightrider (Vincent Gil), who has stolen an MFP pursuit vehicle, a beat-up black 1972 Holden HQ LS Monaro coupe.

Charlie blows the Falcon's horn and whistles, Roop comes fumbling towards the car, and then the incompetent officers bicker over who is going to drive, wasting vital time despite the mission's urgency. *Mad Max* seems to hold a healthy disdain for the police. In another image, an establishing shot at the decrepit arches of the 'Halls of Justice' (MFP headquarters) is a haunting vision of a building and perhaps the entire justice system going to ruins.

The camera cuts between the MFP crew blundering into action and the insouciant Max, calmly prepping himself for the chase. The montage begins with a fetish-like portrait of Max – we see a leather boot, leather gloves, a thigh clad in tight leather pants, he's dressed in all black, and there's his own big, gaudy yellow pursuit car.

The Nightrider screams by with his girlfriend in the passenger seat, relishing in his deranged ecstasy. Shrieking a maniacal monologue out the car's open window, he delivers one of the film's most poignant lines: 'I am the Nightrider! I'm a fuel-injected suicide machine!'

The whole montage is like a series of explosions, a sequence of ruptures, literally driven by the combustion engine. The conversion of fossil fuels into energy, the harnessing of firepower – so crucial to modernity – changes the body's relationship to time, space and death. In describing one of *Mad Max*'s many crash scenes, Martin notes that 'the screen itself is a glass about to shatter under the mounting pressure'.

The physical cutting of film produces the montage's continual breaks in time-space. The intense pace – both the quick succession of shots and the drawn-out time of the entire event – creates a sensation of turbulence. Suspense continues to build, pursuit officers crash out, the Nightrider eludes them. But then, he encounters Max, the MFP's 'top pursuit man'. The Nightrider cannot get away from Max and, fulfilling his own prophecy, he dies in a fiery car wreck, ending the pursuit. *Mad Max* is cinema of destruction; death is the road's only destination.

V

Petrol

give me fuel, give me fire, give me that which I desire

—Metallica

Things to Come (1936) is an old movie, set amidst the residue of war. Telecommunications have broken down and there is no more oil or rubber. In one scene, a gangster pulls up in a Rolls-Royce. Without the petrol needed to fuel the luxury car or rubber for its tyres, the vehicle is pulled by a horse and rolls on bare rims. The Rolls-Royce has devolved, mechanically redundant, but its symbolism – luxury, wealth, freedom – absurd as it is, remains intact.

This scene is clairvoyant in its depiction of the length humans will go to in order to maintain the 'motor age', despite historical oil shortages and the ecological and social damage that cars do. Even now, in fossil fuel–induced catastrophe, novel ways of staying on the road are celebrated. Take the electric car, a more 'environmentally friendly' alternative to the combustion engine. Yet, these battery-powered vehicles simply displace their ecological and social destruction to 'sacrifice zones' that they rely on for the minerals to power their batteries. One such sacrifice zone is the Democratic Republic of Congo (DRC), where mining giant Glencore operates its cobalt mines. Mines in the DRC often run on the labour of enslaved Congolese people whose subservience is ensured by private military corporations, subcontracted by mining companies, and whose land is being degraded.[10]

In his article 'Inhabiting the Car', automobility is for British sociologist John Urry a term that identifies these entwined human–automobile relations. The automobile, or rather automobility, is as 'constitutive of the modern as are the more general processes of urbanization (as Le Corbusier understood in the 1920s)'.[11] The automobile is the quintessential *manufactured object* (perhaps soon to be eclipsed by the computer); a major *individual consumption* item, which provides status to its users; a *symbol* of speed, technological and sexual prowess, masculinity and futurity; and a powerful *machinic complex* constituted through its interrelations with other industries, mining, the state and infrastructure.

The attachment to automobility goes beyond machine-dependence, it is a constitutive hybrid relationship: car and driver form an assemblage 'not simply of autonomous humans but simultaneously of machines, roads, buildings, signs and entire cultures of mobility'.[12]

The power of automobility is such that the car driver is exempt from a certain moral standard. Take a drive into the mountains, along the coast or into the desert plains, even in the city. Roads are flecked with dead native animals: possums, wombats, kangaroos, echidnas and others, run over by cars and trucks and left to die. While it would (in most cases) be against the law and unconscionable to kill these animals in any other circumstances, the car driver's *accidental killing* (though it isn't always) is excused by laws and morality. Animal lives are simply collateral damage, laid to waste so that drivers can arrive at a destination faster.

Not only do animals suffer, but whole cultures, ecosystems. This is exemplified by the Victorian state government's decision to bulldoze birthing trees – some over 350 years old – sacred to Djab Wurrung people, to make way for a highway. The trees are the material memory of fifty generations of cultural practice, and as such they are living participants in and members of Djab Wurrung culture and community.[13] The state argues that the new highway will improve road safety, which is to say protect the car driver from other car drivers, by – as protestors have alleged – trimming approximately three minutes off commute times.[14]

The automobile diminishes accountability. To quote Ward, 'the car is indeed a personal liberation and a social menace'.[15]

The individual is not simply liberated by their freedom to move across the country at high speed; there is also a diminished level of social obligation, such as caring about trees, animals, ecosystem destruction.

Miller worked as an Emergency Department doctor while making *Mad Max*, so had seen firsthand the mangled bodies and trauma caused by car accidents. 'I remember the feeling of working casually at St Vincent's Hospital and being quite disturbed by the violence and the road carnage,' says Miller of his time working in the ED.[16] His experience is reflected in the grim realism of the film's portrayal of road carnage. When Big Bopper is wrecked after crashing into a motorhome, Roop's neck is shredded, pieces of the car's shattered windscreen lodged in his flesh as he tries to grip his gaping throat closed. It is as if the shattered windscreen signals the rupturing of the cinema screen as a protective membrane. The scene is shot on a handheld camera, pulling the viewer into more direct proximity with destruction. Later, Roop is shown using an electrolarynx to talk.

Before *Mad Max*, Miller and Kennedy made a short, gruesome satire on the representation of violence in cinema. It was called *Violence in the Cinema, Part 1* (1972) and portrays a psychologist giving a dry but brutal account of the topic. The collaborators are clearly concerned with violence in cinema and on the road but are politically subtle, never didactic in their presentation of such violence.

Exposure to horrific violence – after he sees the burned flesh of his comatose pal Goose, and his wife and child are killed – leads Max to his final descent into 'madness'. Seeking blood revenge, he pursues and kills Toecutter and his crew.

It was 12 April 1979 when Miller and Kennedy premiered *Mad Max* at Melbourne's East End 1 Cinema. The film was made a few years after the 1973 global oil crisis and the local 'Supercar scare' that occupied 1972 newspaper headlines. Miller hired James McCausland, a journalist who had reported on the oil crisis, to write the script for *Mad Max*. However, the only indication of an oil shortage in the film is a single scene in which Toecutter's gang steal petrol from a moving fuel tanker.

Events like the oil crisis are momentary pangs, reminders of the volatility of capitalism, which relies on extractive circuits that literally crisscross the world. What drives the Interceptor is Max, and 'frictionless' financial flows – which extend through physical infrastructure – alter the land and social organisation, rip through biomes, and through flesh.[17] The 'Supercar scare' was a national controversy concerning a claim that Holden, Ford and Chrysler were each producing new muscle cars able to exceed 250 kilometres per hour. There was fear that this would encourage hoon behaviour and endanger lives. After media and public backlash, each of the manufacturers abandoned their new muscle-car plans.

The violence in *Mad Max* is caused by crashing automobiles, mangling flesh and combusting bodies. The final and absolute human–car entanglement happens when they destroy one another. In our contemporary moment, *Mad Max* conjures a vision not so much of what the apocalypse will look like but rather of what has made the apocalypse a reality. That is, a social system reliant on and celebratory of the extraction and burning of fossil fuels.

The muscle car might be one of the ultimate fulfilments of modernism, with its sleek lines, compact size and large, high-powered motor – a futurist symbol of speed and erotic dynamism, and an absurd masculinist vessel. It's a technologically advanced and beautiful killing machine that, gurgling and revving, physically imbues its driver with joy (as in joy-riding) and potency as they destroy the environment and threaten lives.

VI

Madness

this shit is killing you, too, however much more softly, you stupid motherfucker …

—Fred Moten

The shape of the city has been remade since *Mad Max* premiered in 1979; the intensification of gentrification, real estate and property development across the city have seen the increasing sanitisation of urban environments, continuously cleansed of any signs of atrophy. Where *Mad Max* saw decay as a general condition of dystopia, the reality is much sleeker – it sparkles, and gleams grey. Targeted legislation and rent rises drive Indigenous, migrant, poor and 'deviant' peoples further and further away from the city. Only to have their lifeworlds replaced by buildings and savvy public architecture, made from rectangles of precast concrete in shades of institutional grey interspersed with shiny glass, and inhabited by those who can afford and are inculcated to desire this aspirational, homogenised, hermetic lifestyle.

Tony Birch, in his essay on the history of gentrification in Fitzroy, cites former resident John Kyrious, a Greek migrant who 'continued to experience what he called "emotional vibration"' when he passed through his old neighbourhood, which had been developed into Atherton Gardens estate. This was a place 'that had once held the physical repositories of his identity and memory'. The development had punctured holes in the living membrane that had held his social world together. Kyrious says, 'I can't point to the house that I first saw television in … There isn't a scrap that I can point to that I can say "that's mine."' [18]

Max can't take it anymore. He has been on this brutal trip with the MFP, and he knows it. He tells Fifi he's quitting. He does quit after witnessing Goose's burned body. He takes his young family to the coast – a getaway, but he can't get away.

He ruminates. Max wants to love, but he can't express it – he's a melancholy bro, a product of his social environment.

Toecutter's gang's final revenge is not to kill Max, but his wife and child. Let him suffer the pain of loss like they did when the Nightrider was killed. The score is even. Violence is all there is. Max cannot grieve so he goes mad. Frenzied, he hunts and wipes out Toecutter's gang one by one. There is no 'good' or 'evil', 'villain' or 'hero'. Max is no better or worse than Toecutter. Ambient violence envelopes all in *Mad Max*, its utter aftermath, and we're left questioning what it was like before (or if there even was a 'before') this drawn-out disaster began.

Madness is the correct state of being in such a world, which itself is clearly mad.[19] This film, without any signs of Indigeneity except the land itself, is the colonial nightmare condensed to its barest elements: extractive capitalism, maniacal violence, possessive logic.

Notes

1 Susan Sontag, 'The Imagination of Disaster*', *Against Interpretation and Other Essays*, Picador, New York, 1966, p. 42.

2 Fanny Howe, *The Lyrics*, Graywolf Press, Saint Paul, 2007, p. 16.

3 Pauline Boss, *The Myth of Closure: Ambiguous Loss in a Time of Pandemic and Change*, W.W. Norton & Company, New York, 2021.

4 Édouard Glissant, *The Poetics of Relation*, trans. Betsy Wing, University of Michigan Press, Michigan, 1997, p. 7.

5 Colin Ward, *Freedom to Go: After the Motor Age*, Freedom Press, London, 1991, p. 13.

6 Richard Davis, 'Introduction', *Dislocating the Frontier: Essaying the Mystique of the Outback*, eds Davis & Deborah Bird Rose, ANU Press, Canberra, 2006, pp. 7–22.

7 Ibid.

8 Ibid.

9 Aileen Moreton-Robinson, *The White Possessive: Property, Power, and Indigenous Sovereignty*, University of Minnesota Press, Minnesota, 2015.

10 Ajay Singh Chaudhary, 'The Extractive Circuit', *The Baffler*, no. 60, November 2021.

11 John Urry, 'Inhabiting the Car', *The Sociological Review*, 2006, p. 17.

12 Ibid., p. 18.

13 DW Embassy, 'Why We Are Here', https://dwembassy.com/why-we-are-here/

14 Sian Johnson, 'Key Victorian Highway Project Held Up as Protesters Dig In Over "Sacred" Trees', ABC News, 4 July 2018.

15 Ward, 1991, p. 113.

16 George Miller interviewed in 'Production Report: George Miller', *Cinema Papers*, Issue 21, May–June, 1979, p. 369.

17 Chaudhary, 2021.

18 Tony Birch, 'The Best TV Reception in Melbourne: Fitzroy 'Low-Life' and the Invasion of the Renovator', *Traffic*, (3), 2003, pp. 9–29.

19 Mark Fisher, 'The Privatisation of Stress', *Soundings*, Issue 48, 2011.

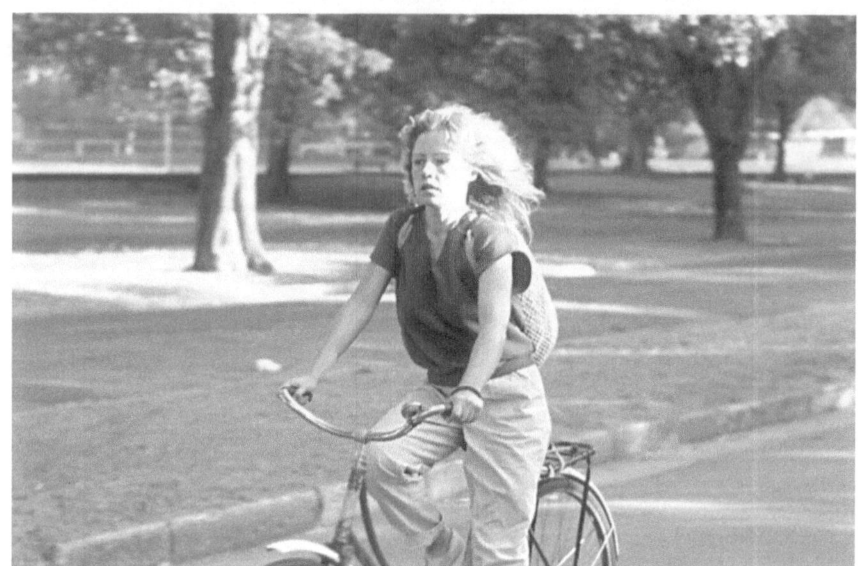

Still from *Monkey Grip* courtesy of Umbrella Entertainment.

Monkey Grip

Ronnie Scott

The woman's name is Nora, and she's getting out of the pool when she goes to look at the guy she's seeing and sees something better: a sexy stranger, Javo, who radiates a type of bruisy depth. He hangs back near the famous sign, AQUA PROFONDA, while Nora and the guy she's seeing, Martin, do their thing. He looks like he'll be trouble, but not the bad kind of trouble; the kind it might be interesting to catch.

Nora learns from a mate that Javo likes heroin, though he seems to have kicked it; the mate is the girlfriend of Nora's housemate, and in the anything-goes manner of the time, Javo is soon hanging out with Nora and Martin, enough that Javo can ask Martin how 'together' they really are, and relay Martin's evasive response straight to Nora – a canny move for such a cruisy guy.

Soon, she's taking him to an art show that she has to cover for the small, busy alternative paper for which she writes reviews. Afterwards, she asks him if he'd like to stay the night. 'That would be good,' he tells her, and it's on.

In the morning, Nora's eleven-year-old daughter, Gracie, finds out; Martin finds out. After Javo heads off, Nora relaxes in the kitchen and says, 'I suppose I've done it again' – the wrong thing, the wrong man – but the story we're talking about, of course, is Ken Cameron's *Monkey Grip* (1982), and the casting of Noni Hazlehurst is one of its great coups. Resignation, pleasure, self-satisfaction, concern: it's all there in the delivery, and it all takes a back seat to a wonderful feeling that it doesn't matter much at all. She supposes she's done it again, and you may now grow aware of a disquieting question that is interesting to this movie the way a mouse is interesting to a cat. Maybe understanding the implications of what you're doing has little to no bearing on whether or not it's actually done? And then the inverse – you can be wise enough to know what's happening to you and have it happen anyway. This suspicion becomes unbearable as the film goes on. Nora's carefree nature, which can be cruel but is rarely nasty, lifts the viewer and carries them over the movie's darkest parts, but there's always the sense that something irrevocable is happening, a little bit past the line of sight, a little way out of control.

The film is based on Helen Garner's 1977 novel, and Garner and Cameron are listed as co-writers. On the indispensable website Ozmovies, where the *Monkey Grip* entry splices an interview with Cameron by Peter Malone and an account of Cameron's DVD commentary into a narrative of how the screenplay was written, Cameron explains that he cut up and re-pasted the novel, typed it up 'so that it resembled a movie', then finessed the adaptation in constant conversation with Garner; he has a collection of letters in which she suggests solutions and scenes. Garner says on the DVD commentary that she saw fourteen or fifteen drafts of the script, and then was there for the filming because Nora's daughter, Gracie, is played by her own daughter, Alice, who is a sharp presence through the film, cheery and watchful, and possessed of slightly eerie wisdom.

Garner disliked the casting of Colin Friels as Javo, telling *The Age*'s Peter Wilmoth in 2008, 'I just can't believe they cast Colin Friels as the junkie. ... He was so healthy, a great big bouncing muscly surfing guy.' We all know people like Javo – if not the heroin, then the sulky mood – and it's true that they're not Colin Friels. But I think of a point that a friend once made about a different kind of story, where two impossibly hot people have a meet-cute on a tram. That doesn't happen in real life, someone at the time complained. But there are people in the world who look like that, my friend explained; when they hook up, it's often with each other, and it has to happen *somewhere*. If Friels's Javo is not realistic to the story, then neither, perhaps, is Hazlehurst's Nora, and you have to have someone like Friels to make the viewer believe that someone like Hazlehurst would give him the time of day. *Monkey Grip* is a movie, and it has to have some glitz. They have to hook up *somewhere*, and they hook up here.

Sex was an issue for this film. At first, nobody liked it, neither the distributors, nor 'most of' the Australian Film Commission, which, speculated producer Patricia Lovell, saw it as pornographic. Stratton had interviewed Lovell for his 1990 book *The Avocado Plantation*, about the turbulent economics of the 1980s in Australian film. The story of *Monkey Grip*'s production is harrowing. It almost found funding, but 'fell over for lack of $150,000'. Lovell moved on and produced *Gallipoli* instead; by the time tax breaks made production more viable, other costs had gone up, so it was still a struggle to fund. When it finally got off the ground, some new funding problem meant that it looked like production might delay for two weeks – sending Lovell to hospital where she spent forty-eight hours under sedation from nervous exhaustion. When the film was done, Lovell heard that Gilles Jacob, director of the Cannes Film Festival, had been told 'by someone in authority' that 'the Australian government would not be pleased if *Monkey Grip* competed at Cannes' (though it did). Lovell screened the movie for three distributors in Melbourne, all of whom turned it down; one told her, 'I loathed it.' Finally, Lovell distributed it herself, and after the first week's takings offered proof of its heft, it was picked up officially by Roadshow.

Lots of films are incredibly sexy or incredibly sexual (dark, yearning, weird); *Monkey Grip* is both. It shows the parts of sex that are all about desperation, habit and distraction as much as those that are about intimacy, spontaneity or fun. The first time Nora has sex with Javo is full-on, but first it's so tentative that you think it might not happen; they get under the covers and at first you think they might just go to sleep. As soon as it's happening, you realise that it was silly to think it might not. The eyes are closed, the clothes are off, the facial expressions work very hard; there's some finger-sucking where the camera doesn't cut away, and a kiss that's more sexual than the finger-sucking.

Cameron told Stratton: 'I had no problem with the actors during the filming of those scenes. I felt it was worth going all the way with them, and I was young enough not to have hangups. The atmosphere on the set was a bit funny: in the end, I had the entire crew, myself included, rehearse naked … we all believed in the novel and the film, so we felt those scenes had to be done that way.' It's great, and sex reappears throughout the film as something that's both absolutely normal – enmeshed in work, time, reading, eating sandwiches, meeting deadlines, having daughters, moving house, writing lyrics, being in bands – and something that's like Javo: on a spectrum between consuming and impossible.

After Javo behaves oddly at a party, he says to Nora, 'You just don't get it, do you?' When he'd told her he was 'stoned' earlier, he meant he was on smack. Nora smiles and kisses him. Javo overdoses. Nora visits him in hospital, where Javo is smoking. He looks at an old man across the room and says, 'Jeez, old people give me the shits.'

Javo comes over to Nora's share house and finds her in the shower and decides that she will be the one to give him outpatient care. Someone who knows how to inject penicillin comes over to show her how it's done. Nora gives the injection; Javo is upset. They make jokes about the penicillin injection that are really jokes about junk; Gracie grabs the needle and says, 'Don't do it – you'll get hooked!' All laugh. Everything in the house appears to settle down. Javo becomes part of the family, presiding over the children Nora lives with and the sharing of gifts.

And then one day Javo's gone. First there is a false bottom, which presages those to come. He's gone, and Nora finds him again, in a kind of drab bohemian lair, a large, dark, brick building with an arched window, where he gets to gesture at a traumatic origin. He has sex with Nora. He says – or sort of says; the line is fed by Nora – that his father is the reason women 'never hit the mark'. That night, Nora wakes up and Javo isn't there. She finds him in another room, in the middle of shooting up, which he finishes doing despite her presence, half meeting her eyes. And then he's really gone; he's off to Singapore, with

Martin (the guy Nora was seeing at the start – played by Tim Burns). Javo sends Nora a postcard. He wrote it on the plane, so there's nothing about the trip itself. The world has swallowed him up.

The seasons change; Nora's place of residence changes. She hears news in the winter that Javo is in Bangkok, in prison for stealing sunglasses (also with Martin). She sends him letters daily. 'I miss him a real lot,' she tells a friend she's hooking up with. 'Like a piece of glass stuck in your foot,' the friend suggests.

And then, one sunny day, he's back – in a garden full of hanging ferns and stag-horns, Nora's new, less-ramshackle share house. They go inside; she touches his face; they have sex slowly. 'Now that he was back all the splinters of my life made sense again,' narrates Nora. But straight away, there are new complications – pasta, women, alternative theatre. Nora takes Javo for coffee and gnocchi with her pension cheque, and Javo ruins it by going to talk to another woman under the obvious pretext that he wants to see what kind of cigarettes they've got behind the counter. The woman is Lillian (Candy Raymond), a co-star in a play he's acting in, and he lurks on the other side of the restaurant chatting her up while the waiter brings the meals out to Nora.

'I mean, she's too much,' Javo tells Nora; but Nora 'feel[s] like she's lining you up'. Later, the play is staged, in an awful and effective little scene, with Javo as the greasy bartender in a shiny vest, while Lillian is playing a 'sight for sore eyes', a 'babe' in a silver slitted dress. He has to throw up, he leaves the stage but doesn't quite make it, getting as far as a prop piano bench. Nora runs down from the audience to tend to him, and he keeps speaking his lines while he's sick.

Now there's a third-act feeling; things begin to escalate. But part of what makes it so hard to watch – so like relationships you've seen people have, relationships you've been in – is that there aren't any climaxes or moments where peace is restored, there's just peaks that mean nothing, moments of understanding that distract from other problems, resolutions that will probably be broken. Garner told Wilmoth that Cameron found her novel hard to adapt for film because 'it hasn't really got a filmic structure. It's like a long-running TV series ... it just starts and it goes on and on and eventually it stops.' The film mirrors the novel, which mirrors life, yes, but it also mirrors Javo, whose personal magnetism is all the more striking because the rest of him is staggering, exhausting. Cameron cast him after Doc Neeson, frontman of the Angels, dropped out and Cameron saw Friels at the Sydney Opera House playing Hamlet. For all his gravity he's also disappointing and ordinary ('Jeez, old people give me the shits'); the story is never allowed to settle around him.

He creeps into Nora's bed for comfort like a sick kid would. She holds him and kisses him. A needle is left out on the dining room table, in the middle of a household scene where the children are hitting Nora in the head with their dolls and asking her to make them cups of Milo. 'I want to stop,' says Javo, 'but I can't do it now. I can't stop while the play's on … I can't perform when I'm coming down.' Nora understands. 'When the play's finished I'll get off it and we'll go away somewhere, go up north.' They'll go to Sydney, see some friends, go to the beach, get a tan. He'll go cold turkey. 'I'm sick of the junk,' he says.

Cut to Javo playing harmonica in the passenger seat of a Mack truck being driven by a stranger, Nora and Gracie in the back. Soon, they're at a diner just outside of Sydney, facing the kinds of problems faced by families on Australian road trips. They can't order pies because the diner microwave's turned off. Perhaps things are going to be all right.

Although Cameron seems sheepish about the fact that *Monkey Grip* was filmed largely in Sydney – he explains in the DVD commentary that he was based in Sydney, as were Lovell, the DOP and the production designer, so by the time casting was done (in Sydney) and they'd secured funding, 'we'd dug a big hole for ourselves in Sydney' – it's a great joke of the movie that it does a pretty good Melbourne. 'I would have loved to have made it in Melbourne,' says Cameron, beyond the one week of exteriors he was able to film: 'it's the plaster that you see outside the window, it's just all sorts of tiny things that you can't reproduce'. But when Nora rides her bike down a wide, leafy street, it feels like a suburb of Melbourne where you just haven't been. Because the film is iconic to Melbourne (as is the novel), it's satisfying that this seems to have no impact on viewers, as little as knowing that *Rear Window* was filmed in LA. It undercuts the seriousness that forms around iconic things; it makes it easier to see the thing itself.

When they get to Sydney – which scenes were also filmed in Sydney – the house they stay in is all pink light. The bed is 'pre-warmed' by a dog. 'What a good idea!' says Javo when Gracie jumps in the bed, and they cuddle up together. It's holiday time. With a clean shirt, Sydney light, and a comb run through his hair, Javo is transformed into a man on the upswing. Nora catches him trying to take money from her purse while she's napping and says 'Jeez, you're good-looking.' He asks if twenty bucks is okay; he's 'just going to see some friends'.

While he's out, Gracie consults the I Ching – big part of the novel, small part of the film – about the likelihood that the three of them will be going as planned to Manly tomorrow. The universe responds and says 'don't count on it, sister'. Nora asks Gracie what she thinks of Javo, who acknowledges that he's a junkie, which of course has its problems, but, 'You should be nicer to him, and leave him alone, that's what I reckon.' When he finally comes home, Nora finds him in the kitchen, suspiciously going to town on a baguette.

'This was supposed to be a holiday,' says Nora. 'What are you doing, what do you want?'

He says, 'I want some Vegemite,' and it's all downhill from there. He converts a fight about doing smack and making empty promises into a discussion about whether or not he's understood. If she understood him, would she like him? A good question at the wrong time.

Later on, in bed, he says, 'I do this over and over. Whenever I get something good, I destroy it.' But just as he's really exhausted your patience (you lose patience with both of them), the film finds something new in the couple, which is one of the pleasures of the looser, TV-like structure, where characters don't have to change and grow; they can surprise you with qualities that disappear, then emerge anew, as if shuffled. When it's obvious that they're done with each other, generosity becomes possible. They have a tender disagreement about which of them is going to leave the trip early and go home to Melbourne. It's him. They kiss. As he rides away in the cab, he plays a little riff on his harmonica and gifts it to Gracie. Gracie and Nora catch the ferry to Manly. 'You'll get over it,' Gracie advises Nora. The ferry's nice at night, she observes. While Javo has been happening to Nora, Gracie has been growing up. How often do you get to see this kind of thing on film, the child turning casually into the adult?

In *The Avocado Plantation*, Stratton points out that Hazlehurst as Nora in 1982 seemed like it would herald a coming age of complex roles for women actors, which the rest of the 1980s turned out to largely squander. He also mentions Wendy

Hughes's role as Vanessa in Carl Schultz's excellent 1983 movie *Careful, He Might Hear You*, another adaptation of a well-loved Australian novel. I got chills when Nora and Gracie went on the Manly Ferry; at the end of *Careful, He Might Hear You*, Vanessa, who's a snob, decides for once in her life to cross the Harbour on the Ferry, gets into a collision, and drowns. Over in Melbourne, Hazlehurst's Nora puts on her lipstick and decides it's time to give her life a little TLC. Her metaphor is a tub that's been draining towards Javo; now it's time to put the plug back in.

She goes to a gig. (It looks like The Corner, but I'm sure it's in Sydney.) One of the odd surprises of the film is that Chrissy Amphlett, Divinyls frontwoman, plays a muso in Nora's circle named Angela; at the gig, she plays 'Boys in Town' from start to finish, but with actors playing the band (the rest of the Divinyls turned down roles in the film). Nora's hair is slicked down and tied back; she's wearing a sleek, feathered dress. She cuts loose, dances, laughs with friends; she reconnects with former housemate Clive (played with warmth by Michael Caton). Nora's world remains spiky and young but it's comfy without Javo. Soon, she's writing in front of an open fire. She's writing on a tram. She writes a short story addressing her feelings towards Lillian and doesn't think there's any particular reason to show it to her before publishing. Her life changes again. She moves house again. There's the sticky business of telling her housemate, but these things are there to be dealt with.

'I just want it quite clear,' she tells the man she's moving in with, 'that we're not moving into this house as a couple.'

She reads books; she looks up words in the dictionary. Around her, children squabble. The framed picture of Virginia Woolf that Nora transports between residences assumes its place above the new workstation, perpetually stately and sentinel.

Then, once again, there he is, in a striped shirt of thin fabric and a ragged, rather fashion-forward open seam.

'You look great,' she says. 'What happened?'

It's Javo's softer side. They go up to her bedroom. He sits in a sunny chair. 'I've been having a really good time these days,' he says. 'I've been knocking around a bit. Seen Lillian a couple of times.' Nora lies on the bed looking deeply unimpressed.

Unprompted, Javo explains that he never loved Nora; he really needed her when he came back from Thailand, but he's starting to feel better again. A tear slides down her cheek. 'Come on, mate, we can outlast the lot of them,' he says. 'We see so little of each other, we're bound to,' she says, as if that's the point.

In another room Nora's housemate sits on the bed, playing guitar in his yellow socks and Volleys. He knows Javo is there but he's being tactful about it. Later, they all go to a party. Life happens around them. A woman at the party observes that men do not like liberated women. People meet for quiet chats by a trellis adorned with green lights. And then the awful moment:

someone's crying in the dark over a can of Fosters and it turns out, incredibly, they're crying about you.

It's Lillian, and she's now read Nora's published story, the one she decided not to tell Lillian about. 'Events don't belong to people,' Nora explains. But everyone knows who the characters are, Lillian argues. 'Twenty people in Carlton do not constitute everybody!' says Nora. Lillian accuses Nora of just publishing her diaries – a critique that famously dogged Garner at the time, as if, she wrote in an essay in 2001 and was still telling Claudia Karvan in an ABC special twenty years later, writing diaries isn't an interesting, challenging, valuable thing to do. But there's no time for that discourse; Javo is inside, and look – he's thrown up on himself again.

'Sorry, Nor!' he says. 'Guess the dope's fucked me liver.'

'Don't be sorry, people have had to do this for me heaps of times,' she fibs, as she picks him up and hauls him away from the party.

Her housemate goes on tour. She rides her bike; she thinks.

She drops a letter round to Lillian's: 'Can you see this gets to Javo?' She keeps riding her bike – one of the skills Hazlehurst had to learn for the film; the other, she told *Women's Weekly*, was swimming – and soon she's at her old share house, where lovely Clive still lives. She cries in his arms. She cries in the arms of a woman she hasn't met. She leaves the house and cries again in front of the cast-iron fence. Was this scene filmed in Melbourne? Again, if not, it's a pretty good fake.

And now we're back at Fitzroy Pool, and it's summer again. In the DVD commentary, Alice Garner points out that the scenes at the pool, which were filmed at Ryde Aquatic Leisure Centre, have done the trick for any Melburnian who's seen the film, and even Cameron says he's 'quite proud' of the recreation. (When I watched it, I took it as self-sighted gospel that the bleachers at the Fitzroy Pool used to be blue on the verticals.) Rachel Ang, whose 2018 comic *Swimsuit* was set at Fitzroy Pool, told me they set the comic there because 'it's really an amphitheatre, this stage for all kinds of emotional drama'. Ang, who is also an architect, was struck by the 'formal power' of the space where the sun acts as a spotlight and shines on 'everything', the dramas and their social implications. Victoria Hannan, whose 2020 novel *Kokomo* also has a critical scene set at the pool, told me that she did so as a 'direct tribute' to *Monkey Grip* – the scene in the novel where Nora tells Clive, 'No-one will understand but this is a paradise.'

I wanted to spend this time with the plot of *Monkey Grip* because I wanted to try to see, if I could, the thing itself. By the end of the movie, what's obvious is that the thing itself extends beyond the characters and past the movie's frame, into the rich shine of the sunshine, the blue soak of the pool. There are fabulous clothes (Nora wears everything from a fuzzy tangerine sweater to a pair of pedal-pushers in animal print; even Martin, at one point, wears a denim jacket and rope-net shirt). It's the yeahs, give-it-a-burls, fair-dinkums, I-think-it's-beauts; a song done well at band practice is described as 'very tasty'. It's the slowness, the detail, the gossip, the repetition. Everyone's always smoking in front of louvres that are always smudgy, and though the men may look unfathomable, they're also always there.

At the pool, Nora gossips with another old housemate. Gracie gossips at the water's edge with the old housemate's kid. Javo is at the pool, under the AQUA PROFONDA sign. Nora approaches him in possibly the best outfit of the film, a red cap and lemon bomber over a one-piece bathing suit. It makes her happy that Javo's doing well, but it's bloody painful, too. It's like watching a kid grow up and take off. She liked him needing her.

'Mate,' Javo says. 'Our relationship's permanent. Maybe we could go out tonight or something.'

But she's seeing a movie with Gracie.

She remembers him the summer before, and it makes her reflect on their world, 'how we thrashed about, swapping and changing partners, like a complicated dance to which the steps hadn't quite been learned, all of us somehow trying to move gracefully, in spite of our ignorance'. A beautiful score rises, quite heavy with strings. Everything is blue. The credits rise. The movie ends.

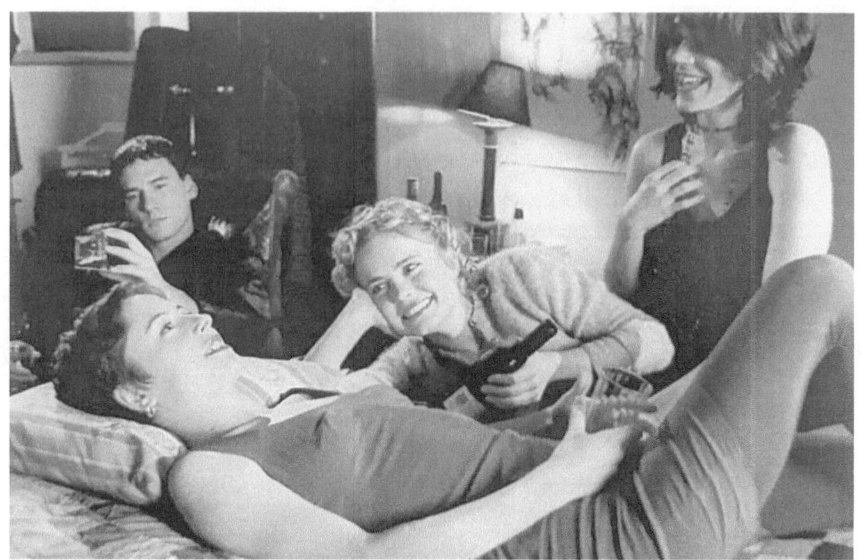

Still from *Love and Other Catastrophes* courtesy of Stavros Kazantzidis.

Love and Other Catastrophes

Jenny Valentish

A crowded student house party, Carlton, mid-'90s.

Film student Alice is recording her peers on a multi-turreted Super-8 camera, weaving through the crowd but particularly zooming in on Ari, a classics student she finds attractive. The protagonist, Mia, is arguing the limitations of monogamy with a friend, but that's just a front. In reality, she's moping over her ex, Danni, who's having a fabulous time in the next room, which is crammed with people dancing to a rave remix of 'Recognise' by the Underground Lovers. Lovelorn medical student Mike looks alienated as he perches on a sofa next to four girls – each dressed in black, with dark eyeliner and red lipstick – who have huddled together in order to deconstruct the faculty staff.

'Wasn't he the lecturer who was a cross-dresser?' asks one girl.

'Nah, you're thinking of Mr Jones from the literature department, who has an alter ego called Maria,' says another, who has two long strands of hair hanging down from her centre part.

'Did you guys hear he's going out with one of his students?'

'Yeah, I know her – Julie's her name. She's really nice, she's in my class.'

'So does that mean Julie's going out with Jones or Maria?'

'She goes out with Maria,' chimes in another girl, who has a nose ring and miniature bunches perched atop her head. 'Jones is asexual, but Maria's a full-on lesbian.'

So begins the final act of 1996's *Love and Other Catastrophes*, shot at the very sandstone university it portrays, the University of Melbourne. Its 23-year-old director and co-writer, Emma-Kate Croghan, was a recent graduate of the VCA's School of Film and Television, then found herself on the dole. She'd made some shorts that were well received at film festivals – *Sexy Girls, Sexy Appliances* and *Desire* – as well as a music video for INXS's 'I'm Only Looking', before basing her first feature at the campus where many of her friends studied, due north of the VCA and across the river, in Parkville.

In part, *Love and Other Catastrophes* is a love letter to Melbourne, or at least to a clique of suburbs: Carlton, Fitzroy and – at a push – Brunswick, where the bulk of the university's students lived. Just as young, arty residents of, say, St Kilda and Richmond often stayed faithful to local crowds and haunts, there was a territorial pride in those living in Carlton, which had a rich history of subversive culture in the forms of La Mama Theatre and the Pram Factory theatre collective.

The film has also become an ethnographic snapshot of a culturally fertile period of DIY fashion, music and movies – the likes of which hadn't been seen since the '70s – and a surge of academic interest in feminism, identity politics and queer culture.

The action is shot over one day and revolves around the calamities of film student Mia (Frances O'Connor, who'd previously had roles in *Blue Heelers* and *The Man from Snowy River*). First, there's the romance troubles – she's a commitment-phobe who's kind-of, sort-of broken up with her girlfriend Danni (Radha Mitchell), who may-or-may-not have moved on to haughty beret-wearing Savita (Suzi Dougherty). Then there's the accommodation: Mia is living in a warehouse with her friend Alice (Alice Garner, who won the Film Critics Circle of Australia award for Best Supporting Actress), but they need a third housemate, stat. Shy medical student Mike (Matt Day) hopes to fill those shoes, partly because he's alarmed by the antics of his current cone-punching roomies and partly because of his crush on Alice.

Most urgently, Mia wants to swap courses to cultural studies, but her current professor (Kym Gyngell) is affronted by this and, as a result, obstructive. In order to qualify, she also needs to pay off an astronomical library fine – for which, awkwardly, she needs the financial assistance of wealthy Danni. Mia has till the end of the day to race around campus securing the right permissions and bumping up against bureaucracy, in an escalating farce that sucks in her friends and involves a major death-by-doughnut setback.

Love and Other Catastrophes was shot on an indie budget, initially of $40,000, which grew to around $500,000 courtesy of post-production funding from the Australian Film Commission. While it undeniably has retro appeal, it did well at the box office, grossing $1,687,929 in Australia, and enjoying some international acclaim, with Croghan joking that she had to explain to her dole officer why she was going to Cannes. The film also screened at Sundance, Toronto and Venice, and was nominated for five AFIs.

On *The Movie Show* on SBS in 1996, David Stratton enthused that he had enjoyed it enormously and 'it made me want to be a student again', while Margaret Pomeranz called it a 'classic romantic comedy'. Writing in the UK's *Independent*, Ryan Gilbey observed: 'Emma-Kate Croghan looks more like the lead singer in an indie band than a film director. But then her first feature, an effervescent comedy entitled *Love and Other*

Catastrophes, often feels more like a pop album than a movie. It is bright and breezy and rough around the edges; it seems to have been made by a bunch of your mates one Sunday afternoon after a mammoth drinking session.'

Famed US film critic Roger Ebert wasn't as keen, giving it two out of five and complaining that Croghan was 'so distracted by stylistic quirks that the characters are forever being upstaged by the shots they're in ... Movies like this are intensely interesting to the people in them, just as people like this are intensely interesting to one another'.

Either way, this was an era in which indie films could actually prove financially viable, which sat uncomfortably with the '90s ethos of not selling out (another '70s throwback). *Reality Bites*, for instance, released in 1994, grossed $33.4 million worldwide, but was written by a 20-year-old about her life post-graduation. Helen Childress got meta when creating Lelaina Pierce (Winona Ryder), a recent college graduate making a documentary about her disaffected friends (Ethan Hawke, Janeane Garofalo, Steve Zahn), and nailed the day's sentiment about not working for The Man. 'I'm not going to work at the Gap, for Chrissake!' Lelaina exclaims about the generic retailer, the implication being that she'd rather be an impoverished artist than a corporate whore.

The gen-X legacy has become lost in the culture battles between Millennials, Boomers and Zoomers, but perhaps it only has its studied apathy to blame. This was a generation characterised by slackers, stoners, latchkey kids (divorce rates were high, and mothers were entering the workforce in larger numbers) and Prozac. Douglas Coupland's 1991 novel *Generation X: Tales for an Accelerated Culture* covered most bases, following three twenty-somethings ('brought up with divorce, Watergate and Three Mile Island, and scarred by the '80s fall-out of yuppies, recession, crack and Ronald Reagan') who would rather work in dead-end 'McJobs' than be capitalist careerists.

The book curated terms that became synonymous with gen X (which covers those born between 1965 and 1980): the Mid-Twenties Breakdown; Now Denial ('To tell oneself that the only time worth living in is the past and that the only time that may ever be interesting again is the future') and its close relative Historical Underdosing (meaning the '90s was a period of time considered to be dull); Option Paralysis ('The tendency, when given unlimited choices, to make none') and Terminal Wanderlust, which was a condition attributed to those constantly trying to find an idealised sense of community.

It was Richard Linklater's *Slacker* (1990) that set the tone for the gen-X film genre. *Slacker* follows socially marginalised, unemployed moochers in Austin, Texas, with the focus passed like a baton from one character to another. Like *Love and Other Catastrophes*, the action takes place over a single day. Shot on 16 mm film when Linklater was twenty-nine, it was made for just US$23,000 but grossed more than a million at the box office. Its lack of structure and emphasis on naturalistic dialogue was considered so influential on a next generation of filmmakers, that in 2012 the film was selected for preservation in the National Film Registry of the Library of Congress for being 'culturally, historically or aesthetically significant'.

Yet the gen-X genre is as blink-and-you'll-miss-it as the generation itself. You can add *Singles* (1992), which revolves around twenty-somethings living in a Seattle apartment building, including a cafe waitress played by Bridget Fonda, who is intrigued by grunge rocker Matt Dillon (his fictional band features real-life members of Pearl Jam). One might wonder, was the equally brooding Matt Dyktynski (Ari in *Love and Other Catastrophes*) being positioned as Australia's answer to America's gen-X poster boy Matt Dillon?

Then there's *Empire Records* (1995), which starred Liv Tyler, Renée Zellweger and Anthony LaPaglia. It may have opened to the undeniably cool tones of The Cruel Sea's 'The Honeymoon Is Over', but it also wanted to cash in on 'the coolest generation', as gen X has been dubbed. It failed by having a distinct plot, but tried to score credibility points by pitting the staff of an indie record store against a corporate giant (to whom they would absolutely not sell out). The irony was the film was made for a budget of US$10 million and grossed only $303,841 at the box office, despite there being plenty of salacious shots of Tyler's midriff (dressed, as she was, in '90s uniform of short kilt and crop top).

The UK was experiencing peak lad culture in the '90s – with Britpop, the rise of novelist Irvine Welsh and the success of *Trainspotting*, and a resurgence of interest in mod fashion – but *Love and Other Catastrophes* clearly takes influence from the United States, right down to the grungy soundtrack. Most pertinent on the film front was Kevin Smith's *Clerks* (1994), about neighbouring convenience-store and video-store workers who slack off to play hockey on the roof and nerd out over movies, and of which Emma-Kate Croghan told a magazine, '*Clerks* had just come out in Australia, and we just thought, if they can do it, so can we.'

In fact, *Love and Other Catastrophes* ticks all the boxes of a classic American gen-X film, which should include dialogue that is naturalistic to the point of being banal, a lack of direction on the career front, and romance typified by non-committal couplings within friendship groups (the term 'friends with benefits' probably made its cultural debut in Alanis Morissette's 1995 track 'Head Over Feet', and the sentiment was equally seen on TV, via *Friends* and *Seinfeld*).

The main point of difference between *Love and Other Catastrophes* and the wider cultural trends of the '90s is its charm. From the splicing-in of cutesy hand-shot footage, to the often deliberately contrived dialogue, it's a world apart from the decade's fascination with the underbelly of serious drug use. Tarantino, Irvine Welsh and Bret Easton Ellis were all preoccupied with the topic, and Melbourne itself had a 'healthy' heroin scene, but *Love and Other Catastrophes* is distinctly wholesome.

Dr Greg Dolgopolov, who teaches and researches at the University of New South Wales in video production, film festivals and film theory and literacy, remembers *Love and Other Catastrophes* being filmed on campus at the University of Melbourne when he was doing his PhD there.

'The great thing about *Love and Other Catastrophes* was it's quite a hopeful, positive film, and we were seeing a lot of dark and gothic,' he says. 'It came out around the time Jane Campion's *Sweetie* came out. They made a good combination of new independent female voices that were speaking to their audience and their audience was not unlike that. They're kind of neo-gothic, dirty and grungy, and hopeful.'

The students would never have taken the route to the Arts faculty they did in the film, Dolgopolov notes, but other than that, campus life was faithfully portrayed. 'The police were not allowed on campus and there was a general atmosphere that you really could do anything you liked,' he says. 'If you were told off it would probably be a maintenance worker rather than anyone in any position of authority.'

In fact, he says, the University of Melbourne was second only to La Trobe in permissiveness: 'La Trobe probably had the most ratbag proto-fascist left-wingers and hardcore anarchists,' he says. 'If you weren't with them you were against them.'

Elly Varrenti was a classmate of Dolgopolov's who now teaches part-time at the university as well as being a writer, broadcaster and actor. 'I remember when I was complaining about some overdue essay or other and a friend of mine said, "Oh come on El, you can get a degree from Melbourne University just by reading a paperback in [local cafe] Johnny's Green Room,"' she says of the institution's laid-back reputation.

Varrenti remembers the enrolment process involved running manically back and forth all over campus the way Mia does in the film, with bureaucracy actually having a face – such as that of the gatekeeper of a department – rather than taking the form of an online portal as it does today. Similarly, the campus was a social locus, whereas contemporary students tend to come in for lectures and then leave.

'There was a lot of theatre stuff happening on campus back then and plenty of people from those days including Greg and me were also doing stuff outside the uni environment,' Varrenti says. 'Greg actually got a small, but to us a mind-blowing amount of money via a government grant to start our own theatre company. Those were the days when arts funding bodies didn't require you have a Masters in form filling and box ticking but when a great idea and plenty of energy was enough. We had the kind of chaotic creative confidence I've come to associate with making art in the '90s.'

Offsite, Varrenti spent quality time in the Italian cafes on Lygon Street, such as Tiamo and Brunetti's, or in the foyer of the Carlton Cinema on Faraday Street. Readings was good – then more of a record shop than a bookstore – and of course there was La Mama. Students drank at The Clyde and caught up for coffee at Rumbarella's, the latter making a cameo in the film. Sometimes they'd stray further to Fitzroy's Night Cat or Black Cat Cafe. Many girls took waitressing jobs at Genevieve's or Paradiso.

Glenn D'Cruz has now retired from academia – he was most recently Associate Professor of Art and Performance at Deakin University – but he taught Varrenti and Dolgopolov in the '90s, having been hired at the tender age of twenty-five.

He often mingled with students – which wouldn't happen now, as he notes – and remembers parties that would amass up to 500 people in large Fitzroy houses. 'Staff and students would mix socially and I made a lot of friends amongst the students I taught,' he says. 'Sometimes I'd be off my face at the Punter's Club and students would come up to me. I'd think, can I access my lecturer persona? Absolutely not!'

Being Anglo-Indian and from East London, D'Cruz's first thought upon arriving at the University of Melbourne was how white and privileged the students were, something he thinks is reflected in *Love and Other Catastrophes*, deliberately or not. 'Even the title; I thought, give me a break. Catastrophes like dealing with a university's bureaucracy?' he says.

Take the scene in which Alice joins Ari, who she has a

crush on, for coffee and tells him about her long overdue thesis, *Doris Day: Feminist Warrior.*

'You're into popular culture and all that,' Ari nods.

'I bet you're really brainy and deep and read Socrates when you're relaxing,' Alice gushes in response. 'I suppose your parents are in publishing or academia and you all speak Ancient Greek around the table.'

The character of Ari reminds Varrenti of French New Wave cinema with a punky twist. 'He self-identifies as an intellectual, philosophical one of the group, and it reminded me of Godard stuff,' she says. 'There's always one of those characters.'

D'Cruz thinks *Love and Other Catastrophes* is more a homage to screwball comedies of the '30s and '40s, hence the references to Doris Day, and Croghan herself told *Cinema Papers* in 1996 about her love of romantic comedies from that era, such as *The Shop Around The Corner*, *Holiday* and *The Awful Truth.*

'There are a few jump cuts at the start, but it's a very conventional narrative,' D'Cruz says. 'There are also the remnants of post-punk culture; the idea that anyone can play and anyone can participate.'

In 1997, US film critic Ruthe Stein reported on a 'new wave' of Australian cinema – including *Shine*, *Hotel de Love*, *Angel Baby*, *Cosi*, *Children of the Revolution*, *Love Serenade* and *Love and Other Catastrophes* – and Croghan told Stein, 'My generation was the first to be brought up on video, so we had access to all the American films. We could watch horror films – anything we could get our hands on. That will mark the difference between my generation and filmmakers like Peter Weir, who were more influenced by art house repertory.'

Certainly, *Love and Other Catastrophes* wears its deep love of film on its sleeve. It was shot on Super 16 mm, blown up to 35 mm for theatrical release; real-life film critics Adrian Martin and Paul Harris make fleeting appearances; and an interview with Croghan in the UK's *Independent* newspaper ran with the headline: 'Food I Could Live Without. But Film … Never'. In one scene, Gyngell's character, Professor Leach, wants his class to study Hitchcock, which is met with groans. He suddenly sees the students separated into tribes: the Quentin Tarantino tribe, the Woody Allen tribe, the Spike Lee tribe – and dressed accordingly.

'In Melbourne in the '90s there was a real buzz around film culture,' says D'Cruz. 'With my course I made sure they were aware of Paul Harris on RRR and Cinémathèque at RMIT. What dominated film theory was this idea that experimental film could have some kind of political impact on culture. It was a revolutionary act in itself.'

D'Cruz references Laura Mulvey's seminal 1975 essay 'Visual Pleasure in Narrative Cinema' in terms of prejudices of patriarchy being encoded into film. 'In the '90s there was a more critical approach to that,' he says. 'People started to question the theorists of the '70s, but nevertheless there was still this idea that film was critical. Attention was starting to be paid to working-class culture and non-white culture.'

In *Love and Other Catastrophes*, Mia is desperate to switch from film to cultural studies, which was a relatively new concept in Australian universities – and actually, the University of Melbourne was particularly late to the party, according to D'Cruz.

'There was a strong sense of activism from students – protests on campus, marches – and cultural studies was cool and hip because it directly engaged with politics,' he says. 'A lot of middle-class kids got seduced by the idea of applying semiotics to subcultures and to music culture, and excited by the idea that consumption could be a political act. Not only that, but it explicitly gave you a political costume. You could engage in a bit of political cosplay and rebel against Mummy and Daddy a bit.'

There's one scene where a female student has cornered Mike and is pontificating on Milan Kundera's take on Parmenides' perception that the world is divided into pairs of opposites. It is, of course, deliberately pretentious dialogue, but Varrenti insists, 'We *did* talk like that!'

D'Cruz agrees. 'Although maybe it was just the parties I went to. It was trying on identities in the same way that in the film [Mia and Alice] try on different outfits. There's one scene where the uncool lecturer, played by Kym Gyngell, starts using unintelligible psychoanalytic jargon, and people did have those conversations.'

Varrenti says that in 1996, post-structuralist theory would have been colonising every social science and humanities subject – and there was a hunger for it. 'I remember the word "phallocentric" being a revelation for me and suddenly looking at the world through a phallocentric lens,' she says. And then there was David Bennett's course, Art, Pornography, Blasphemy and Propaganda, which every student wanted to take.

'A lot of us did that subject and were horrified at how hard and incomprehensible it was, and how little we got to read about fucking,' Varrenti says. 'It was actually one of the toughest subjects you could do, and David was intellectually rigorous, running a very serious cultural subject. I can't imagine a subject like that would even get through the front door now because there is so much censoriousness in the university system; there'd be so many trigger warnings.'

In Chuck Klosterman's book *The Nineties*, published in 2022, the essayist writes, 'Many of the polarising issues that dominate contemporary discourse were already in play, but ensconced as thought experiments in academic circles. It was, in retrospect, a remarkably easy time to be alive.' The discourse brewing on campuses, though, was about to surge beyond the sandstone surrounds. As Croghan herself put it, in an interview with *Senses of Cinema* in 2018: 'there was stuff in the air about universities and students, strangely enough because of scandals that had happened at Melbourne Uni … Helen Garner had released the book *The First Stone*, which is completely unrelated [to *Love and Other Catastrophes*] but there was just stuff in the air about university life, and being a recent graduate it was in the air for me.'

She's referring to the incident that Garner (whose daughter Alice plays Alice in the film) turned her focus to, in which two University of Melbourne students accused the master of Ormond College of groping them. Alan Gregory was found guilty at the Melbourne Magistrates Court and subsequently resigned. D'Cruz thinks the controversy generated by the book had a huge impact on campus culture and the way students spoke about gender. Alice Garner was in her third year at the university at the time, but had hardly been aware of the furore until her mother wrote about it. As she told *The Sydney Morning Herald* in an article titled 'The Good Daughter', the colleges were a separate world. Varrenti describes there being an 'apartheid' between campus life and college life, the latter of which attracted 'monied or country kids, and on both counts, daggy'.

Dolgopolov agrees with that. 'Some of my friends had spent a year in college and run screaming because they'd been sexually harassed or had experienced things they never wanted to experience again,' he says. 'Some colleges had religious affiliations; there was a women-only college; there was extra tutoring. It felt a bit like mollycoddling. Why would you send your kid to live in a college and not in a shared house?'

Having rewatched *Love and Other Catastrophes*, Varrenti has some grief for those long-gone days of self-expression and for the enjoyment of debate. 'I felt sad, possibly nostalgic, for a life I took for granted,' she says, 'but mostly I felt sad for my nineteen-year-old son who is about to start an arts degree at Melbourne University, because campus life back then was just more creatively shambolic and intellectually loose. In a good way.'

As Croghan herself told *Cinema Papers* in 1996, 'You go to this place to learn, but really it's about getting the social thing happening, finding your place in the world.'

The ensuing change of culture feels so demoralising to D'Cruz that he decided to leave academia early; one reason being that university students must now partake in a compulsory unit ensuring they are work-ready. 'You're eighteen years old, and the first course you do is to sketch out a plan for your life,' he says in disgust. 'The humanities are especially for play; you don't do a drama degree or film degree and then just waltz into a film position. So all the things I enjoyed about *Love and Other Catastrophes* are gone – the playfulness and experimentation.'

Even Douglas Coupland, who defined gen X to a large degree, thinks that individuality is moot in the current digital age. He wrote in *The Guardian* in 2021 that he cannot remember what his pre-internet brain felt like. 'I find comfort in the fact that brains all over the planet have been rewired similarly to mine. In fact, I'd go as far as to say that our species has never been as neurally homogenised as it is now.' In his new book, *The Extreme Self,* he defines 'autophobia' as 'fear of individuality', adding 'it's easier just to subcontract your identity to QAnon or Antifa'.

Emma-Kate Croghan, of course, could never have known that her film would become a time capsule for academia-as-rite-of-passage. She went on to make another feature, *Strange Planet*, starring Claudia Karvan and Naomi Watts, in 1999, and then moved to Los Angeles, then New York – where, as she says on her blog, 'I became a better writer and collected some great development hell stories; I once had a development executive ask me to explain what "solipsistic" meant.'

It's not what you'd call the most self-promoting bio, particularly for someone who moved to the United States to be in the heartland of filmmaking, but then the very generation she immortalised has all but faded into cultural obscurity.

As Klosterman put it in *The Nineties*, 'it's hard to exaggerate the pervasion of self-constructed, self-aware apathy that would come to delineate the caricature of a time period that already feels forgotten, mostly because those who embodied it would feel embarrassed to insist it was important.'

This is precisely what makes *Love and Other Catastrophes* all the more precious.

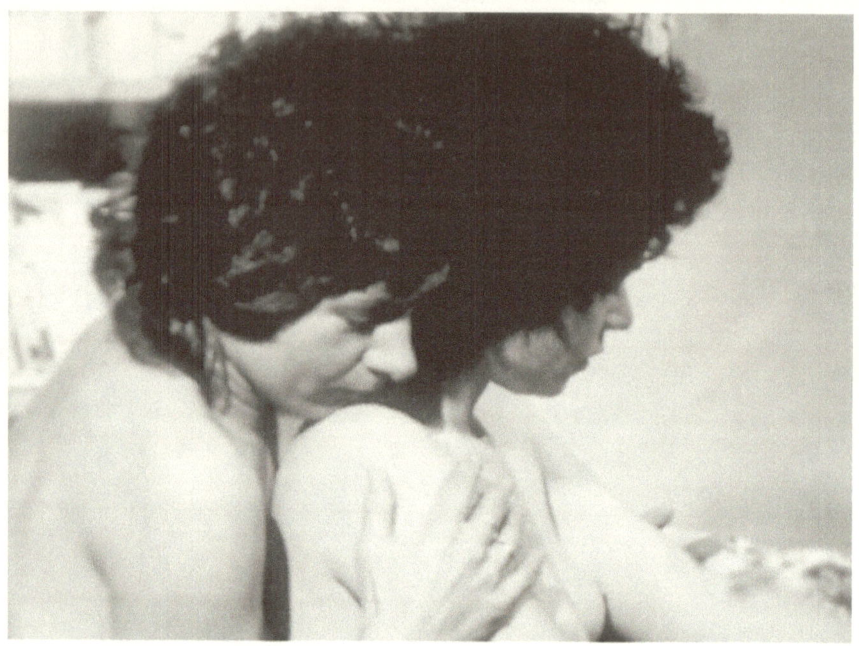

Still from *Homosexuality: A Film for Discussion* courtesy of Barbara Creed.

Homosexuality: A Film for Discussion

Kate Jinx

Two women, naked, caress. They're lying atop a heavily patterned blanket on a bed, cluttered bookshelves are in the background, and a large woven artwork dangles from a wall. The woman closest to the camera has her back to us, as gentle guitar strings play. Folk music and lesbianism, a classic combination. I've just hit play on a digitised copy of Barbara Creed's 1975 film, *Homosexuality: A Film for Discussion*, at the Melbourne outpost of the National Film & Sound Archives. At this point, it's 2015, and I'm about nine months deep into my PhD candidature looking at the (deep breath) documentation-of-queer-history-on-screen-in-Australia-in-relation-to-what-was-happening-in-the-USA-UK-and-Canada-between-1962-and-1994-ina-non-narrative-setting (exhale). Seven years have passed since then, and yet I know that one-sentence summary as well as I remember my parents' landline circa 1985 and the Pizza Hut delivery number of my childhood. I'm ashamed to say that I still have absolutely no idea what my girlfriend's mobile number is and we've been together for coming up twelve years – I'll no doubt be in trouble if I'm ever arrested and only granted that one call, unless I'm in the mood for a vegetarian supreme.

As one woman gently strokes the other's back, her mouth appearing to be hovering over the other's breast, I nervously look behind me to see if anyone else in the archival room is watching me watch this, a frisson of queer romance emanating from my little monitor in a dark room in Federation Square. No-one is, and by the time I turn back around in my seat, the women on screen are gone and a simple title card appears. The first few seconds of the film remind me of a particularly condensed sex scene (the only one) in Radclyffe Hall's infamous queer novel *The Well of Loneliness*, which appears here in its entirety, be warned!

… and that night they were not divided.

The audacity. In 1928, however, this led to an obscenity trial, a subsequent banning, and an order that all copies be pulped. The book, still hotly debated, is rather depressing but it thrilled me upon first read, as does almost any little whiff of queer representation from before my own '90s teen dyke heyday.

At that point in my candidature research, I'd watched many, many hours of so-called queer representation on screen, much of it negative. News anchors unable to keep their homophobic revulsion from live television in a simple account of a community gathering, fixations on gay beats, and clearly fetishistic hosts probing trans women about their bodies (not that this has changed much). At one point I began to focus more fully on queer documentation made by queer documentarians, a personal salve, a little ray of light between the usually straight-faced grimaces and disapproving tsk-tsks. Canadian activist and academic Thomas Waugh once wrote, 'if films are to be instrumental in the process of change, they must be made not only about people directly implicated in change but with and for those people as well'.[1] Creed's *Homosexuality: A Film for Discussion* does precisely that.

Originally intended as an educational film to screen in schools, it is a 43-minute black-and-white work featuring frank discussions between 'out' gay men and women about their lived experiences, and two mothers (one, not mentioned within the film, is Creed's) of gay children, who speak about their emotional support and changes – if any – with their children after they came out. These considered segments are sensitively spliced between street interviews, or vox pops, conducted by Creed with the general public of Melbourne, who are asked varying questions about their thoughts on homosexuality – some positive, some negative, but all with great candour (some, perhaps a little too much). For me, first seeing it forty years after its initial release, it was not a time capsule but some proof of community, of existence and resistance. Interviewed in 2017 for *i-D Magazine*, Creed spoke of the importance of documentation: 'Without [these records], gay people, or any other marginalised group, don't have their own history. If marginalised groups can't access their own history it makes them feel impotent, invisible and without a voice.'[2]

Here, in her film, everyone has a voice – and it is a delight to see so many gay Melburnians happily allowing themselves to be explicitly recorded on camera, no mean feat considering sodomy laws were not repealed in Victoria until 1981, aversion therapy was rampant, and the threat of being outed could mean job loss or worse. Creed, now a widely published author and Screen Studies Professor Emeritus at the University of Melbourne, was a founding member of the early 1970s Melbourne gay liberation movement and co-founder of the Melbourne Women's Filmmaking Group. Though, for the most part, only her voice is present in *Homosexuality*, she had already outed herself on national television during Gay Pride Week in 1973 – one of the few members of the gay liberation movement unafraid of this being the way their parents found out. On a recent sunny

March afternoon at her home in Melbourne's inner north, Creed recalls this experience for me: 'I rang her up and I said, "Mum, remember how you've always told me, never, ever worry about what the neighbours think? Well, if you turn on the television tonight ..."'

I like to think of queer archives as living archives, buffering timelines and creating dialogues between past and present, a proof of concept for our very existence. The nature of my PhD research combined with the need for copyright security (no cameras!) meant that I found myself many times in open-plan libraries and centres around the world watching queer people across time in various stages of undress, performing for or being observed by the camera. It's nice to think that nobody is watching you, but I could never resist clocking what other researchers had pulled to view. So much war! So many newsreels! And on one particularly good trip to some archives in California, I saw a small group wade through dozens of Bill Cosby videos. 'What do they want with that?' I thought, as I returned to my community-access television coverage about a gay sex-on-premises site being closed due to a mould outbreak. Quite different to the time I accidentally stitched up my girlfriend when I sent her, early on in our relationship, to see *Community Action Center* by A.L. Steiner and A.K. Burns, a 'sociosexual' video work made by some artists I'd met in New York. She dutifully went to see it and sat, red-faced, while some male tradies stomped back and forth through the room to fix the Manhattan gallery's boiler while on screen one person masturbated with a large crystal and another used their large breasts to wipe foam off a car window. The artists weren't the only ones exposed.

Coming out in one's personal life is already a multi-layered process, and so coming out in public – and in this case, on screen – adds an extra element. Putting a visible face or an audible voice on members of the queer community shines a further light on the act of 'coming out' itself. The stakes were particularly high in the 1970s, and as Waugh points out, 'our filmmakers can never forget that the single act of filming a gay person can expose them to eviction, firing, family rejection, violence, loss of child custody, and even criminal charges'.[3] There are only a handful of Australian television shows and documentary films that feature interviews with gay people that predate Creed's film, but the track record of workplace acceptance from those is not particularly cheering.

One of the earliest examples of lived homosexuality appearing on Australian screens is current affairs program *7 Days: Love is Love : Lesbians*, presented by the late journalist Anne Deveson, and broadcast on the ABC in 1964. It was a benchmark half-hour program that examined lesbian lives in Sydney through a series of interviews with women, all only halfway out of the closet – in that their voices were coming out but their faces were not. I like to think of it as 'coming out but staying in'.

One of those voices belonged to the unnamed Dawn O'Donnell, a notorious queer Sydney character and influential lesbian entrepreneur who is recognised as kickstarting the queer NSW nightlife scene in the late 1960s. She speaks openly about her need to live a double life, occasionally making reference to her involvement in a 'secret society', adding, 'You would be amazed at who, where, what and when.' As it turns out, her voice was as distinctive as her opinions, and the day after the program aired, she was immediately fired from her job as a figure-skating coach at a Sydney ice rink – as revealed in Fiona Cunningham Reid's 1994 documentary *Croc-A-Dyke Dundee*, in which O'Donnell adds, 'He did me the biggest favour in the world. That's how I got into bars.'

In 1972, an episode of ABC's social affairs program *Chequerboard* aired, subtitled 'This Just Happens To Be Part of Me'. It features the beloved Peter de Waal and his partner, the late Peter Bonsall-Boone, both involved in early Sydney gay-rights group CAMP (Campaign Against Moral Persecution). It opens with the first real male-homosexual kiss on Australian screens, and aside from discussing the issues they have growing native flora, this episode is notable in that all participants are fully visible. Soon after *Chequerboard* aired, Bonsall-Boone was fired from his job as Secretary of St Clements Anglican Church in Mosman, who until then had turned a blind eye to his homosexuality. Much about the social views of the time can be gleaned from a 1972 review in *The Bulletin*, which backhandedly commended the program, 'Perhaps most important was just to see and hear them on television. Contrary to popular belief, they did not have two heads, did not lisp, mince or have limp wrists, and looked just like you and me.'[4]

During one television appearance in 1972, Creed was asked if she herself had concerns about repercussions when she returned to work after the show had aired. She says she hadn't actually considered it beforehand, but responded that her colleagues were far too intelligent to have any such issues. They weren't all as supportive as she'd hoped, however, and she found that upon her return to the Coburg Teachers' College, there was a heated debate in the staff lounge. One female colleague reported her to the school's principal, claiming Creed had made a pass at her in the cafeteria. It turned out that she had reported a male lecturer for the same thing a week before, and was doing a master's degree involving biblical prophecy. Her claims were taken with a grain of salt, but her boss ultimately removed Creed from the school visits she undertook as part of her job, watching and reporting on student teachers. He claimed initially that it was because she was overworked, but in reality it was out of fear that parents might protest: 'If they'd seen me on television, how dare they let this monstrous person into the schools?!' Her loyal students at the college revolted of their own volition, demonstrating with placards that she be allowed to fully do her job. They were successful.

Two years later, Creed received funding from the Experimental Film Fund (EFF), which was then administered by the Australian Film Institute. The fund was set up to enable young filmmakers with small grants, and little in the way of specification guidelines. Her intention for *Homosexuality: A Film for Discussion* was to create a film to be taken into schools, where each screening would be followed by a robust discussion with the students. The title is a nod to the 1973 work *Film for Discussion* made by the Sydney Women's Film Group, also funded by the EFF, which highlighted the burgeoning plight of the women's liberation movement. Of course, we all know that the 1970s was a hothouse for progressive leanings, consciousness-raising, and great hair – or as Creed describes it, 'a very radical, political period'. Accordingly, it was also a particularly fertile time for the funding of film projects in Australia – both by governmental bodies and community groups.

A year after Creed's film premiered, the Gay Film Fund (GFF) was set up in Sydney, raising money for new projects through dances, screenings and barbeques. One film that was partly funded through the GFF was another iconically Australian queer documentary – One in Seven Collective's *Witches, Faggots, Dykes and Poofters* (1978), produced by Digby Duncan. It is well known for its footage of the first Mardi Gras, the subsequent violent police intervention and its political, social and emotional aftermath. In the documentary, one of the participants (unnamed in the film but now widely known as Robyn

Plaister) speaks about an interrogation by the headmistress at the independent school she was teaching at, following the publication of a now-famous photograph of her arrest at Mardi Gras in a newspaper. Though she could not legally be fired as her name had been omitted, Plaister and her classes were now under scrutiny: 'what that really says to me is the fact that there are so many gay teachers within schools that have to be quiet, that are not allowed to expose their lifestyle, and that can't be true to themselves, and what that does to one'.

Prior to making her first funded film, Creed had documented gay liberation and women's liberation marches in Melbourne in the early '70s on Super8. Often the marches would be held on Friday evenings, with members walking through the city, holding hands, chanting, or kissing, 'you know, trying to shock people into awareness that there were other forms of sexual desire apart from straight … and that was always fun actually'. When it came to putting together *Homosexuality*, shot on 16 mm, the self-taught Creed would edit her footage covertly at night at the Coburg Teachers' College, locking herself in the women's toilets after the cleaners had been through, before editing on the college's hefty Steenbeck machine.

The actual 'casting' of the documentary was similarly close to home for Creed and it was mostly filmed where she was living in Fitzroy. The bulk of the conversation footage features two couples: Ross Moore and Simeon Kronenberg (who were in the same gay mixed-consciousness raising group as Creed) chatting informally with Anne Houlihan and Gael Waldron. All gay participants in *Homosexuality* have their full names in the end credits. Creed had asked them to talk about four or five main themes: growing up, family life, school, coming out, and relationships. This aided the film to be structured in a way that, when taken into schools, Creed could stop the projector at the end of each section to speak with students about what they had just seen. Quite literally a film for discussion.

The vox pops were conducted by Creed, wearing a suit, and wielding a small microphone on Flinders and Swanston Streets in the city, with a few more done in Carlton. She'd tell her prospective interviewees she was making a film on homosexuality and what the people of Melbourne think about it. Everyone agreed to appear, and all had unwaveringly strong views – positive or negative. So as not to shape their answers, Creed did not offer that she herself was a lesbian.

> Do you think laws against homosexuals should be changed?
> Do you think homosexuality is natural?
> Do you know any homosexuals?
> Do you usually assume that people you meet at first are heterosexual?
> How would you feel if you saw two men kissing in the street?

Do you think homosexuals look different from other
people?

How would you describe what a typical lesbian or homosexual looks like?

How would you feel if you had children and they told you
they were homosexual?

Do you think homosexuals are happy?

Interestingly, the responses do not align with any one age group of those interviewed, and for the most part are delivered in earnest. Some are staunchly supportive of queer rights, while others invoke *Sodom and Gomorrah*, and one creepy pastor type with a distinctly hellmouth-from-*Buffy* vibe mentions demonic possession. Only one man employs a little mimicry, waving his hand around and commenting on 'funny accents'. Beautifully, his own accent is quite distinctive among the rest of the interviewees.

There were several cinematic little jewels that struck and delighted me when I first encountered this documentary, one of which I have returned to many times over the years. These include the openness with which the interviewees speak, offering their personal histories with seemingly no sense of a need for self-preservation in an unjust society; the fact that one of the men interviewed on the street looks uncannily like a young Bryan Brown; and the sensitivity of the filmmaking, which pairs romance, progressive politicism and pride with a cross-section of viewpoints by a larger public. And then there are the cutest little homophobes in all of Melbourne who appear around eleven minutes in. When Creed saw them she says she rushed over with her mic, 'and it was like manna from heaven'. Four boys, maybe ten or eleven years old, simultaneously angle for and try to dodge Creed's camera. When she asks if the laws around homosexuality should be changed, the boy closest to the camera chortles, 'Nah, kick 'em out!' Creed, audibly bemused or perhaps exasperated, says 'Well … why should we kick them out?' and the first boy replies, ''Cause they're poofs!' before emitting a high-pitched squeal that sets off all the other boys to pipe up with their thoughts: 'Because they're queers and idiots and everything!', 'Dress like sheilas!', 'Carry handbags!'. Their word-for-word dialogue has become a near-daily recital in my household. Creed says, 'Every time I managed to interview someone like those boys who say such astonishing things, you realise how early the prejudice sets in.' On a damaged roll of film that was ultimately left out, Creed captured a young man who said that homosexuals should all be flushed down the toilet.

The closest thing to any queer education at my suburban public high school in the 1990s was a Health sex-education class package that covered the AIDS epidemic. My teacher, however, decided to skip the content that week, brushing it off with, 'The only people who get that are drug addicts and gays and I hope that doesn't include any of you.' I lodged a complaint but nothing happened, so I started selling red ribbons at recess and lunch instead – clearly intent on being bullied, just in case the cat collars (bought from the local pet store) and pointedly kissing my girlfriend in the quadrangle wasn't quite enough. It's quite hard to imagine (particularly with the challenges facing the more recent Safe Schools program and religious discrimination bill), a group of out homosexuals, filmmakers and activists, rolling a projector into a Victorian classroom in the mid 1970s, ready to openly discuss sexuality with high-school students. Creed recalls that students were eager to engage with the material, mostly asking straightforward questions about what it was like growing up, how did their parents react to them coming out, how did they find partners, and if they'd ever been attacked for being gay. A visit to Preshil (an alternative school) posed different responses, with 'out' lesbian and gay students who already had their own spin on things.

'We thought it was really important for the students to actually meet gay people,' offers Creed. 'Eventually conservative sections found out we were doing this … and before we knew it, there was a huge debate going on about whether or not schools – just like the debate now – were the right place to teach students about sexuality.' The controversy trickled into televisions and newspaper spreads. Creed's film and the 1978 educational booklet *Young, Gay and Proud* published by the

Melbourne Gay Teachers and Students Group are mentioned together in numerous articles throughout the late 1970s, the target of a petition objecting to 'the efforts being made within government schools to promote homosexual behaviour as a valid lifestyle'. It all sounds so familiar. Over email correspondence earlier this year, Creed wrote: 'it becomes very clear that we are still going over the same ground – LGBTI students are still being isolated, discriminated against, bullied and left without proper support, sometimes with tragic consequences. I made the film to take into Schools in the 1970s in order to give support to gay students, to let them see they were not alone, that they were not sick or unnatural and that they had rights.' Ultimately the Director General of Education stated that if teachers were to invite screenings of Creed's film, then he could see no issue. The school visits continued.

Homosexuality: A Film for Discussion also had a life outside of the education system, playing in numerous cinemas and festivals, and was screened at ten p.m. nightly on 4–16 November 1975 as part of a local gay line-up at the former Co-Op Cinema in Carlton known as 'Melbourne's theatre for the thoughtful', alongside Maya Frankel's *Turkish Baths* and Don McLennan's *A Point of Departure*. A review in *Campaign* magazine notes that the sold-out season was reprised at the Playbox Theatre. The article also takes pains to mention that the critic found it 'entertaining, instructive, thought provoking. It demolishes previous limitations in presenting the realities of homosexual experience, oppression ... and hope.'[5] Hope is what I continue to find in it too.

Leaving Barb's house after prodding her for minute details on a film she made nearly half a century ago, I thought about what ratio of positive to negative responses she would receive now from people on the streets of Melbourne. I'd like to think more of the former than the latter, but thinking too much about statistics brings up the still-stinging wounds from 2017's Australian Marriage Law Postal Survey. Everything's changed and nothing's changed and everything's changed.

After I turned back around to continue my first encounter with *Homosexuality: A Film for Discussion* at the NFSA archives, (I never did finish that PhD; life – as it tends to – got in the way), no longer caring who saw me watching it, those embracing women do return to the screen after the initial title cards. Creed says she started with these affectionate displays because 'the greatest mystery around desire, particularly if you're talking about same-sex desire, is what do homosexuals do?' It enabled the viewer to see for themselves, and come to terms with it. The women are followed by two men kissing softly, two more women talking and going for a walk and a quick peck in Edinburgh Gardens, and more couples laughing with each other, talking, drinking, strolling, and a bit more kissing. These images accurately sum up much of my own lived queer history (particularly the bit about Edinburgh Gardens). That said, if anyone featured had two heads, lisped, minced, or looked nothing like you or me, that's great too.

Notes

1 Thomas Waugh, 'Why Do Documentary Filmmakers Keep Trying to Change the World (1984)' in *The Right to Play Oneself: Looking Back on Documentary Film*, University of Minnesota Press, Minneapolis, 2011.
2 Alexandra Manatakis, 'inside the video archives of gay liberation, melbourne's first queer student group', *i-d*, 28 April 2017.
3 Thomas Waugh, 'Lesbian and Gay Documentary: Minority Self-Imagine, Oppositional Film Practice, and the Question of Image Ethics (1984)' in *The Right to Play Oneself: Looking Back on Documentary Film*, University of Minnesota Press, Minneapolis, 2011.
4 D. Anderson, 'Coming Out', *The Bulletin*, vol. 094, no. 4829, 11 November 1972.
5 A. Roberts, 'Melbourne: Films on Homosexuality by Melbourne Film–Makers', *Campaign*, no. 41, March 1979.

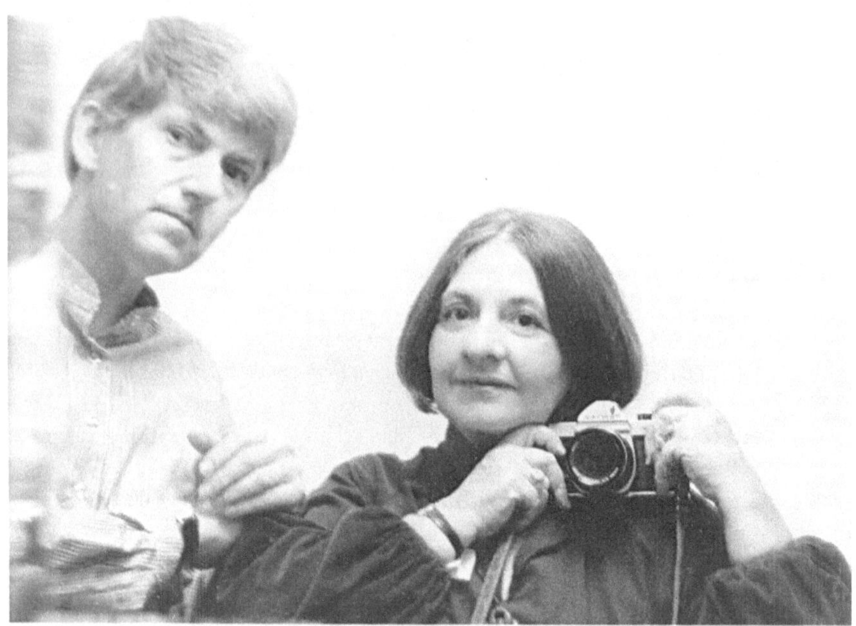

Still from *In This Life's Body* courtesy of Arthur Cantrill.

In This Life's Body

Rebecca Harkins-Cross

'Everyone who is born holds dual citizenship, in the kingdom of the well and in the kingdom of the sick,' wrote Susan Sontag, not long after she'd first been diagnosed with breast cancer. 'Although we all prefer to use only the good passport, sooner or later each of us is obliged, at least for a spell, to identify ourselves as citizens of that other place.'[1]

Sontag's famous metaphor was partially ironic, among the few figurative indulgences she yielded to in *Illness as Metaphor* (1978). In later work she described this introduction as her 'mock exorcism of the seductiveness of metaphorical thinking'.[2] Demon expelled, Sontag remained the arch critic expounding on the language of illness, refusing the temptation not only of metaphor but also of confessing to readers the subjective experience from which her study emerged.

In This Life's Body (1984) is also a missive from 'that other place', made when filmmaker Corinne Cantrill was afflicted by an illness she doesn't name, originating in her womb, that doctors insisted required invasive surgery. Unlike Sontag's steadfast commitment to critical objectivity, Cantrill's visit to what Sontag called 'the night-side of life'[3] saw Australia's *grande dame* of avant-garde cinema take a stylistic detour.

This autobiographical essay film, a cinematic künstlerroman, remains an outlier in Cantrill's sizeable body of work – all made in collaboration with her husband, Arthur (who also shares co-directing credit for *In This Life's Body*, though she later said it was her individual creation)[4] – which largely eschews mainstream cinema's narrative cornerstones of plot and character. Moreover, it directly contradicts the Cantrills' self-declared war on humanism, storytelling and the tyranny of content over form.

'Our films have no story because all the stories have been told and retold, on the grey pages of literature until they are meaningless,'* the Cantrills wrote in their 'Cinema Manifesto',

---

* *In This Life's Body* takes as much from literature's 'grey pages' as from the cinema, with Cantrill citing (in the voiceover) Anais Nin, Ania Walwicz and Laleen Jayamanne's writings as key influences. For further exploration of the Cantrills' relationship with literature, see: Giles Fielke, 'Direct Action on Things: Harry Hooton and Artist Film in Australia', *Cordite*, 1 October 2020.

published in 1971, which prefaced the first edition of their journal *Cantrills Filmnotes*. Ardently devoted to celluloid's materiality, they wanted to create 'films which defy analysis, which present a surface so clean, so hard, that it defies the dissector's blade'.[5]

When faced with the surgeon's scalpel, however, Cantrill's central act of defiance is to return to the origin story of self-narrativisation: the family triangle. This psychoanalytic premise is an odd one for filmmakers who had, in that same manifesto, declared that 'Marx and Freud are dead', in an outright rejection of the depth models of hermeneutics then dominating film studies and, more broadly, what they called 'the morgue of the Universities'.[6]

Suspecting that her physical malady may in fact stem from some psychical injury, the filmmaker returns to the photographic evidence of her existence. Can trauma's traces be glimpsed in a portrait of the artist as a fat baby, wide-eyed and grinning at the unseen parent behind the camera?

'My mother tells me that I was an unwanted child,' Cantrill says in her lyrical voiceover. 'She probably meant unplanned, but she always said unwanted.'

●●●

In This Life's Body opens with one of the few moving images in a film constructed largely from still photography. The camera pans up and down a rippling pool. Shown in negative, the white, shimmering mass is supernatural. In this uncanny mirror we spy the likeness of a naked woman, upside down, a reflection of an inversion.

In the next shot, the woman (now recognisable as Cantrill) reclines on the shore, the soft mounds of her body merging with the riverbank's undulations, as if her physical form is returning to the earth. Occupying the no-man's-land between life and death, the body seems unmoored from chronological time, suspended in Chronos's gyre. 'Neither flesh nor fleshless,' as T.S. Eliot wrote in his poem 'Burnt Norton'. 'Neither arrest nor movement. And do not call it fixity, where the past and future are gathered.'[7]

Cut to an ultrasound of her uterus. Viewed through the male doctor's gaze, her womb is an image of living death, the wellspring of creation turned necrotic. Presented alongside the previous landscape, however, Cantrill highlights the shapely echoes of body and earth. These static images are remapped as the interior's rolling terrains, in which she sees 'beauty', 'eroticism', 'the source of female desire'.

This opening sequence can be read as rejoinder to those who conflate the autobiographer with Narcissus. Female artists who use their lived reality as material are invariably charged with self-absorption, as Chris Kraus showed in *I Love Dick*: 'As if the only reason for a woman to publicly reveal herself could be self-therapeutic. As if the point was not to reveal the circumstances of one's own objectification.'[8]

Faced with physical dissolution, Cantrill seeks out the records of her body as whole.

'The integrity of the body was vital,' she says. And so she pours over a personal archive of family photographs, happy snaps, press shots, film stills; posed studies by artists, friends, lovers; excised footage; self-portraits that render the self as she wants to be seen. In an accompanying essay published in *Cantrills Filmnotes*, she explains that she let the available images act as 'the structure on which to form my story'.[9]

Watching these photographic traces of a life accumulate, I find myself haunted by that woman reflected in the shimmering surface. Reversed and refracted, her image suggests this portrait of the self will be multivalent. Cantrill's voiceover moves between 'I', 'she' and 'we', suggesting that her personal experience might speak to that of woman more broadly.

The film's most vulnerable moments of self-inquiry are spoken through a disembodied third person pronoun: 'She said, "I will live in this body or die with it."'

●●●

In This Life's Body is primarily a work of autobiography, so it would be remiss of me to skimp on the facts.

Corinne Cantrill (née Joseph) is born in Sydney, just

before the Great Depression. The eldest of two girls. Anglo Irish/German mother, Sephardic Jewish father (Iraqi heritage, born in Singapore, arriving to Australia via China). A theosophist and a communist respectively, Cantrill calls her parents' ill-starred marriage 'one of life's unexplained mysteries'.

In photographs of a smiling baby, Cantrill sees the pains of a Jewish child living through World War II; dark features in a racist colony; childhood poverty, family violence, a broken home. In the smiling baby, she sees a woman 'destined to be inherently insecure, restless, dissatisfied, wanting everything, wanting it both ways, outside the rules, open to possibilities'.

Hers is an unhappy childhood, where even as a girl she feels herself marked as an outsider. In the face of perceived parental indifference, she instead finds validation at school, where teachers recognise her curiosity and studiousness.

But in adolescence, another kind of knowledge beckons – a longing inchoate but potent. Cantrill's narration switches from first to third person to speak of her 'powerful sexual desire': 'She was drawn to men in an extraordinary way. Sexual desire, but no idea what sex was.' And so she quits school to become an autodidact in the discipline of love.

In one photograph, this teen on life's cusp poses in her backyard. Lipstick, short hair in waves, budding breasts protruding beneath her tight sweater. A half smile, an unwavering gaze. With one hand on hip and the other resting on a pitchfork, it's a teenager's charmingly guileless attempt at self-fashioning via self-portrait, playing dress-ups as seductress.

Meanwhile, her mother quits her father, taking up with a bohemian who frequents Pakie's Club – Sydney's answer to Parisian cafe culture. The teenager falls into the scene, too, enraptured by 'an older, European, sophisticated crowd. All free thinking, free love.' Here, the desire to escape the philistine outpost also takes hold, and like any good Antipodean with artistic dreams, she begins plotting her passage to the old continent.

Amid flings with older intellectuals and budding artists, she saves money working as a life-drawing model and then as a botanist.* Somewhere in the Indian Ocean, she tosses all her plant samples from the ship's stern, a grand gesture as she sails toward her future: London, Paris, Rome, Yugoslavia. She works, studies music and languages, and falls in love, again and again, which her mother would say was writ in her auspicious astrology: 'Saturn square to the house of love.'

Eventually she returns to Sydney where she meets Jacob, a writer who shares her Iraqi heritage, with whom she moves to Brisbane. Marriage, home ownership, motherhood. But Jacob is moody, saturnine, increasingly resentful, and only grows more so when she starts setting up a Children's Creative Leisure Centre.

---

* She explains in the narration that she is able to study as a non-matriculated student at Sydney University, and gets her first jobs in wartime when many male scientists have been deployed.

This is where she meets Arthur Cantrill, and where the more familiar part of her story – at least to Australian cinephiles – begins: 'Soon after he met me, he started making passionate advances. I thought, "He's very bold. I'm supposed to be a married woman!"

'It was our fate. Such an unlikely relationship could only be fate.'

•••

For a filmmaker whose dedication to celluloid is borderline fetishistic, it seems strange that Cantrill's most personal film is intent on denying the pleasure of movement from the moving image.

Cantrill even refuses the documentary cliche of panning across an archival image. At best, repeating particular photographs gives a sense of motion – say, cutting from a portrait image centre frame to a close-up on details; or, recontextualising earlier photos by juxtaposing them with new ones – but the camera mostly lingers too long to build necessary rhythm.

Her voiceover self-reflexively questions this formal decision. 'Did the filming of photographs transform them into another medium?' she asks. 'The movement of the film grain from frame to frame, the varied framings of the image, the length of shots, the cuts, fades, dissolves, the large projected image in the dark room. How did these elements transform photographs into film?'

I look to Chris Marker's *La Jetée* (1962), perhaps the most celebrated film made from stills, for elucidation. The French New Wave director's existential sci-fi follows an astral traveller haunted by an image from childhood. In a war-ravaged Paris, he takes part in an experiment 'to send an emissary into time to summon the past and future to the aid of the present'. Marker's mortal anti-hero must learn the same lesson taught to the guinea pigs sacrificed before him: 'one cannot escape time'.

La Jetée implicitly reveals the rub of photography. Each picture attempts to intervene in time's slipstream. But as soon as the photograph is taken, the moment it captures belongs to a past already out of reach. Each picture paradoxically proves such yearnings futile.

Is it a coincidence that when Sontag was writing *Illness as Metaphor*, she was also writing *On Photography* (1977)? Here, Sontag too observes how the photograph's attempt to wrest control over the present signifies an all-too-human helplessness. For the photograph is always a *memento mori*, testament to 'time's relentless melt'.[10]

Similarly, Roland Barthes' *Camera Lucida* (1980) was written in the wake of his beloved mother's death.* His study of photography contains many comparable ideas about the

---

* Barthes lived with his mother for most of his adult life. He detailed his overwhelming grief in a posthumously published diary. See: Roland Barthes, *Mourning Diary*, trans. Richard Howard, Hill and Wang, New York, 2010.

photograph as a reminder of mortality. His melancholy thesis of the photograph's temporality – that the photograph represents 'the return of the dead'[11] – takes on different shades when read with knowledge of his grief.

So, too, does Barthes' longing for photography to give him 'a neutral, anatomic body, a body which signifies nothing!'[12] – another futile yearning (not least for an overdetermined subject like Cantrill, as a Jewish woman). Through grief's lens, the 'body which signifies nothing' reads like a longing for death's oblivion.*

●●●

In the early 1960s, the Cantrills begin experimenting with filmmaking. They collaborate on short documentaries about the Children's Library and Craft Movement, which Corinne sells to television stations, but they soon grow frustrated by the generic constraints of both television and traditional documentary forms.

While Corinne is falling in love with Arthur, and discovering the medium that would become her life's great passion, the 'I' and 'she' of the film's earlier narration start to be strong-armed

---

* Barthes died the same year the book was published, after being hit by a laundry truck in the streets of Paris.

by a 'we' – firstly, of the artistic/romantic partnership, and soon enough, the family unit.

After giving birth to a second son, Ivor, she notes how few photographs of her are taken, 'as though we thought of the children as being extensions of ourselves'. Ivor is later diagnosed with autism, and for the first time another voice interjects, in tapes of Cantrill patiently teaching Ivor to talk (another rejection of medical experts, who had insisted Ivor never would).

Seeking broader horizons as filmmakers, plus better educational opportunities for Ivor, the family relocate to 'Swinging' London in 1965. Arthur works as an editor at the BBC, while Corinne looks after the children, and in their spare time they continue making films together. Corinne is overcome by a deep depression, visualised through a series of photos where she's turning her back to the camera.

In one photograph, the boys are playing in a park. She stands between them, her hair obscuring her face. Framed in wrought iron, two chains down the centre of the image dismember her body, as if the family has become a cage in which the mother is ensnared. For Cantrill, London is a place and time of 'she': 'Perhaps her depression was to do with the dirt and greyness and the class resentment,' she says in the voiceover.

Cantrill would be the first to refuse typecasting as the artist mother whose desires have been subsumed by her children.

She insists the constraints imposed upon their life by Ivor's diagnosis were key to their artistic vision's evolution – making films independently, at home, integrating everyday life into their work. When Cantrill wrote about *In This Life's Body* for a book on women's independent filmmaking, she stressed, 'I don't have any tales of woe about being a bored housewife tied to small children.'[13]

The film's emphasis not only on artmaking as a record of daily existence, but also on the artistic potential of the personal, has clear roots in feminist practice.* But as much as Cantrill has been a pioneering female filmmaker in Australia, making films with Arthur for two decades before Gillian Armstrong would be lauded as such for *My Brilliant Career* (1979), there are moments where *In This Life's Body* actively resists feminist reading.

As if to pre-emptively reject being lumped in with her second-wave sisters – say, the experimental short *We Aim to Please* (1976) or the labour documentary *For Love or Money* (1983) – Cantrill places her romantic history at the centre of her story, which she describes as 'a blessing, as though it was given to me to understand human nature and myself through the medium of loving men'.

---

* It's important to note the influence of the New American Cinema, too, which the Cantrills' work was in direct dialogue with – say, Jonas Mekas' diary films like *Walden* (1968) or *Reminisces of a Journey to Lithuania* (1972); and Stan Brakhage's record of his child's birth, *Window Water Baby Moving* (1959).

Still, *In This Life's Body* carved out space for autobiographical feminist cinema in Australia.* You can see its traces in Gillian Leahy's essay film, *My Life Without Steve* (1986), and later Margot Nash's story of familial mental illness, *The Silences* (2015), who has written about how Cantrill's work offered her permission.[14]

●●●

The Cantrills return from London for Arthur to take up a fellowship at the Australian National University in Canberra from 1969 to 1970. With a bursary and no distractions, it's the most fruitful era of their career.

Here they devise their Expanded Cinema programs, integrating film with live performance and visual art, with projections on unconventional screens – including kettle steam (*Concert for Electric Jugs*, 1981), a silver disc (*Milky Way Special*, 1971), and a screen-turned-canvas, painted in real time (*Calligraphy Contest for the New Year*, 1969).**

---

* You can glimpse *In This Life's Body*'s legacy internationally, too, though perhaps more obliquely, in Sarah Polley's *Stories We Tell* (2002), the actor-turned-filmmaker's investigation of family secrets; Agnes Varda's *The Beaches of Agnes* (2008), in which the filmmaker turns the camera on herself; and Chantal Akerman's final film *No Home Movie* (2015), a portrait of her mother made in grief, not long before the filmmaker's suicide.

** After some showings in Canberra, they were performed at The Age gallery at National Gallery of Victoria in 1971, and later restaged for the Other Film Festival in Brisbane in 2006 and at La Mama in 2009. Otherwise, they've rarely been seen.

The fellowship culminates in their first feature-length film, *Harry Hooton* (1970), an experimental biography of the outsider poet, philosopher and mutual friend, constructed around audio recordings of Hooton reading his work and pontificating from his deathbed. Rather than narrating his life, they illustrate his materialist philosophy through an abrasive symphony of nature and machine.

(What impressions I retain are fragmentary: the wings of the Sydney Opera House, under construction; a painfully blue ocean in flux; sparks raining like fireworks from a welder's gun; the mad tango of whirling cogs; a woman's face superimposed to show her full frontal and in profile simultaneously, like a cubist painting.)

In This Life's Body is a more conventional documentary than *Harry Hooton*, but when compared they reveal the former isn't quite the outlier I originally claimed. Indeed, both films' aesthetic and thematic resonances echo throughout the Cantrills' expansive oeuvre: the repetition of images/footage (*Home Movie: A Day in the Bush*, 1969); the way that repetition can reveal the limits of our perception (*4000 Frames*, 1970; *Myself When 14*, 1989); the primacy of sensuality (*Corporeal*, 1978); the untapped possibility of the domestic (*Garden of Chromatic Disturbance*, 1998; *The Room of Chromatic Mystery*, 2006); the life force of the bush (*The Native Trees of Stradbroke Island*, 1963; the 1977 *Touching the Earth* series; *Waterfall*, 1984; *The Land is Not Empty*, 2000); the portrait of the artist (*Robert Klippel Sculpture Studies*, 1964–1965; *Dream*, 1966 [which animated Charles Lloyd's dry points]; *Henri Gaudier-Brzeska*, 1968); and the repurposing of personal archival footage (*Red Stone Dancer*, 1968; *Island Fuse*, 1971).

Dare I say that the subjects of *Harry Hooton* and *In This Life's Body* also share a penchant for self-mythologisation? I'm not the first[15] to note that the film's final act lags when it begins repeating a familiar tale of the Cantrills' prolific output, cutting-edge experimentation, contributions to an indifferent local film culture, and deserved validation from overseas counterparts.

In This Life's Body adds to this legend the toll, for Corinne at least, of such ambition: the pains of an exhausted body, too long out of balance. 'Over the years so much energy had gone into the work, the films, the magazine, screenings, special events. So often it seemed futile, a waste of time,' she says.

●●●

If I were to indulge in my own bout of metaphorical thinking, it would be hard to resist the symbolic lures of the womb.

In This Life's Body originates in a malady of that wayward organ the ancients deemed the site of female hysteria. Our humanity is engendered only when we're expelled from our first home, the place of plenty, where all our needs are met before we have the consciousness to ask for them. This first exile is the primary wound of subjectivity.

A sense of unbelonging recurs throughout Cantrill's telling of her life, and the film is haunted by the figure of the mother: the mother the child perceives has driven the father away; the mother who did not, or could not, love enough; and her echoes in the mother the unloved child herself becomes – literally, cinematically.

When Cantrill returns to childhood photographs, however, she's forced to recognise other stories. The unhappy upbringing of memory is disturbed by forgotten photographs of the smiling baby, who is confident and at ease. A series of beach snaps shows an ecstatic toddler frolicking in the shallows, watched by adoring parents.

'Are the three of us faking happiness for the camera?' she asks. 'Are these photos just posed illusion? Or are the feelings as genuine as they seem?'

Sontag notes how the act of photographing is itself a form of evidence. 'Through photographs, each family constructs a portrait-chronicle of itself – a portable kit of images that bears witness to its connectedness.'[16] To take photographs of one's children is to declare that they are seen.

Cantrill herself repeats the ritual when her first son, Aaron, is born. She is embarrassed upon returning to these self-conscious images. She looks so achingly young, dressed in evening gown and lipstick, incongruous in her suburban home, as she feeds and bathes her boy. 'I'm embarrassed by the overwhelming intensity of my proud mother manner,' she says.

Towards the film's end, Cantrill places images of herself and her family members side by side, at similar ages. It's one of the only moments in a film running two and a half hours when her voiceover recedes, allowing viewers to glean for themselves the echoes between her face and theirs. The uncannily similar poses of two proud mothers showing off their babies for the camera.

Cantrill returns to a photo of her mother as a teen, a frizzy-haired backyard ballerina *en pointe*, looking directly into the camera. Beside it, that image of rouged self with pitchfork. Both girls look so hopeful about the life to come. To tell one's own story invariably precludes others', including that of another aspiring artist who, before children, before a violent marriage, is practically levitating with dreams of her own.*

It exceeds my meagre qualifications to analyse this story's emotional echoes – how the language of rejection, indifference and outsider-ness are used to describe both the family triangle and the local film scene – but I'd be lying if I claimed it hadn't crossed my mind.

●●●

---

* It also allows us to conceive of the resentments she might foist upon a daughter who realises the artistic life she only imagined.

The Cantrills are aliens in the highly territorialised history of Australian cinema, refusing to be corralled into any neat narrative or group. As Judy Annear and Kiffy Rubbo wrote in the catalogue for *Mid-Stream*, a 1979 survey exhibition of the duo's work to date, 'the Cantrills are eccentric and view themselves as such'.[17] For over sixty years, they've made resolutely independent work, outside of government film funding, outside of the filmmaking co-ops, and outside of the universities.*

That said, the Cantrills have always fostered their own cinematic communities. They programmed avant-garde cinema in Canberra; after moving to Melbourne in 1971, presented Expanded Cinema events and other screenings at underground venue The Maze, and later at La Mama; championed obscure and emerging filmmakers in *Cantrills Filmnotes* – the longest running journal of its kind, published from 1971 to 2000; and hosted screenings and salons at their homes in Brunswick, Moonee Ponds and, nowadays, Castlemaine. New generations of Australian filmmakers and cinephiles continue to make pilgrimages to the rural town, seeking their guidance or to view their work.

---

* Michael Koller's description of Waterfall as 'a true film maudit' speaks to so much of their body of work: 'an Australian film in an art form dominated by "entertainment" films from America or "serious" works from Europe; a short film in a culture which evaluates and discusses mainly feature films; a serious, formal, experimental work at a time when structural works are in disrepute'. See: Michael Koller, 'Waterfall', *Senses of Cinema*, 56 (Oct 2010).

Yet, for all the Cantrills' (warranted) frustration about institutional neglect and lacklustre enthusiasm in the wider culture, they also make it very difficult for interested audiences to access their films. They are uncompromising about how their work is projected, rarely yielding to digitisation. Their rigid parameters regarding the films' presentation and contextualisation have simultaneously enshrined their mythic reputation and further limited their reach.

Long after *Cantrills Filmnotes* evolved from an impassioned zine to a respected journal of experimental cinema, the Cantrills continued to write and publish extended essays on their own work. Depending on your vantage, it's either an act of artistic generosity or an attempt to stifle diverging interpretations. Corinne's essay on *In This Life's Body* is prefaced with a warning: 'This is a very personal film – not a "product" to be distributed, exhibited, loaned out in the usual ways.'[18]

●●●

'To photograph people is to violate them,' wrote Sontag, 'by seeing them as they never see themselves.'[19] To reframe the photographs of one's life, then, is to wrest back control of one's own image.

At the heart of *In This Life's Body* – perhaps of all autobiography – lie two conflicting desires: to be seen by others, and to control the other's gaze. Yet what the eye is drawn to in an image – what Barthes called the *punctum*, 'that accident which pricks me (but also bruises me, is poignant to me)'[20] – is unique to each spectator, who brings to the photographic encounter their own past, stories and hurts. To truly show oneself to another is to accept the possibility that we may not recognise the person reflected in their gaze.

As much as Cantrill seeks a sovereign self-image, however, she knows that revealing the self does not mean to yield, indulge, seduce or tempt. As if speaking of the self was a weakness. As if divulging the personal was a tawdry trick to get an audience onside. She recognises in the film's later moments that such vulnerability might also proffer communion: 'My friends found this project of value to themselves in thinking about their lives. Many of them shared childhood unhappiness. I was not as alone as I had thought.'

When the writing day is done, I ride home along the Yarra River, and see familiar scenes anew as if through the botanist-turned-filmmaker's eyes. Last light dancing on the shimmering water. A summer breeze animating the parched leaves. Not images of death, but of life.

Notes

1   Susan Sontag, *Illness as Metaphor & Aids and its Metaphors*, Penguin, London, 2002, p. 3.
2   Ibid., p. 91.
3   Ibid., p. 3.

4   Corinne Cantrill, 'Personal Statement: Corinne Cantrill', *Don't Shoot Darling: Women's Independent Filmmaking in Australia*, eds Annette Blonski, Barbara Creed & Freda Freiberg, Greenhouse, Melbourne, p. 189.

5   Arthur & Corinne Cantrill, 'Cinema Manifesto', *Cantrills Filmnotes*, 1 (March 1971), p. 3.

6   Ibid., p. 3.

7   T.S. Eliot, 'Burnt Norton', *Four Quartets*, Faber, London, 1944, p. 15.

8   Chris Kraus, *I Love Dick*, Semiotext(e), Los Angeles, 2006 [1997], p. 215.

9   Corinne Cantrill, 'Notes on *In This Life's Body*', *Cantrills Filmnotes*, 45/46 (October 1984), p. 55.

10 Susan Sontag, *On Photography*, Penguin, London, 2008 [1997], p. 15.

11 Roland Barthes, *Camera Lucinda: Reflections on Photography*, trans. Richard Howard, Vintage, London, 1980, p. 9.

12 Ibid., p. 12.

13 Corinne Cantrill, 1987, p. 186.

14 Margot Nash, 'Corinne Cantrill's *In This Life's Body*: A Personal Experience', *Senses of Cinema*, 99 (July 2021).

15 See: Freda Freiberg, 'Time's Relentless Melt: Corinne Cantrill's *In This Life's Body*', *Don't Shoot Darling: Women's Independent Filmmaking in Australia*, eds Annette Blonski, Barbara Creed & Freda Freiberg, Greenhouse, Melbourne, 1987, p. 336.

16 Sontag, 2008, p. 8.

17 Rubbo, Kiffy & Judy Annear, 'Introduction', *Mid-Stream: A Survey Exhibition of the Filmwork by Arthur and Corinne Cantrill, 1963–1979*, Ewing and George Paton Galleries, Melbourne, 1979, p. 1.

18 Corinne Cantrill, 1984, p. 54.

19 Sontag, 2008, p. 14.

20 Barthes, 2000, p. 27.

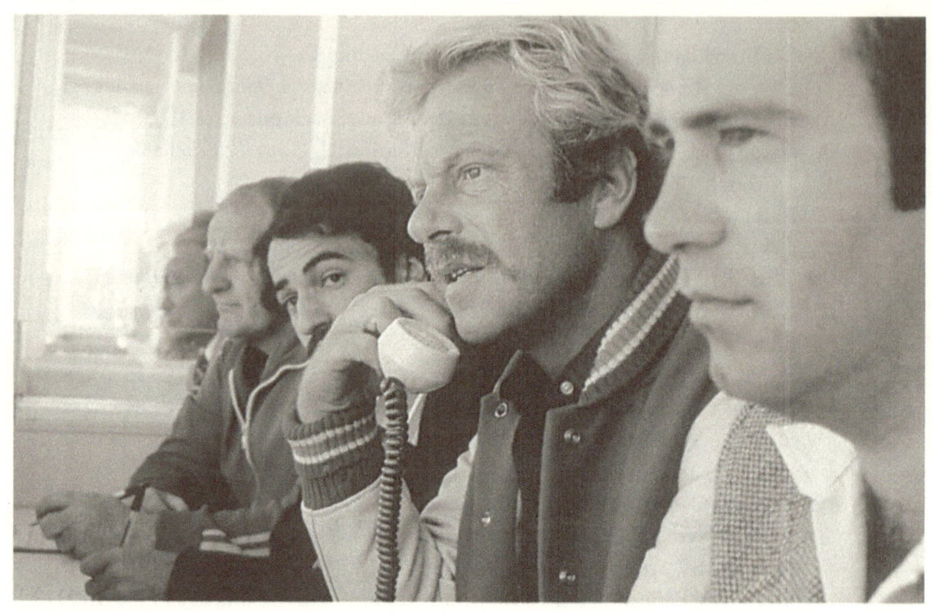

Still from *The Club* courtesy of Umbrella Entertainment.

The Club

Kylie Maslen

As a child, many of our family holidays were spent driving our brown Ford Falcon station wagon across the Dukes then Western Highways, from Adelaide to Melbourne. The big city to the east promised the cosmopolitan – art galleries, bookshops and restaurants – but also carried the lure of being the football capital of Australia. Dreary winter afternoons were spent at the grounds of Victorian Football League (VFL) clubs, watching our team lose time and again. But no matter how grim the day had been, footy was always the first activity to get pencilled in for the next holiday.

This fanaticism within footy culture is at the heart of *The Club* (1980) – the screen adaptation of David Williamson's play of the same name. The film centres on a football club in disarray, and the ruling committee who have decided to take action to turn the recent poor performances around. They sign Geoff Hayward (John Howard), a football wunderkind from Tasmania, for a sum so hefty the president (Ted Parker, played by Graham Kennedy) drains the remains of his personal bank account to seal the deal. Committee member, ex-coach and club champion Jock Riley (Frank Wilson) baulks at the process. Back in his day, men were queueing up to come to 'this great club'. But new administrator Gerry Cooper (Alan Cassell) sees the way the game is changing, and the Hayward trade is just the first step in his grand plans. However, no-one informed the coach, Laurie Holden (Jack Thompson), or the captain, Danny Rowe (Harold Hopkins). As the season unfurls, Laurie, Danny and the players fight the committee to win back control of the club and work their way into premiership contention.

The Club sits firmly within the Australian New Wave, a movement that celebrated – rather than cringed at – Australian culture on screen. Over the late 1960s and early 1970s the Gorton and Whitlam governments moved to revive the Australian film industry, which was languishing after the Second World War. The establishment of the Australian Film, Television and Radio

School (AFTRS) gave space for Australian filmmakers to not only learn their craft, but to showcase Australian life.

Beginning with films *Stork* (1971) and *Walkabout* (1971) through to *Crocodile Dundee 2* (1988) and *Young Einstein* (1988), the movement became a breeding ground for local directors such as Gillian Armstrong, Bruce Beresford and Peter Weir, as well as actors who quickly became household names – Bryan Brown, Judy Davis, Mel Gibson, David Gulpilli, Paul Hogan, Nicole Kidman, Sam Neill, Jack Thompson and Jacki Weaver among them.

The South Australian Film Corporation (SAFC) is a production company established by the state's progressive premier, Don Dunstan, during this era. Dunstan's impact on South Australian culture remains prominent to this day, with the SAFC (who continue to fund projects and provide facilities for local talent) among his legacies, beginning with *Sunday Too Far Away* (1975), the first New Wave feature film to be funded by the SAFC.

The Club may seem a thoroughly Melbourne story, but it was produced by the SAFC. Bruce Beresford, the film's director, had made several films with the SAFC by the time *The Club* came along. The most well known and well received is *Breaker Morant* (1980), which was: nominated for the Palme d'Or and for an Academy Award for Best Adapted Screenplay; winner of the Cannes Film Festival Best Supporting Actor for Jack

Thompson; nominated for the Golden Globe for Best Foreign Film; and, locally, winner of ten Australian Film Institute Awards. Six months later, *The Club* was released. Though a thoroughly different film to *Breaker Morant*, it helps to demonstrate the prolific nature of Beresford and Thompson's work during this era.

David Williamson would also play a large role in Australian New Wave with his screenplays *Stork* (1971), *Don's Party* (1976), *Gallipoli* (1981), *The Club* (1980) and *The Year of Living Dangerously* (1982) all produced during the period. In a review of Williamson's autobiography, *Home Truths*, literary critic Peter Craven writes, '[m]aybe he spends too much time saying what a money-spinner he was, maybe he talks about success as a value in itself in a way that would embarrass the Stoppards of this world',[1] but Williamson undeniably remains Australia's 'most familiar and formidable' writer for both stage and screen.

There is a posturing theatricality that dates *The Club* to the New Wave era, captured at its best by Frank Wilson as Jock Riley. Club great, games record holder, former coach, drunk, failing businessman and vocal sexist, Jock symbolises the old guard of football and of society more broadly. Early on he casually recalls 'I thumped her one' when speaking of his wife, he's quick to point out that Hayward has landed himself 'a good-looking sheila', and he uses a 'stripper' employed for the club's annual ball to bring down Ted's presidency for his own gain.

But Jock is the fool, never more so than during a visit to Geoff's home where he hopes to solve the recruit's poor playing form in a heart-to-heart. Geoff – a peace-loving inner-city economics student – tricks Jock into smoking hash by telling him it's a hand-rolled cigarette. As Jock tries to level with him, Geoff invents a sordid tale of incest and impotence. Jock, high enough to believe him, is played with cough-spluttering, wide-eyed comedic excellence.

As much as Williamson's characters ring true, followers of Australian Rules may find the gameplay in *The Club* to be about as camp as *Priscilla: Queen of the Desert* (1994). Slowed down to demonstrate the 360-degree of movement required, Victoria Park becomes a venue for an unintentional masterclass in Kabuki theatre. Highly stylised, Geoff is shown scooping the ball off the ground, evading the opposition and punting it through the goals from seemingly as far as the defensive end, 100 metres away (a herculean feat when kicks fetching 60 metres are seen as monstrous). Footage of players taking marks is slowed, which would make the skill far more difficult than doing so in real time, then quickly reverted to pace as cameras cut away to the applause of the crowd. The effect is jarring and unnecessary; the game is spectacular in its natural state, pedestrian at half-pace.

●●●

Just as Geoff moves from Tasmania to Melbourne in pursuit of career opportunities and cosmopolitanism, so do thousands of twenty-somethings from outside the big cities every year, including me. It was a job in the arts that lured me in, but the promise of football helped me to stay. With only a handful of friends away from home, my team gave me a sense of familiarity. In the early months I often felt out of place among colleagues who grew up in Melbourne and had school friends to spend weekends with, or those also from out of town who had been there long enough to have built friendship groups of their own. But walking from Jolimont or Richmond station over to the MCG, I had a place to belong.

There's something special about the journey to the game that is at the heart of the sports-crazed city of Melbourne. Walking to the train station and slowly seeing others in club colours swarm around you. On the platform there are those going about lives not structured around the football fixture, who sink at the revelation of the loud, busy carriages they're soon to face. Inside, the train is awash with colour. Kids chatter away to their parents about their favourite players. Knowing smiles are exchanged, conversations are struck in an organic way that feels easy. 'What are our chances today?', 'Do you reckon he'll be okay to play on that dodgy knee?', 'I've got a bad feeling about this match.' And then, the train emerges at the station. A polite farewell is bid to your new friends, 'Enjoy the game, mate,' and the surge towards the ground begins.

As much as I enjoy the large crowds and atmosphere of seeing my team play at the MCG, I, like many others around me, grew up on matches played at local venues like *The Club*'s Victoria Park. Seeing the old-fashioned turnstiles as fans arrive at the oval in the film, the concrete steps around the ground often slick with rain, the old-fashioned grandstands that are somehow still standing despite being old and creaky in the 1970s and '80s – this is what football still looks like for so many today. I spent much of my childhood climbing those concrete steps at suburban ovals, with my stuffed toy tiger under one arm and the *Footy Budget* (the South Australian equivalent of Victoria's *Footy Record*) in the other. I learnt players' names by reading their profiles and noting down goals kicked, and I absorbed by osmosis all my favourite combinations of swear words and sledges by hearing the fans around me when things weren't going our way. Seeing fans of the Collingwood Magpies filling the seats in *The Club*, this same fanaticism is evident.

In the original stage version of *The Club*, there are no scenes outside of the club rooms. While the few that take place outside Victoria Park in the film add to the characters' backstories, particularly Geoff's, the inner sanctum of the club is maintained.

While Ted doesn't sit on the team selection panel, Danny is keen to point out that he 'take[s] two-thirds of 'em into the bar and talk[s] for four hours every Wednesday night'.

'The team's barely discussed,' Ted proffers.

Danny laughs. 'Well, that's not what I heard.'

My family would go to training at the Glenelg Football Club every Thursday evening when I was a kid to see the main session. My grandfather, a 'club man', and his friends would trade in banter about the team, their chances against the upcoming opponent, and the age and abilities of those sitting around the table compared to those slogging it out in the rain on the oval. The scenes in *The Club* where Ted is propping up the bar take me straight back to those evenings. Even the foyer of Victoria Park in the film reminds me of my brother and I asking for coins so we could buy packets of chips from the vending machine. In so many respects, *The Club* captures Australian Rules football not just in Melbourne, but around the country (with the exception of the rugby league states of Queensland and New South Wales).

While my state club, Glenelg, has renovated its rooms since I was a child in the 1980s, it – like Victoria Park – remains a working oval. The Collingwood Football Club in the AFL (Australian Football League) now has training facilities closer to the MCG. The Holden Centre, which cost $25 million to redevelop, sits in Melbourne's Olympic Park, approximately 4 kilometres down Hoddle Street from Victoria Park. The last AFL match played at Victoria Park was in 1999. Writing for *Guardian Australia* twenty years later, Cheryl Critchley from the AFL Fans Association reminisced:

Depending on who you follow, Victoria Park was the holy grail or hell on earth. The rickety terraces of the AFL's most feared suburban venue gave the Magpie army a sense of belonging and power for more than 100 years. Opposition fans entered Vic Park at their peril and not just due to the menacing atmosphere, prehistoric toilets, cigarette smoke and lack of seats.[2]

I remember one of those childhood trips to Melbourne, seated in a train with my family. Like many from the country or interstate, the big city provided a multitude of reasons for getting lost or completely bungling right-hand turns. This time, we had missed our stop. I was elbow-deep in an Enid Blyton book when my parents saw the sign for Victoria Park station and subsequently freaked out, tightly gripping my brother and me as if bracing for impact. Amid the panic it was quickly agreed that we should travel a few more stops before catching a train back in the right direction. For my parents, Victoria Park meant crime. It meant danger. The dirty, gritty, inner-city suburb was a long way away from our comfortable Adelaide suburban life.

Critchley, speaking to Collingwood's history and archives manager Michael Roberts in 2019, offers a reminder of the 'tribal atmosphere and connection at grounds like Victoria Park' that fuelled millions of childhoods like mine at Glenelg Oval, across Victoria and around the country.

'It was raw,' [Roberts] says. 'You kind of breathed every-thing in … the sounds and the atmosphere and the closeness of the players to the fence. It was a complete sensory experience.

'You grew up here. People formed lifelong friendships. Victoria Park was not just a place where you came and watched footy. It was our place. It was full of meaning and it was full of connections.'[3]

In recent years, Collingwood's women's side have brought life back to the suburban oval that's home to *The Club*. Regularly hosting AFL Women's games, the grandstands are a little worse for wear but still provide shelter from the sun and rain, the gates remain the same, and the 1990s paint job is faded but yet to be hidden. It may feel impossible to think of Jock Riley turning up to watch the 'sheilas' play, but it's a special kind of wonderful to know that the progress of the women's game is what's keeping the bastions of old grounds like Victoria Park alive.

●●●

Collingwood has its own particular legend within Australian folklore that Williamson taps into. This is implicit for football fans in the play, but explicit in the film through the guern-seys worn, the setting and the use of then-active players and coaches among the cast. A working-class team from inner-city Melbourne, Collingwood carries a reputation for being particularly physical. Often the victim of classist judgements, fans are ridiculed for their lack of education, their fiery nature and the quality of their teeth. Richmond legend Jack Dyer – a featured commentator in *The Club* – opined: 'An Essendon supporter is a Collingwood supporter who can read and write.'[4]

In his book *The Football Solution*, political journalist (and fellow Tigers supporter) George Megalogenis writes of the era when the fledgling competition began to build against a backdrop of enormous change in Melbourne's inner suburbs: 'When the depression of the 1890s hit, the middle class moved out to the leafy suburbs, or left Melbourne altogether. Almost 50,000 people – around 10 per cent of Melbourne's total population – fled the capital between 1891 and 1893. Most headed to the Western Australian gold rush, taking football with them.'[5]

Suburbs like Collingwood were left like ghost towns, inhabited only by the poorest residents. With a cessation of industry in favour of mining gold in the country, inner-city mansions became slums, unemployment rates climbed exponentially and charities were overrun with people seeking food and basic supplies. Although Collingwood today is highly gentrified, the suburb – as well as the football team – has never altogether shaken its working-class roots. Megalogenis writes: '[W]e started playing [Aussie Rules] in the long boom of the nineteenth century, when Melbourne and Victoria were marvellous, but it was the bust that taught us how to barrack.'[6]

Australians are never more invested in sport than when battling – a sentiment reflected in the recent Covid-riddled football seasons. A Roy Morgan survey released in September 2021 found that '[o]ver 8.8 million Australians now support an AFL club, up over 1.3 million on a year ago'.[7] It is the teams like Collingwood, whose fanatical members and fans turn up week after week, rain or shine, that sustain the league. When wealthier teams' fans retreat to the snow season as their side starts to slump (a regular jibe directed at followers of the Melbourne Demons), supporters of working-class sides such as Collingwood and Western Bulldogs keep the competition alight.

Collingwood hasn't always rewarded the loyalty and ferocity of its fans on the field, but that only adds to their folklore. Club legend Lou Richards – who appears alongside Dyer in *The Club* as a commentator – coined the term 'Colliwobbles' for the particular curse that is said to haunt the team. The Colliwobbles were at their peak just as *The Club* is set, with 1977 (the year of the first stage production, by the Melbourne Theatre Company) providing a drawn grand final followed by a loss in the decider the following week, and 1979, 1980 and 1981 seeing Collingwood lose in grand finals. When Collingwood finally beat their own curse and won a premiership in 1990, Richards staged a burial of the Colliwobbles at Victoria Park. I remember watching as a child and feeling overawed at the mysticism involved. With Collingwood's reputation for being especially brutish, the juxtaposition of laying this curse to rest right where their players' spiked boots pivot, their bodies crunch in tackles, their water is spat into muddy puddles, has stayed with me ever since.

In 2018, after leading the West Coast Eagles for the majority of the premiership decider, Collingwood lost by five points after a miraculous, technically astounding goal by Dom Sheed sealed the win with less than two minutes left to play. *The Age*'s match summary that evening is titled 'Colliwobbles Return as Eagles Claim Grand Final for the Ages'.[8]

●●●

The Club draws on the Mike Brady song 'Up There Cazaly' as its primary soundtrack. Written to advertise VFL on Channel Seven in 1979, it is an ode to the high-leaping ruck Roy Cazaly who played 198 games for St Kilda and South Melbourne from 1911 to 1927. As iconically Australian as the game itself, the tune is an original anthem, unlike the military songs many of the Aussie Rules clubs repurposed to create their own victory celebrations. Indeed, writing about the song in *Guardian Australia* in 2014, sportswriter Geoff Lemon reports the phrase 'Up There Cazaly' was used by Australian soldiers on the Kokoda Trail and while on duty in North Africa. Lemon writes that while these claims 'have an apocryphal tinge, [the] mythology did Cazaly's folk hero status no harm. Brady performed its final act of confirmation.'[9]

The song is – like much of *The Club* – a celebration of the game before it became a professional pursuit. It is an ode to weekend warriors, players and fans alike, summated in the first and only verse. 'Up There Cazaly' opens with a reflection that weekdays are 'to earn a living'; while Brady doesn't make the distinction clear, there is a homey sentiment to this line that separates itself from the upper class and managers of the workplace. Weekdays are for 'the man', an endless grind to support one's family. Weekends, however, are for workers to do as they please. Footy, being the ultimate recreation for players and fans alike, is a balm against demanding bosses, long hours and financial concerns.

In the years immediately following *The Club*'s release, the VFL became increasingly professional. Players from around the country were fetching increasing wages and bonuses, not dissimilar to Geoff Hayward's signing in the film. Clubs with wealthy benefactors such as Ted Parker were able to stay afloat. Big-name players brought interest from fans and large numbers of supporters through the turnstiles, reaping financial rewards in return for the risk taken. Buying players is 'good economics', as Jock tells Laurie. Better players mean a greater chance of winning premierships, and 'if we win a premiership,' Jock says, 'it will arrest the membership decline, and members mean money!'

Outside the film, smaller clubs in the VFL – Fitzroy and South Melbourne in particular – were unable to keep up. Fitzroy was eventually forced to merge with Brisbane in 1996 after

South Melbourne was relocated to Sydney in 1982. Throughout the late 1980s and across the 1990s more and more teams from outside Victoria were created so that the VFL became a national competition and was subsequently renamed the Australian Football League in 1990. Despite the league going national, Victoria retains its stronghold on the administration of the sport.

With this professionalism, players gained more and more power. In *The Club*, we see the team storm into the boardroom to fight for their coach. One by one they remove the photos adorning the walls of years gone by, making a statement that the club will never regain those heights if they do not listen to the men who take the bumps and bruises in the name of entertainment. It is in line with action seen in club rooms, beginning in the 1970s, when Essendon player Geoff Pryor steeped himself in research into players' unions in sports outside Australia.[10] Pryor began to speak to competitors from outside his club about protecting players from the game's administration. The VFL Players' Association was formed in December 1973, before changing its name to the AFL Players' Association (AFLPA) in 1990 in line with the national competition.

The year 1990 also saw the start of the Collective Bargaining Agreement reached between the league and the AFLPA, a move that no doubt would have been an affront to the Teds and Jocks of the world. Since coming into action, players are less likely to have part-time or indeed full-time jobs in order to supplement their income from playing. This battle is currently at its peak in the AFLW, and it is a move foreshadowed in *The Club* when Geoff Hayward and his management sit at the boardroom table negotiating his payment. Geoff refuses to take the fee originally on offer because he will see so little of it. A shrewd self-advocate, football is his primary source of income – something that differentiates him from many of his teammates (including his captain, Danny) who, it's bandied, play for pride in the jumper and little else. *The Club* not only reflects this era of the game; it acts as a historical record, albeit a farcical one.

●●●

In April 2019, I sat in Adelaide's Space Theatre wearing a Richmond sweatshirt, uncharacteristically attired for the theatre. As the rest of the audience filed in, I saw someone point to a man seated on the opposite side of the stalls. In a town obsessed with Australian Rules football such an act is not uncommon. Tall men, whose heads float above the crowds, are treated like gods. 'Is that ...?', 'I think that's ...', 'Look!', are the muffled queries that permeate cafes and shopping centres, but rarely theatres. Here was a giant, clearly revered, spending a Friday evening at the Adelaide Festival Centre. But this time there was no follow-up 'Who does he play for again?'. Here was the playwright, David Williamson. As imposing as a retired foot-baller, the slim 213 cm now eighty-year-old quietly took his seat alongside his wife. It was opening night of *The Club*, although this time his satirical jibe at the masculine culture of Australian Rules football would be performed by feminist theatre group isthisyours? in an 'all-female, three actor version'. As the lights went down and the play began, I couldn't stop myself from occasionally glancing back in Williamson's direction. Just as the film ends with Ted watching the team run out from his couch at home, Williamson was inextricably tied to the play, but had relinquished control. Forty-five years after the first theatre pro-duction and its subsequent film adaptation, *The Club* – whether on stage or screen – remains as subversive as ever.

Notes

1   Peter Craven, 'The Irresistible Rise and Occasional Fall of David Williamson', *The Sydney Morning Herald*, 20 October 2021.
2   Cheryl Critchley, 'Tears on the Terraces: 20 Years On, Collingwood Fans Still Miss "Vic Park"', *Guardian Australia*, 28 August 2019.
3   Ibid.
4   Richmond Football Club, 'Jack's "Dyerisms"', 14 November 2014.
5   George Megalogenis, *The Football Solution: How Richmond's Premiership Can Save Australia*, Penguin Books, Melbourne, 2019.
6   Ibid.
7   Roy Morgan, 'AFL supporter bases boom in 2020/21 as lockdowns keep people at home and "glued" to the action on TV', 21 September 2021.
8   Andrew Wu, 'Colliwobbles Return as Eagles Claim Grand Final for the Ages', *The Age*, 29 September 2018.
9   Geoff Lemon, '"Up There Cazaly" by Mike Brady – an AFL Anthem that Isn't Awful', *Guardian Australia*, 4 November 2014.
10 AFL Players, 'About', https://www.aflplayers.com.au/about, accessed 12 February 2022.

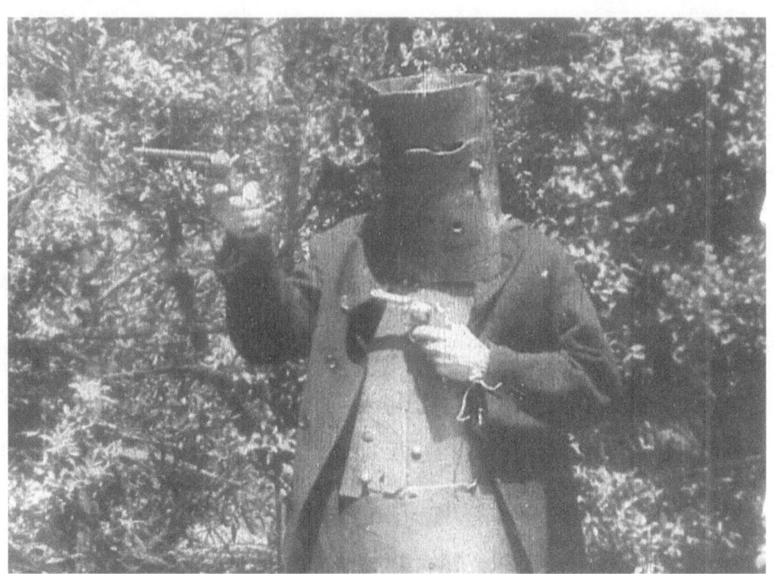

Still from *The Story of the Kelly Gang* courtesy of the National Film and Sound Archive of Australia (NFSA).

The Story of the Kelly Gang

Martin Flanagan

When Ned Kelly was hanged in the Old Melbourne Gaol on 11 November 1880, my grandfather, Patrick Flanagan, was eleven years old. Patrick's grandfather had been an Irish convict transported to Van Diemen's Land around the same time Ned's father was. My father once told me that the Kelly saga was the great romantic story of Patrick's boyhood.

When *The Story of the Kelly Gang* premiered at Melbourne's Athenaeum Theatre on Boxing Day 1906, my grandfather was thirty-seven. So that's one perspective from which to view the phenomenon of *The Story of the Kelly Gang* – much of its audience had a detailed living memory of the story, in the way that much of the audience had a detailed living memory of the Lindy

Chamberlain story when the Fred Schepisi movie *Evil Angels* opened in 1988. In 1906, Ned's mother was still alive, as was his brother Jim.

The Story of the Kelly Gang, commonly described as the world's first full-length feature film, had live commentary between the scenes, so the final product is perhaps more accurately described as a documentary with reconstructions than a feature film. It was hugely successful, returning £25,000 on an investment of £1000. As American Westerns had yet to arrive in Australia, the film established a genre and has been likened to D.W. Griffith's *Birth of a Nation* in terms of 'giving birth' to a sense of national identity. Within six years, however, it was banned in Victoria. New South Wales went further, banning 'bushranger' films altogether – a ban that apparently stood until the 1940s, by which time the print of *The Story of the Kelly Gang* was thought lost.

Ned Kelly's critics ritually dismiss him as a common criminal. He was anything but common. In a 1911 interview in Sydney newspaper *The Sun*, Alexander Fitzpatrick, the policeman with whom the Kelly Outbreak began, said of Ned, 'Considering his environment, he was a superior man. He possessed great natural ability and under favourable circumstances would probably have become a leader of good men in society.'[1] A bank manager who Ned robbed described him as 'a splendid specimen of the human kind, tall, active, rather handsome'.[2]

He was in trouble with the police from the age of fourteen. At sixteen, he was pulled from a horse by a policeman. They wrestled on the ground. Ned won. He got the policeman face-down in the dirt and dug his spurs into the trooper's thighs – in Ned's words, the trooper 'roared like a big calf attacked by dogs and shifted several yards of the fence'. Ned was pistol-whipped for that.

Aaron Sherritt was the member of the 'flash mob' from Greta who could best match Ned within the realm of his special abilities – bushcraft, horse riding, bare-knuckle fighting. Sherritt told a senior Victorian police officer, 'I look upon Ned Kelly as an extraordinary man, there is no man in the world like him – he is superhuman. I look on him as invulnerable; you can do nothing with him.'[3] The Kelly gang would eventually murder Sherritt, believing him – possibly wrongly – to be a police informer.

Ned's skill in the bush was the reason the police took so long – two years – to capture him. It's also why a major turning point in the saga was the Victorian police bringing in a detachment of native police from Queensland in March 1879. After that, Ned was no longer in his element – he was in their element. Ned and his three companions became the hunted, having to ride long distances every night to give them a day's space on the trackers. That's when Ned decided to make a stand and planned the operation remembered as the Glenrowan Siege, employing tactics used by Boer farmers in their war against the British in South Africa the following decade.

As the police learnt to their detriment at Stringybark Creek, Ned was a crack shot. He was a highly accomplished horseman – he could gallop a horse with his feet out of the stirrups and held to the sides of the animal's neck.[4] He was also a boxing champion. That's one of the few photos we have of him – in boxing pose. He wears long white underwear, a pair of silk shorts over the top. As a sportswriter I can't help noting he holds his fists low – halfway down his chest. It's the pose of one who has the confidence to invite his enemy towards him. He looks fierce. He'd just done three years in prison for being in possession of a stolen horse. Ned claimed he didn't know it was stolen; he was looking after it for Wild Wright, who didn't tell him it was stolen. At the age of nineteen, Ned fought Wild Wright out the back of a Beechworth pub and was declared champion of North East Victoria.

Ned's father, John 'Red' Kelly, was an Irish convict sentenced to Van Diemen's Land (now Tasmania) in 1842 for stealing a pig. He was tall and handsome, but he drank too much and there is speculation that he had acted as a police informer back in Tipperary.[5] Red Kelly died in 1866 after a spell of imprisonment for stealing meat, leaving twelve-year-old Ned as the man of the house.

Red Kelly can be seen as a man broken by the convict system and the attitudes that surrounded it. In 1853, *The Argus* newspaper observed of Victoria's senior judge Sir Redmond Barry, an Irish Protestant, that he gave ex-convicts one-and-a-half times the penalty that he gave men who had arrived as free settlers, 'so convinced is he of the hideousness of having the land overridden with fugitive convicts'.[6] Sir Redmond saw himself as a nation builder. He was integral to the establishment of the University of Melbourne and the State Library of Victoria, his statue standing outside the latter. The colony, now state of Victoria is very much a product of the Victorian Age. Sir Redmond is one of the pre-eminent Victorians. Ned Kelly is his antithesis.

The dominant personality in Ned's life was his mother, Ellen Kelly (nee Quinn). Significantly, Ellen was not a product of convict culture – however, she was forged in sectarian politics. The Quinns were free settlers from Northern Ireland; what's more, they came from the same town as the Protestant firebrand of the 1970s, the reverend Ian Paisley. In the wake of the gold rush, the most significant sub-group in the Victorian police was Irish Protestants, but it must be noted that of the three policemen Ned shot and killed at Stringybark Creek on 25 October 1878, two were not Protestants. Two were Irish Catholics.

The incident that sparked the Kelly Outbreak occurred on 15 April 1878, when Constable Alexander Fitzpatrick, some say in an inebriated state, rode up to the Kelly shanty in Greta. The Kellys claimed Constable Fitzpatrick, who had a reputation as a womaniser, made an improper approach towards Ned's fifteen-year-old sister, Kate. In the scuffle that ensued, Fitzpatrick claimed Ned grazed him with a shot from two yards. Ned scoffed at the idea that he'd miss anyone from two yards and claimed he wasn't there. Constable Fitzpatrick was sacked from the force two years later, the Chief Commissioner of Victoria Police, Frederick Standish, saying, 'The ex-Constable's conduct during the time he was a member of the force was generally bad and discreditable to the force.'[7] On the basis of Fitzpatrick's evidence, Sir Redmond Barry sentenced Ned's mother to three years hard labour, separating her from her newborn baby. Kelly biographer Ian Jones reports that, upon being returned to her cell, Ellen remarked ominously, 'There will be murder now.'[8]

In the 1920s, following the release of a book titled *The Girl Who Helped Ned Kelly*, Ned's brother Jim (who lived until 1946) declared dismissively, 'My brother was so devoted to his mother he had no "girl".'[9] J.J. Kenneally, who wrote *The Inner History of the Kelly Gang* in 1929 with the assistance of relatives, reported that upon hearing of his mother's imprisonment on Fitzpatrick's evidence, Ned declared, 'I will make the name of Ned Kelly ring for generations.' One hundred and twenty years later, songwriters Paul Kelly and Mick Thomas put it this way in their song 'Our Sunshine':

There came a man on a stolen horse

And he rode right onto the page

Burning bright but not for long

Lit up with a holy rage ...

Ned was an original. As Booker prize winner Peter Carey recognised when he read Ned's manifesto, known as the Jerilderie Letter, it represents a novel literary style – Carey declared he beheld 'an avant-garde artist without a comma to his name'.[10] Reading the Jerilderie Letter is like reading *Huckleberry Finn* if it were written by American outlaw Jesse James. Then there's the costume: the armour and helmet. Ned had a sense of theatre. When he was eleven, he saved a child from drowning and the grateful family awarded him a green sash. He wore the sash under his armour at Glenrowan.

When Ned staggered out of the dawn mist, banging on his armour with his pistol, and clanked towards the small army of troopers surrounding the Glenrowan hotel on 29 June 1880, no-one knew who or what he was. One of the journalists present, Thomas Carrington of *The Australasian Sketcher*, described it thus: 'Presently we noticed a very tall figure in white stalking slowly along in the direction of the hotel. There was no head visible, and in the dim light of morning, with the steam rising from the ground, it looked, for all the world, like the ghost of Hamlet's father with no head, only a very long, thick neck ...'[11]

Another witness to the day, a Scottish bank clerk from nearby Oxley, wrote, 'Ned Kelly, from his appearance in the imperfect light, looked like some unearthly being, on whom bullets had no effect ... The police thought he was a fiend, seeing their rifle bullets were sliding off him like hail'.[12] According to the Scotsman's account, 'they were firing into him at about ten yards'.

Several hours earlier, Ned had been wounded three times during what has since been called 'the first volley'. He now advanced on sixty armed men, pistol resting on his useless left arm, his intention being to draw their fire away from the besieged hotel where his three companions were, not knowing one of them was already dead. When a policeman aimed and fired at Ned's legs, he toppled and fell beneath the weight of his armour, which the Scottish bank clerk wrote amounted to 97 pounds (44 kilograms).

The fact that there were journalists present at Glenrowan meant Ned's last stand amounted to a press conference. A telegraph wire to Perth, which had been connected only three years earlier, meant the story flashed around Australia. Melbourne's *The Age* had just converted to technology that allowed for the printing of black-and-white drawings. If Vietnam was, as is said, the first television war, Ned was the first illustrated bushranger.

Through Shane Carmody's essay in the autumn 2004 edition of *The La Trobe Journal*, I learnt of a manuscript written by Thomas McIntyre, the only policeman to survive the shoot-out with the Kelly gang at Stringybark Creek. It seems that McIntyre left the force the following year with what would now be called PTSD.[13] At the time, McIntyre's courage was publicly questioned. Ironically, the person who declared he was not a coward was Ned. In the Jerilderie Letter, Ned wrote, 'he is as good a man, as wears the (police) jacket'.

McIntyre was one of four heavily armed policemen, with body straps on their horses, who had come looking for the Kellys. Ned believed their intention was to return him and his brother to the nearby town of Mansfield as 'masses of animated gore'. When the police party split up, Ned held up the two remaining at camp. What followed is the subject of ongoing controversy, but Thomas McIntyre was left with one of his companions, Thomas Lonigan, dead nearby, and was talking to Ned.

McIntyre made a 'strong appeal' on behalf of the two absent policemen, Kennedy and Scanlon:

I told him that they were both countrymen and co-religionists of his own. That one of them was the father of a large family, and that the other was a good-natured inoffensive man liked by everybody. This statement that they were countrymen of Kelly's was not strictly true, for Kelly was Australian born, but his father came from Tipperary and his mother from Armagh, and I thought he might be possessed of some of that patriotic-religious feeling which is such a bond of sympathy amongst the Irish people. My opinion is that he possessed none of this feeling. On the question of religion I believe he was apathetic, and like a great many young bushmen he prided himself more on his Australian birth than he did upon his extraction from any particular race. A favourite expression of his was: 'I will let them see what one native can do'.

Ned was, to use the expression of the day, native-born. He had a native style – it was called being 'flash'. It was a style of the post-convict generation – a generation that saw the world anew, in a way that was wholly unlike their cowed parents. When Ned was asked where the gang was headed after robbing the Euroa bank, he replied, 'Oh, the country belongs to us. We can go where we like.'[14] The police explicitly sought to take 'the flashness' out of the Kellys. The original police order to harass the Kellys said they were to be subjected to a campaign that robbed them of their 'prestige' – their 'flashness' – in the eyes of people in the district.[15]

Over the years, some have insisted the Kelly saga is an expression of 'the Irish civil war' acted out in a foreign land. It's more than that – Ned is about a whole new idea of Australia. If you want to immerse yourself in the psychology of a penal colony, read Franz Kafka's short story *In the Penal Colony* – it's a whole other world permeated with fear where order is cruelly and imaginatively enforced. Ned's generation is the first one beyond that – in Ned's words, they determined to live 'bold and fearless and free'.

To me, as someone who comes from convict culture, whose family history is rooted in that nineteenth-century group known as Vandemonians and whose great-grandfather was a bushranger, Ned is the person who says, louder and more articulately than any other, 'You're not treating me as a convict. I'm free born.' It's a cry that native-born kids of subsequent waves of migrants can identify with. The people Ned grew up among wanted what they called 'equal justice'.

In the 1940s, while on the run as an army deserter, Sidney Nolan painted his famous series of Ned Kelly paintings. He wrote, in 1948, 'I find the desire to paint the landscape involves a wish to hear more of the stories that take place in the landscape ... which persist in the memory, to find expression in such household sayings as "game as Ned Kelly".'[16] Through Ned, he found a way of painting the Australian landscape. He found a figure that fitted: this man in a mask whose face we never see. Nolan is not concerned with the man, he's concerned with the legend, with the story stamped on the landscape.

Artist David Band borrowed Nolan's image for the cover of Paul Kelly's 1994 album, *Wanted Man*. It's a double pun – the guitar in the illustration is Nolan's helmeted Kelly figure held vertically. Ned keeps morphing, keeps jumping cultures. I once found a way to describe Ned to a Muslim friend by using the word 'jihad'. In her 1992 book, *Dingo Makes Us Human*, Deborah Bird Rose states that in north-western Australia the Yarralin people told a story that Captain Cook took Ned Kelly back to England where his throat was cut. The story continues: 'They bury him. Leave him. Sun go down, little bit dark now, he left this world. BOOOOOMMMMM! Go longa top. This world shaking. All the white men been shaking. They all been frightened.'

In 1997, I spent a day with two traditional artists from the Kimberley, Gidja men Paddy Bedford and Hector Jandany. They had come to Melbourne to see two things – the MCG and where Ned Kelly was hanged. Standing beneath the steel trap-door at Old Melbourne Gaol, Hector had tears running down his face. He told me his mother used to sing the song that Ned Kelly sang the night before he died.

The showdown between Sir Redmond Barry and Ned came on 29 October 1880, the second day of Ned's trial for the murder of Constable Thomas Lonigan at Stringybark Creek. The court transcript shows their exchange was fierce and nakedly open.[17]

Upon being advised of the jury's guilty finding, Ned insisted he could have cleared himself of the charge had he questioned the witnesses. Barry barked back: 'The verdict of the jury is irresistible!'

Ned said this was only the first trial – there would be a second trial 'in another place' where both he and Sir Redmond would be judged. Sir Redmond sought to end the exchange. This is from the court transcript:

Sir Redmond: 'It is painful in the extreme to perform the duty which I now have to discharge, and I will confine myself strictly to it. I do not think anything I can say would aggravate the pain you must now be suffering.'

Kelly: 'No! I declare before you, God and man that my mind is as easy and clear as it can possibly be.' (uproar in Court)

Crier: 'Silence in the Court!'

Sir Redmond: 'It is blasphemy to say so.'

Sir Redmond proceeded to pass the sentence that Ned be taken to another place and hanged by the neck until dead. In doing so, he laid out what he considered to be the moral of the story:

Unfortunately, in a new community, where society is not bound together so closely as it should be, there is a class which disregards the consequences of crime and looks upon the perpetrators of crimes as heroes.

These unfortunate youths, said Sir Redmond, are led astray by felons they regard as self-made heroes. Sir Redmond then defined a felon as someone who has

cut himself off from all the affections, charities and obligations of society [and] is as helpless and degraded as a wild beast of the field. He has nowhere to lay his head, he has no-one to prepare for him the comforts of life. He suspects his friends, he dreads his enemies, he is in constant alarm lest his pursuers should reach him … that is the life of the outlaw or felon.

Kelly: 'An outlaw!'

That is, he is not a felon.

Sir Redmond pronounced the awful sentence of death, normally delivered to hushed courtrooms. He had scarcely finished when Ned said: 'I will go a little further than that and say I will see you there where I go.'

Ned Kelly, aged twenty-five and with his limbs pinioned, fell 8 feet before the hangman's rope snapped tight and broke his neck. He took four minutes to die. His mother, in the prison laundry, heard the clang of the trapdoor open. Sir Redmond Barry died twelve days later of blood poisoning from a boil on his neck.

In the 1890s, a Melbourne lawyer claimed he had a tobacco pouch made of Ned's scrotum. A skull purporting to be his turned up in the Kimberley in the 2000s. In 2013, after Ned's remains were handed back to his descendants, he was buried beside his mother in Greta cemetery under a thick layer of concrete to deter souvenir-seekers.

Identifying him simply as a common criminal serves to eliminate the social and political dimensions of the story. Realising Ned had a network of supporters, the government locked up those they termed 'Kelly sympathisers'. Even after Ned was hanged, there was fear of further outbreaks in the region. Kelly biographer Ian Jones takes seriously stories that there were plans afoot to create a Republic of North Eastern Victoria. In the twelve days between Sir Redmond sentencing Ned to death and the actual execution, a Melbourne petition calling for clemency got 32,000 signatures.

The Ned Kelly story is like live ammunition. You can hide it and you can put it away but it can always go off. In 1883, three years after Ned was hanged, two juvenile delinquents aged eighteen and nineteen were hanged in Hobart after a double murder in which the perpetrators fancied themselves members of the Kelly gang. When captured, they sang Kelly songs and maintained what they considered an outlaw demeanour in court. They had lost their bravado by the time they mounted the scaffold. Launceston's *The Examiner* published a graphic account of the 'execution' (a euphemism for a grotesque and unnatural death), the mother of one of the delinquents quoted as blaming their fate on them reading a history of the Kelly gang.

At the same time, more than 100 Kelly folk songs emerged. This one was recorded in 2010 by Shane Howard, writer of iconic Australian song 'Solid Rock':

Farewell Dan and Edward Kelly,

Farewell Stevie Hart and Joe Byrne too,

With the poor your memory lingers.

Those who blame you are but few.

That special witness to the Kelly saga, the former Constable MacIntyre, wrote in 1900, 'The press records of the Kelly gang in the Melbourne public library are very much mutilated and if the character and career of the outlaws depended upon tradition I imagine that in course of time Kelly would come to occupy a position in history similar to that occupied by Robin Hood ...'

It was the success of Ned Kelly stage shows that persuaded two theatre entrepreneurs, John and Nevin Tait, to make *The Story of the Kelly Gang*. Such was their confidence, they went beyond the accepted format of one scene equalling one film and put together a sequence of six scenes.

The opening scene would have made Redmond Barry turn in his grave. To some extent – a considerable extent, in fact – he had lost the argument. The filmmakers took their plot from what Constable McIntyre called 'the tradition', by starting with Constable Alexander Fitzpatrick turning up at the Kelly hut in Greta and making a pass at Kate Kennedy, thus bringing the credibility of the police – and the authority of the state – immediately into question.

I have only read general accounts, but it seems the Victorian government wasn't happy with the film. The government banned it from being shown in two towns where Kelly support was strong – Beechworth, where Ned became boxing champion of the North East, and Wangaratta. The film was shown in Ballarat. It's said that a group of kids saw the film, robbed a pharmacy, and held another group of kids at gunpoint. *The Story of the Kelly Gang*, six years after it premiered to enthusiastic audiences and drew crowds wherever it went, was banned in Victoria. In New South Wales, it started a genre of 'bushranger' pictures. In 1915, New South Wales banned the genre.

If the poet Lord Byron, an outlaw in his way, can be described as England's first rock star, then Ned Kelly is Australia's first rock star. They both became overnight sensations by assaulting head-on the way their societies depicted themselves. I don't claim to know who Ned was – not really. I'm like Sidney Nolan, I can't see his face. I never get to the end of understanding him – there's always something else to learn and, with that, the picture changes. But I do dare to suggest he's the most powerful whitefella story this land has produced – what other story has travelled as far, to as many places, to as many different people, and remains vital today? It's primal stuff – mother/son, rebel/outlaw. Opinions about him are as divided as ever, but the issues he embodies are timeless – that's his power. The first film about him was shut down, but no matter. The Ned Kelly story is live.

Notes

1　National Museum of Australia and Ryebuck Media, 'In Search of Ned Kelly'.

2　Ian Jones, *Ned Kelly: A Short Life*, Hachette Australia, Sydney, 2008, p. 171.

3　Ibid., p. 205.

4　Ibid., p. 170.

5　Ibid., p. 3.

6　State Library of Victoria, 'Sir Redmond Barry in Court', Ergo.

7　Creative Victoria and CV Content Contributors, 'The Fitzpatrick Incident', Culture Victoria, 2016.

8　Jones, 2008, p. 124.

9　J.J. Kenneally, *The Inner History of the Kelly Gang*, Melbourne, 1929, p. 201.

10　Peter Carey, 'Peter Carey on *True History of the Kelly Gang*', *The Guardian*, 9 February 2020.

11　Peter FitzSimons, 'Iron Man: The Story of Ned Kelly's Last Stand', *The Sydney Morning Herald*, 3 November 2013.

12　'"Police thought he was a fiend, seeing rifle bullets slide off him": Letter written by man who witnessed death of legendary criminal Ned Kelly reveals details of his last stand', *Daily Mail Australia*, 9 October 2013.

13　Shane Carmody, 'Through Green-Tinted Glasses: Barry, Kelly and Irish Settlement', *The La Trobe Journal: Redmond Barry Number*, no. 73, Autumn 2004.

14　Jones, 2008, p. 171.

15　Kenneally, 1946 [1929], p. 23.

16　Shira Wolfe, 'Lost (and Found) Artist Series: Sidney Nolan, Australia's (Almost) Forgotten Art Superstar', *Artland*.

17　Ed. Jess O'Brien, 'The Trial of Ned Kelly by John P. Suta, Principal – John Suta Legal', ALA National Conference, 25 October 2013 [May 2017].

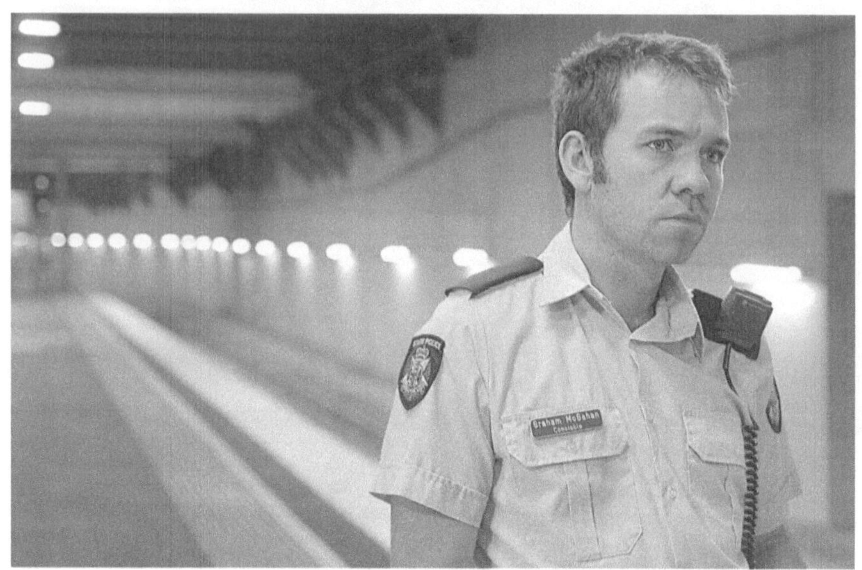

Still from *Noise* courtesy of Madman Entertainment.

Noise

Fiona Murphy

As a child I wanted to be a nun. I longed to wear the habit: a peaked white cap; layers of black; a garland of glass rosary beads, pale blue, strung together with silver and rhythmically passing between my index finger and thumb. Most of all, I wanted to sleep in a small cell. A room that I pictured furnished with a single bunk and a round porthole window to let in light. My daydream wasn't fuelled by any desire to live by the words of the Bible. Or to even to live a life steeped in holy ritual. Mine was an agonistic impression of a nun's life: orderly, peaceful and immense.

At twenty-two years old, following a year of backpacking, I returned to Sydney and moved back into my parents' house where my three siblings still lived. Within hours, I began to look for a share house in earnest. I found an ad for a room for rent. Tucked behind a large Catholic church in Sydney's inner west, the ad specified that the single room was only available to females. Applicants could be of any religious persuasion, as long as they were respectful of living on church grounds. The find felt fortuitous. Sight unseen, I made up my mind quickly and decisively. That afternoon, I told my mother about my plans to move.

'A convent?'

'The rent is cheap and it's only a short walk to the train station. Plus, there's wi-fi included.'

'But a convent?'

I showed her the ad. 'I think it's a former convent that still houses some working nuns. I reckon it'd be more like a boarding house.'

'But Fiona, it says no visitors,' Mum said after closely reading the newspaper ad.

'I can easily hop on the train and visit you on the weekends.'

'Yes, but what about other visitors?'

Her point was salient and corrupting. What was I thinking? Why was I trying to cut myself off from other people? Why was I trying to make my life smaller, more contained?

Within a month or so, I moved into a terrace in Stanmore with three others. The house sat under a flight path and the front door swung open onto a congested road. My room was located at the back of the house, directly above the kitchen. On the floorplan, my room was classified as a study. Even with my bed pushed into the corner and my wardrobe stowed on the stairway landing, I needed to shuffle sideways, crab-like, to move around my new room. But when I pulled the bedroom door shut that night, I experienced a wellspring of feeling. *This* is what I had been searching for since childhood: silence.

•••

Depending on the circumstances, silence can be considered reverent, suspicious, pregnant or withholding. A preamble, a pause, a promise of something to come. A void, an erasure, a space waiting to be filled. For me, silence has always meant safety, both physical and psychic. Born profoundly deaf in my left ear, my relationship with noise has always been confused and vexed. It requires constant vigilance and guesswork for me to decode sounds. Conversations demand a steady gaze and sweat-inducing attentiveness, whereas silence has always offered comfort, security, certainty. It gives me the chance to *think* rather than strain. A chance to daydream, selfishly and with great pleasure. In the words of the poet Judith Wright – whose hearing dipped lower and lower as the bones in her ears, the smallest ones in the entire human body, ossified from otosclerosis – *silence is my habitat.*

●●●

While I felt most comfortable in silence, throughout my twenties I seldom dwelled inside that habitat. I lived and worked and played in the world of sound. As I moved from share house to share house, my desire for silence remained unsatiated. This hunger dictated my days, informing hundreds of decisions: choosing to walk alone through backstreets instead of commuting via public transport; messaging friends instead of calling; forgoing TV shows or films in favour of books; running outside in the cold, the wet, the dark, instead of inside the large, sterile gym where heavy bass music bellowed day and night. It would take deliberate, conscious work to secure stretches of silence within each day. But without it, I risked tumbling into terrible moods, labile and extreme.

●●●

I am not alone in my obsessions. Acoustic ecologist Gordan Hempton has spent over forty years travelling the globe, recording natural soundscapes. He suggests that 'quietness', or natural silence, is rapidly becoming extinct. Noise is most commonly described as unwanted sound.

Some of the implications of noise can be masked in a kind of distressing beauty. Research from the University of Melbourne shows that birds living in urban environments sing differently to members of the same species living in rural locations. Their songs and calls have become louder, slower and higher pitched to be heard over the din of traffic.

The impact on humans can be somewhat more mundane, but insidious and cascading: headaches, raised blood pressure, heart disease, sleep disturbances, annoyance, depression, anxiety, cognitive impairment. If exposed for long enough or in excessive quantities, it can truncate your lifespan. Perhaps, this is not surprising. The word 'noise' is most readily paired with either complaint or pollution. Some suggest that it is derived from the Latin word *nausea* ('disgust, annoyance, discomfort'), whereas others suggest its origins lie in *noxia* ('hurting, injury, damage'). And, when held in the mouth, the word, at least for me, has the sticky residue of trouble and ill will.

Matthew Saville's decision to call his debut feature film *Noise* feels both playful and assertive. It is a title that demands attention. And the film is exactly what it says on the tin, the score is a mess of sound: confusing, relentless, and aggressively pushing itself to the foreground. Simply put, the film's soundscape is the stuff of life.

●●●

Inspired by musique concrète, sound designer Emma Bortignon composed the film's score by layering hundreds of recorded sounds. In an interview with The National Film and Sound Archive (NFSA), Bortignon explained that she enjoyed the 'data management' aspect of the creative process. This is a rather gentle, workaday description for a composition that pushed the boundaries of Australian film and earnt Bortignon an AACTA/ AFI Award. It implies a neatness, a clean order, that does not exist within the film.

Here, sound takes centre stage. Arising from the murk of darkness, before any images appear, the film opens with the distant squeal and clatter of a train running along tracks. The sound is discordant and distorted. It carries all the qualities of an omen: vague but alerting. What follows is the discovery of seven murdered commuters. Their bodies slashed and bobbing along in a train doing laps around Melbourne. Within seconds an association between noise and violence has been seeded in the viewer. From there, commonplace items are amplified, becoming sonically charged: the clink of a teaspoon along the lip of a porcelain mug; footsteps, heavy on concrete or dragged through grass and gravel; the high-pitched whine of a toy car; the filthy suck of a cigarette.

'Sound finds those little pockets and can fill them in,' explains Bortignon. 'They are the sort of moments that I'm always looking for – what's happening off-screen that can inform the story? What's the sound of this character's handbag? [How] can [it] aid some sort of aspect of who they are, or their inner thinking or inner working at this moment?'

And this is where the score hews staggeringly close to real life – as viewers, we are pulled inside Constable Graham McGahan's head. A place that he is finding increasingly difficult, even torturous, to inhabit.

●●

We meet Constable Graham McGahan, hollow-eyed and slouched, on a train platform. The station is just down the line from the massacre. The fluorescent lights illuminate the weary green tinge in McGahan's skin. His radio crackles, a dispatcher requests an update. When McGahan doesn't respond the dispatcher asks again and again: *Melbourne East 818. Melbourne East 818.* McGahan continues to slouch along, looking up and down the empty platform. Eventually, as he circles back to the escalator, his partner in blue yells, 'Can't you hear?'

●●

Silence has never felt isolating to me. It has never implied a sense of solitude, rather the opposite. I feel enlivened by the rush and ease of silence. My body feels expansive, loose, bold. It is less of a yearning, more an inherent or essential need. A way to recover from the daily assault of noise. In seeking silence, my gestures became grander as I entered my late twenties. I now knew what

I wanted. I lost my sense of shyness about desiring quietness, stillness. I began to avoid cafes and pubs and beer gardens. I quit jobs that felt too noisy and that demanded focused listening for hours at a stretch. I eventually moved to Melbourne. With great swaths of the city low-lying, the skyline felt wide and mercifully free of flight paths.

Even after relocating, I continued to seek silence. That was until my early thirties, when silence became a destination that I could no longer cross into, let alone reside within. My body had changed.

It started as a hum. A small nuisance that began in the summer of 2018. At first, I mistook it for a neighbour's over-worked air-conditioning unit. And then a failing fridge. And then a wheezing vacuum cleaner. I switched off power points, slammed my apartment windows closed and drew the curtains. Its persistence rattled me, then rankled me. I spent hours, days, weeks, hunting for the source of the noise. I began to consider leaving Melbourne, moving somewhere quieter. Somewhere I could sink into silence.

The hum shadowed me all summer, insistent and inescapable. I complained to friends that the city was changing. That it was becoming noisier. I looked for places to move to, jobs to apply for. I downloaded a meditation app. Eventually, after several weeks and a brief trip away from the city, I realised that only I was hearing the noise. The hum was coming from within me.

●●●

After a sudden collapse at the train station, his head slamming off the rolling steps of the escalator, McGahan is taken to the hospital. He tells the doctor that he has been experiencing blackouts and dizziness for months. He is diagnosed with tinnitus. There is talk about whether he has a tumour. The small gash on his forehead is cleaned and dressed with a single stitch. And it sits there, prominent and red, giving shape to his invisible torment for the duration of the film. Sometimes I wished I had a mark to point to and say: *Look, this is happening to me inside.*

●●●

'In an evolutionary sense, being able to hear warns us of danger, so the ear has to stay open,' explains audiologist and tinnitus therapist Myriam Westcott. 'That's why we can't close our ears, the way we can close our eyes if we don't want to see something.'

Our conversation happens in 2021, just hours after Melbourne is shaken by an earthquake. I had spent the preceding weeks interviewing people with tinnitus. Those who were born with the noise alive within them, never knowing silence. And those who described it as an 'alien presence', something foreign and invasive, something that just arrived one day. Without prompting, each person I interviewed attempted to recreate the sounds they could hear inside their heads: humming, hissing, clicking, whining, droning, whistling, screeching. It's just like that, they would often say, only worse.

As we talk, Westcott explains the neurophysiological model of tinnitus, which suggests that the body's central nervous system is generating the noise. She speaks at length about how our bodies can respond and reverberate to danger. The subconscious, she explains, 'is almost like the third party in the room, in a way. That part of the brain is very preoccupied with feeling safe.'

Tinnitus, while benign, commonly provokes feelings of distress, grief, rage. It cannot be switched off. Westcott explains that as yet there is no way to eliminate or cure the condition, one can only habituate to the sound. 'And if the tinnitus is seen as a sinister invasion, it's always there,' she says. 'That really does stir the brain up a lot.'

McGahan's tinnitus vaults forward in moments of acute stress. The viewer is not spared from the experience of the unwieldly, high-pitched tone. It appears when McGahan is holding a can of pepper spray. His arms are stretched long, his anger directed towards a drunk man kneeling on the road in front of him. The high-pitched tone returns, but this time he is holding a gun, his body charged with noise.

As the film progresses, McGahan's mood becomes monotone, tightly gripped. He can't even be careless in sleep. Following a night shift, he throws himself on his bed. His arms stretch above him, bone and muscle barricading his ears. The noise unabating.

●●

Bortignon described working on *Noise* as a 'dream job'. She says, 'If I can work on a film where sound drives a character, I probably have the most fun.'

I watch the film in small twenty-minute increments. The score, which is both frightening and awe-inspiring, stays within me. It awakens the hum that somehow in the past two or three years has folded itself into my body. How did Bortignon create something so stirring?

'I had more time than I ever would have imagined,' explains Bortignon, during her interview with the National Film and Sound Archive. 'I had support. I had resources. I had just endless encouragement and I was pushed.'

'Sometimes I thought it was loud enough, and then the director Michael Seville was like, "no, let's turn it up more". And you know it's [with] those kinds of encouragement that you are able to push to the edge and then make a judgement [about the score]. And then pull it back a little bit [if necessary].'

Bortignon admits that going to the edge is 'sort of a little bit scary', but she is always trying to push her work there. '[Sound] can be so driving. It is very much like music, but without being music. It can lead your perception and it can influence story. It can occupy part of the frame that image cannot.'

Sound can speak to something within all of us. As my interview with Westcott wraps up, she tells me, 'The reality is that in the right circumstances, we will all hear the humming of our body.'

It is only when sounds become noise that they can cause terrible discomfort or damage. Westcott explains that most people 'are able to spontaneously habituate to their tinnitus over time'. Even those who are highly distressed, even traumatised, by their tinnitus can be helped to coexist with it.

'The tinnitus gets judged more and more subconsciously, as a boring sound, like any other boring sound,' says Westcott.

There is nothing boring about *Noise*. The tinnitus has texture and truth. It shimmers, hisses, strikes.

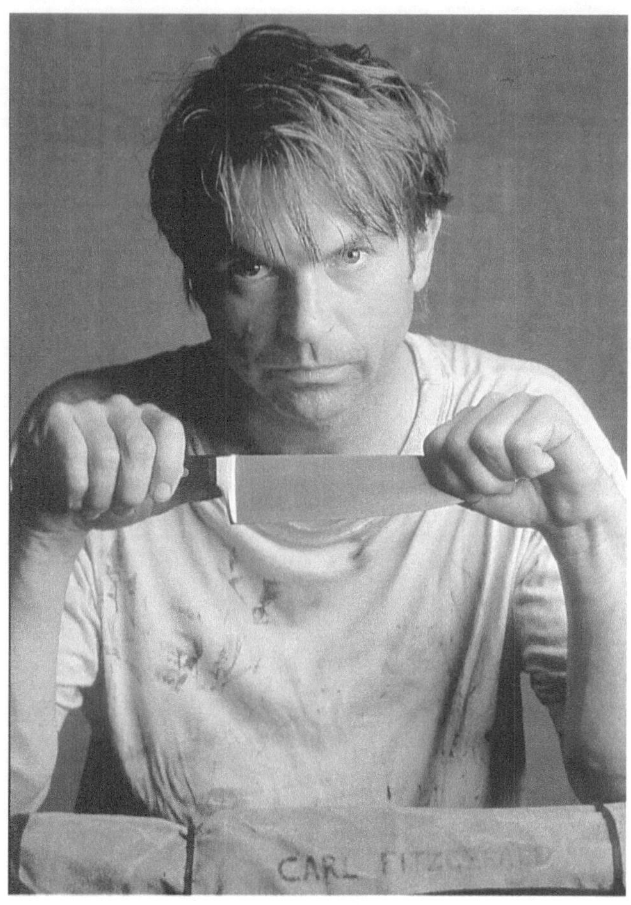

Still from *Death in Brunswick* courtesy of Umbrella Entertainment.
Photographed by Jennifer Mitchell.

Death in Brunswick

Mish Grigor

Our metropolitan streets, our offices and furnished rooms, our railroad stations and our factories appeared to have us locked up hopelessly. Then came the film and burst this prison-world asunder … so that now, in the midst of its far-flung ruins and debris, we calmly and adventurously go travelling.

Walter Benjamin, *The Work of Art in the Age of Mechanical Reproduction*

I can't wait to get out. This place is a hole.

—Me in my diary, talking about Western Sydney, circa 1998

Marooned in Mount Gambier

I once met a bush poet who told me that there are two poets in Australia who make enough money to live from their writing, and they both write about Australia. He also told me that his wife has a lisp, and that he once met Al Pacino.

'It's very important that we keep telling ourselves who we are,' he said. 'That's why *Neighbours* is important. And *Home and Away*. And *The Footy Show*.'

I was marooned in Mount Gambier, waiting for a flight, and though I hated to admit that he and I had something in common, I agreed.

Lost in Brume

Representation is a word that gets thrown around a lot. It's lonely-making when you can't see your likeness anywhere. When you're unsuccessfully looking for yourself on screen, stage and page, it feels like you're lost in a brume, that thick fog with no detectable edges.

I had forgotten the encounter with the poet until one day, deep in Melbourne's long lockdowns, when some masked friend, on some grey perambulation, mentioned to me and my boyfriend that the 1990 movie *Death in Brunswick* was shot round the corner from where we stood.

We rushed home. We made popcorn. My boyfriend excitedly closed the blinds 'for a cinema-like experience'. Our Brunswick. On the big screen!!!

Click Go the Suburbs

Since Australia started being called Australia, we've been nervously obsessed with life 'on the land'. And by land, we mean land outside the cities where most of us live. I remember singing 'Click Go The Shears' in primary school, long before I had any idea what a 'bare-bellied yoe' was.* I feel like every time I turn on Aussie TV, drone shots are sucking up lush coastal spans. You can almost hear the screenwriter purr, 'The landscape is a charming character of its own.' The bush is well represented. It has meaning, it's a personality. But the suburbs? My suburb, Brunswick? Not so well represented. Maybe it needs a better agent.

In *Death in Brunswick*, the story is framed by cheap houses and dirty streets rather than eucalyptus trees and wind-carved rock. Seeing this version of Melbourne on screen is pretty rare. Sure, there's a bunch of films shot here, but the city is rarely the main *thing*, like LA is for *L.A. Story*, Berlin is for *Wings of Desire*, Hong Kong is for *Chungking Express*. This film wasn't just shot in Brunswick, it was about Brunswick, the suburb we couldn't leave.

According to John Clarke, who plays Dave, when the film was screened at the Progress Cinema in Coburg, the location for Carl and Sophie's awkward date, audiences 'stood and applauded

---

* The original line was apparently 'bare-belled ewe', but in the great tradition of poetry we sing bare-bellied yoe. Because it rhymes.

the car driving down Sydney Road'.[1] They were clapping at a representation of their streets.

According to me and my boyfriend, when we watched it in our apartment in Brunswick in the middle of a pandemic lockdown, it was like catching your reflection on the day you've had a new haircut. *Hey, that looks familiar – oh wait! It's me. There I am, huh!*

The Shit Bit of the City

The opening shot of *Death in Brunswick* is of two women clad in black, one pushing a shopping cart that is also black, walking swiftly up a suburban street. The houses on either side of the street are squat, green shrubbery escapes from fences. There's an abandoned car stuffed with a long-dead Christmas tree. The hot asphalt glistens.

It reminds me of Western Sydney, where I grew up. It's the edge of the city; the shit bit. Suburbs built to house a growing population, but not planned with love. Scant parks, everything built quick and on the cheap. At university in Sydney I remember a fellow student saying to me, with a wrinkled nose, 'Well I've never been further west than Central Station. I mean, why would I go out there?' It pissed me off. Although I agreed with the nose, only I was allowed to say that sort of thing, I was from there.

When you live in the shit bit of a city, you know that everyone thinks where you live is a bit shit, and you know that you're a bit shit for being from there.

As a teen, I was desperate to escape. I did, and I enjoyed my twenties in Potts Point, where I had a tiny flat with a glimpse of one of the wires of Sydney Harbour Bridge from the shower window. Then I moved to Brunswick, for a boy, in 2019. I settled in just in time for the pandemic, during which Melbourne gained a reputation for having the longest lockdown in the world.

Fuck Off Home

The lockdown wasn't death in Brunswick, but it wasn't quite life either.

It started slowly. First, playgrounds were cordoned off by faintly threatening strips of hazard tape, then teams of cleaners were employed by the council to traipse up and down the suburb, wiping down poles and pedestrian crossing buttons. Then we were unable to leave a 5-kilometre radius from our homes. Then the army was at the park.

We were only allowed out for an hour of masked exercise a day, and we weren't allowed to stop walking. We dutifully took endless strolls along the Merri Creek, drank long blacks on Sydney Road (hurriedly replacing our masks between sips), and meandered through rows of dead Italians at the Carlton cemetery.

One afternoon, deep in lockdown brain fog and desperate for human interaction, before picnics were officially reinstated and we were allowed to socialise outside, we arranged to 'bump into' some friends at a park. Thousands of Melburnians had the same idea that sunny day, bending the rules by sitting down, chatting, and cracking open tins of beer. It was the first time I heard the hubbub of human chat in months.

We leaned transgressively against a tree for two hours before the cops drove off the road and started zigzagging through the grass, yelling into their police-car microphones: 'Everyone go home! Seriously guys, fuck off home.' We bolted like teenagers caught smoking bongs.

Death in Brunswick Brunswick

I love my Brunswick life in the normal times – I zip between art galleries, theatres, ten zillion cafes, and good bars. But in lockdown I hated it. It was just walking, and looking at houses. So many poky old houses. Once again, I tried to manifest escape.

The bush poet had said to me: 'Next time you're in the bush, stand near a tree. Try to reflect the shape of the tree back to itself. If the tree can see you, showing it what it is, it will feel good. Doubled – even in our clumsy, imperfect way – we give the tree an echo, and it will shimmer back to us. It will stand taller.'

Watching *Death in Brunswick*, seeing the nonnas, we began to shimmer.

The Brunswick of 1990 we see in the film is not that different to Brunswick now. The nonnas and the yiayias still dominate the suburb. My boyfriend and I call our two closest neighbours Nonna 1 and Nonna 2. We can see their backyards from our tiny lounge room. They keep a breezeblock on the concrete near their shared fence so they can climb up and chat, or pass over oranges. They both always seem to have stockings drying on the Hills Hoist.

When we encounter them on the street, they talk to us in speedy southern dialect while we nod helplessly. I can make out a few words from when I spent three months with a family in Napoli in 2002. Something something stupid fucking boys something girls something rubbish bin something my daughter something something something. I translate for my boyfriend, mildly gloating. He raises his eyebrows suspiciously.

By the *Death in Brunswick* point in the lockdown, my boyfriend and I had looked at everything there was to look at in our 5-kilometre circle: the Free Speech monument near the Retreat Hotel (Brunswick's oldest pub), the weird blobby gold monument on Sydney Road (a cast of the biggest nugget found on the Victorian goldfields), the chimneys of the old brick factories, the *Terminator 2*–style storm drain under the freeway in Pascoe Vale. Everything, every day, over and over. Our eyes were fatigued by the sameness.

Finding a film shot right here in our area, everything looked new again. We had an idea: we could re-enact some of the scenes in the very places they were shot! Would this be life imitating art? Or life imitating art imitating life? Whatever it was, it gave us a project, complete with an opening sequence of cranky can-crushing – great for expressing pandemic vexations.

Sam Neill Is My Brother's Bestie

I already felt close to Sam Neill through my brother, Will, a VIP Concierge at a high-end hotel in Sydney who looks after the famous guests in the penthouse suite. Will's job requires discretion, and absolutely no gushing over celebs. This isn't a problem for Will, because he has no idea who anyone is – his interests are strictly planes, *Titanic* and *Jurassic Park*.

One day Sean Connery was 'his' guest. 'Are you in town for work? Mr … Connery?' asks Will, as they ascend to the penthouse in the 'special' lift.

'Yesh, I'm here for a moofie,' says Sean Connery, absolutely nailing the James Bond voice.

'Oh cool! That must be fun. So, are you an actor, or a director, or?' Sean Connery had been extremely famous for a LONG TIME, so in my mind he is finding this pretty funny.

'Yeesh. Asch a matter of fact, I'm an actor.'

'Really? Anything I would've seen?' asks Will.

'Do you know the Bond films?'

'Oh yes! Pierce Brosnan? Cool! You were in those?'

Sean Connery laughed. 'Maybe you could ask your mother – schee may have sheen me in shomething.'

They step out of the lift and walk across plush carpet to the suite.

'Well, Mr Connery, this is your room, please don't hesitate to let us know if you need anything. And good luck with your acting!'

A day later, a script arrives. Will knocks on the heavy wooden door to hand-deliver it.

'Mr Connery. Here is a … script.' I imagine he says it kindly, not wanting the budding actor to get nervous.

'Thansch,' says Sean Connery.

And then Will sees Mr Connery has a guest – Sam Neill.

Jurassic Park Sam Neill.

'OH MY GOD!' squeals my brother, hands to his face. He grabs at the doorframe to steady himself, limbs flopping.

'Ohmygodohmygodohmygod. Mr … Mr Neill! Or should I say, Alan! Alan Grant! Oh my gawd. I'm just – oh my GAWD! I love, I like, like, I really love *Jurassic Park*. Like I am, oh my gawd. Hi! HELLO!'

Presumably, Sam Neill is doing that trademark one eyebrow, half smiling, floppy hair thing.

'This must happen to you all the time!' spurts Will, on the verge of spontaneous combustion.

International superstar Sean Connery watches my brother worship at the feet of 'Kiwi-guy-we-claim-as-our-own-who-has-done-pretty-bloody-well-in-the-flicks' Sam Neill.

Eventually William regains his strength.

'Mr Neill. It is my honour to have you here,' says Will, aware of how hot his face feels. He scrambles around Mr Connery's room, grabs a notepad, and gets Sam Neill's autograph on the hotel stationery.

This story has entered Grigor family lore, told regularly at birthdays or to invited guests at family 'do's. It's also a good connection should I ever have to play 'six degrees of separation' at a dinner party, because if I'm two degrees from Sean Connery, I'm pretty much part of Hollywood society. For Will, however, the story is all about the hand brush he had with the handsome Sam Neill in the exchange of the cheap hotel biro.

It's hard to imagine that suave, five-star hotel superstar pal Mr Neill is the same insalubrious ne'er-do-well of *Death in Brunswick* – but then again, that's acting for you.

Life in Western Sydney

In the film, the women-in-black add another dead Christmas tree to the car, stepping over broken glass and abandoned tinsel, and go about their day. We cut to some rubbish rattling around in a gutter, the cans that Carl (Sam Neill) stomps. I'm still thinking about Western Sydney.

Chontelle Butcher (her real name) and I met at high school and clicked straight away because we loved being wasted enough to forget the trauma at home. We laughed and danced and hung out with a bunch of weird guys (drug dealers who lived with their mums and constantly got entangled with bigger, more violent drug dealers). Mr McCauley stood at the front of our class in Year 9.

'Raise your hands who is planning on going to uni.' He looked around – about half of us. Some, like me, with tense, determined arms. Others were softer, diffidently interested.

'Think again! Most of you will end up pregnant, unemployed, or both. This is Western Sydney. Look at your parents. Only 7 per cent of you will end up at uni, and hardly anyone will finish. Let's save the world some trouble.' We were told stuff like that all the time. At home, at school, by the local cops.

Chontelle and I would tell each other stories of places we would go once we got out of there. Paris, or Thailand, we'd be rich, and we'd never speak to most of these people again.

At the time I thought our misspent youth was tied up in our location – we were Westies, who smoke bongs, flunk out of school, join gangs, set fire to stuff, get bashed. This stuff is normal for poor people. One day, when I was sixteen, I escaped to Canberra to stay with my middle-class cousins. I went out with Sarah, the closest to me in age. Sarah and her friends went to an expensive grammar school. We went to a party and I looked around, all agog – it was just like a normal party! Girls crawling through the flowerbeds vomiting, someone crying, couples disappearing into cupboards and alleyways, people passed out in the garden. Sure, their clothes are different – nobody has to tuck an anti-theft clip still attached to a stolen shirt into their jeans – but they pass out on the floor too. There are small variations – they drink their parents' Cointreau and take coke instead of cask wine and cheap speed, but I was willing to look beyond that. We all did a dance move called 'Big Fish, Little Fish, Cardboard Box' to 'Vengabus'. I could see myself in them.

I'm still Facebook friends with Chontelle Butcher. She lives a few streets from my mum, and works at the local tax office. To her, Brunswick is an escape.

'Wow,' she says, when I chat to her through lockdown malaise. 'Melbourne. Wow. I mean – you got out. Melbourne! It's arty there! And the coffee culture and stuff … yeah, you really did it, mate. You did it.'

Yeah, I think. I came here, and now I'm stuck here.

Fly in the Souvlaki

In the film, it's 1990, Carl (Sam Neill) is in bed. At thirty-four, he lives with his dominating mother in a crumbling Brunswick weatherboard. He rolls out of his unmade bed. Newspapers are piled up at the door.

Cut to his mother with her head in the stove, legs sticking out like the wicked witch … is this the eponymous death in Brunswick?

Carl's mother: 'I know you think it's bohemian, all this filth.'

Mother is alive. She's cleaning the oven.

Carl gets a job in a cockroach-infested kitchen at what passes as a nightclub in 1990 (hair metal / toxic masculinity). On his first day, he falls in love with Sophie (Zoe Carides), fifteen years his junior, for no discernible reason.

Carl: 'I'm in love with her Dave … I met her yesterday.'

Dave (deadpan): 'It's fairly serious then.'

The fly in the souvlaki is that Greek-Cypriot-Australian Sophie is being set up to marry the Greek-Australian Yianni, the owner of the club and no stranger to various Brunswick baddies. Things get worse for Carl when he accidentally stabs (and kills) kitchen hand / criminal Mustafa (Nico Lathouris). Don't you hate it when that happens? He rings his mate Dave (John Clarke), and they dispose of the body by hiding it in a coffin with another body, in a grave due to be filled in the next day.

The death sets off a gang war that threatens to engulf Carl, but with a few quick (and convenient) narrative moves he gets an inheritance, and Carl gets the girl. Well, he gets punched, then he gets the girl. There's a big Greek-Cypriot wedding. The end.

Death in Brunswick feels like a lot of movies – loser white dude schleps around his local area, is tormented by various life challenges, until he eventually gets a house, a babe, and a happy ending through bloke luck – whatever that is (vaguely misogynistic serendipity?). It's in the style of *He Died with a Felafel in His Hand* – anyone who has been young, lost and poor can easily relate to our protagonist. Well, almost everyone.

As a woman and a working-class person, I'm irked.

There is something of the privileged private-school man-boy in our lead – like many fuckbois I made my way through in my twenties. They are soppy and lack direction, but someone's paying the rent, so they have no real urgency about getting their shit together. They've read a lot and can talk to you about queer theory. They have been to university. I remember going home with a guy in New York at age twenty-one, gaping at his massive, spotlessly clean apartment, at odds with the squalor of the dive bar I had seen him play that night. 'So, what, your parents are just loaded?' It was years later that I discovered I had a 'type'. Sigh.

The 'accurate representation of multicultural Melbourne' the film was applauded for on its release now seems like a parade of clunky, dated racial and gender stereotypes. It's not quite Con the fruiterer, but it's not far off. I try to remember the first time I saw myself on screen – was it Kylie Mole in *The Comedy Company*?

She Goes

Kylie Mole. I was a gum-chewing bogan schoolgirl, just like her. She was grumpy, unkempt, and furious at the world. I loved it! Everything to her was 'so excellent!' Her second-best friend was Kylie Minogue, and she was planning to do her work experience on the dole. Was my class, age and gender being lampooned? I didn't care, all I wanted was to celebrate in giddy recognition. Ah, that poet's tree again!

Non-Load-Bearing Ionic Columns

On the couch I pause the film to look over Sam's shoulder, peering at the architecture behind.

'That bridge is still there!' my boyfriend says, watching Sam Neill walk over the Phoenix Street railway crossing with his bike. 'And so's that,' as Sam/Carl peers through the window of Istanbul Meats, eating a kebab. Again and again we rubberneck around the actors to see where we live – the Bombay nightclub,* Brunswick Baths, the end of Victoria Street, the non-load-bearing ionic columns, the faces of saintly icons looking on. The shimmering is back.

The next day's hour of exercise was a re-enactment journey. First, we visited Carl's house, for can-crushing catharsis, a la Sam Neill in the first scene. Then to Sophie's dad's house, just around the corner on Marks Street. It's been painted sky blue.

'What are you doing?' asks Carl, retching by the open grave.

'We're going to give Mrs De Marco some company before her husband drops in in the morning,' says Dave as he matter-of-factly stomps on her ribcage to make room for Mustafa's body.

---

* Bombay Rock was a real club on Sydney Road that played host to acts as varied as Bo Diddley to Cold Chisel and INXS, it 'was to the working class what Billboard (a club in the city) was to the middle class' (*The Age*, 29 February 1980, p. 42) It has recently reopened with different owners under the same name.

Class in Brunswick

As Shane Maloney writes in the introduction to the novel *Death in Brunswick* by Boyd Oxlade, on which the film is based, 'the title alone is worth the price of admission. Forget Venice, it declares. Step aside Mann and Mahler, Visconti and Bogarde. Here is a book primed to take the mickey.'[2]

The idea that the great Australian ugliness of working-class, multicultural Brunswick would be equivalent to the classical heights of Thomas Mann's highbrow *Death in Venice* (or the incandescent film adaptation by Visconti) is the joke. It's an example of the self-deprecating gag that permeates Australian movies of the '70s and '80s. We're the unpolished, uncultured hooligans of *Crocodile Dundee*, *Wake in Fright*, and *The Cars that Ate Paris*. We're not novelists or bloody aesthetes. Strewth no!

For us in 2020, plonked on couch cushions now intimately moulded to our rear ends from hour upon hour of lockdown usage, the comparison between the two 'Death ins' is less of a joke. *Death in Venice* concerns life in a city slowly beset by a cholera epidemic, as well as protagonist Von Aschenbach's impending – spoiler alert – death. The resulting atmosphere of wistful claustrophobia as disease creeps through the streets felt very familiar. There *was* real death in our Brunswick, and it wasn't funny at all. But for Boyd Oxlade, working a series of low-paying hospitality jobs in the working-class inner north in the '70s, Venice was a world away.

Carl's mum bathes in the music of Mahler when stressed by his life choices. We see, not once but twice, that her favourite record is the soundtrack to *Death in Venice*. Her blue-rinsed twinset-clad body is mocked for the sin of pretentiousness.

She closes her eyes in order to be swept away to the lofty European idyll of Venice and Visconti, but we see that she remains in the knockabout Australian reality of Carl's Brunswick weatherboard shack, replete with bohemian filth. She, like us decades later, is stuck.

Rat King

My boyfriend found all the reviews of *Death in Brunswick*.[3] We watched it again. He read *Death in Venice*. I watched *Death in Venice*. If anyone else lived through the lockdowns in a balcony-less apartment with their partner, you will know that eighteen months spent knowing each other's every breath and thought, hearing every wee, dividing a lounge room into two 'work areas', overhearing every Zoom meeting and then finishing every day by commuting to your 'TV area', is intimate.

Our brains started twisting into one, like a rat king, tails entwined. Some couples broke up. Others, like us, melded into one person, a messy whole, like poor old Mustafa and Mrs De Marco sharing that coffin.

At Home She's a Tourist

We are both performers, so in our lives before the pandemic, we hopped from place to place, festival gig to festival gig, blissfully fed by constant stimulation.

In the lockdowns, that ground to a halt. We knew we were lucky – we had health, we hadn't caught Covid, and, unlike our parents and siblings, we aren't frontline workers – so we were home. Home was safe, but darkly mundane.

The film was evidence that something had happened in Brunswick that wasn't case numbers and press conferences and contact tracing, or just ordinary life. A movie had been made in Brunswick. Brunswick, like me, had 'made it'.

Watching *Death in Brunswick* we saw our place, reflected back to us. We saw ourselves doubled, Brunswick's streetscapes opened up anew.

Exploring the locations of the film, playing out scenes and actions, we travelled in a new way. When our cramped brains knitted together into one we had a project that enlivened us, split us apart into characters in a duetting re-enactment tour. I came to realise that we were doing the same thing Chontelle and I had done: using stories and art to imagine ourselves out of a situation we wanted to run from.

I remembered the bush poet, and vowed to try it with a gum tree sometime too – stand slightly awkwardly tall, echo its shape, see if I can help it understand itself better. The poet was describing something that is hard to articulate about representation, about the ways it makes us shimmer, radiate, live bigger than we are. It's not always perfect; and like me seeing my likeness at a fancy teenage party in Canberra, it can hit you at unexpected times. It always feels good when we peer over Sean Connery's shoulder, emerge from the brume and see the real magic: clear lines, reflections, ourselves.

Notes

1   John Clarke says this in the 'Making of' documentary included in the deluxe DVD set (https://www.ozmovies.com.au/movie/about/death-in-brunswick#about).
2   Shane Maloney, 'Grave Laughter' in Boyd Oxlade, *Death in Brunswick*, Text Publishing, Melbourne, 2012 [1987], p. 10.
3   Greg Burchall, 'Film's Comic Saga', *The Age*, 26 April 1991 (https://www.ozmovies.com.au/movie/about/death-in-brunswick#about).

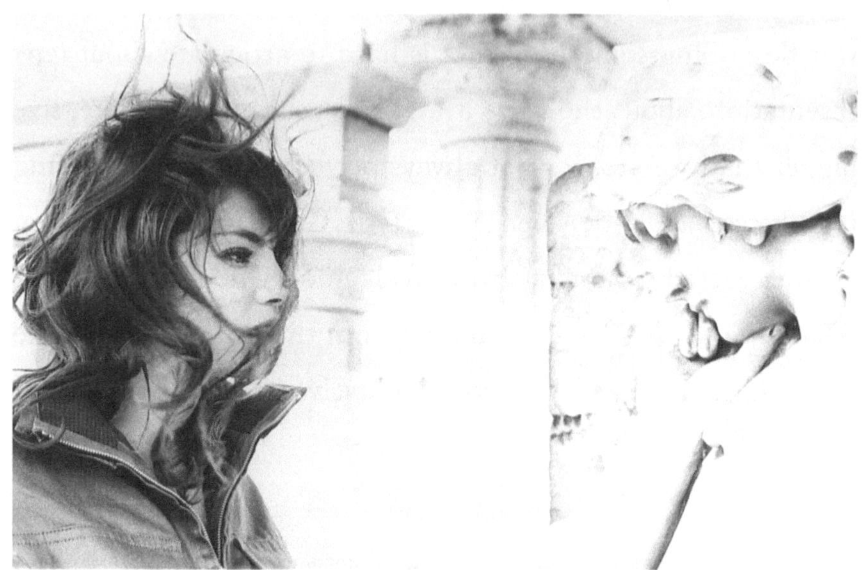

Still from *2000 Weeks* courtesy of Dominic Ryan.

Carlton New Wave

Isabella Trimboli

It's an odd, repetitive element: wreckage. A bunch of unemployed men line up among mounds of gravel and brick, in a place that looks like a bombed-out, abandoned city. Two men climb into a semi-demolished stately mansion – sliced in two like a derelict dollhouse – lamenting a childhood long gone. Two university students rush through a crumbling, detritus-laden landscape: youth and ruin merging into a single image.

These depictions of disrepair and decay appear in several films made in and around Carlton during the '60s, a ferment of filmmaking activity by students, immigrants and artists, defined primarily by its outward gaze. Unsatisfied with the parochialism and sparsity of Australian mainstream cinema, they began making their own films independently, inspired by the artistic upheaval of European arthouse cinema, which too was renouncing tradition and the past. But even as these Melbourne filmmakers attempted to forge new ideas, new visions, they remained preoccupied with remembrance, reverie – their films cannot help but hover over what used to be there before.

This was in an era before government intervention or funding bodies, and just as the first cohort would graduate from newly set-up film school programs. It was also the period preceding the film boom of the '70s and, consequently, remains in its shadow. 'Australian film culture in the 1960s and even beyond is indeed a "secret" largely forgotten, deliberately effaced as to suggest a clean slate, a blank or void or interval – all terms used by certain film historians when summing up this decade,' writes academic Adrian Danks, who goes on to state that only seventeen features of any kind were made in Australia during the decade. But this number doesn't account for the many low-budget, formally inventive short films made using newly accessible 16 mm cameras.

Those working around Carlton were not a tight-knit, collaborative group. It was not a cohesive movement, nor a single scene. There were different pockets, working within their own circles. But overlap – especially between disciplines – was rife. 'There was a lot of interaction and cross-fertilisation of skills between different art forms, such as music and performance and playwriting and group-devised work,' says actor and director

Robin Laurie. But some worked alone, possibilities never realised because of this isolation. 'Our activity was very insular,' says filmmaker Ettore Siracusa. 'We never sought to advertise or to publicise what we were doing.'

But what binds together these disparate filmmakers and their limited output is their brash experimentation, exciting failures, and a desire to produce intelligent, challenging films during a time when Australian cinema was practically a wasteland. Here is a fragmented survey of this culture, or four small glimpses.

1953

The film is mute, abandoned and never finished, but it is easy to piece together a narrative on images alone: men disembark a ship, pore over ads in a newspaper, line up in the hope of procuring menial employment. Their faces – weary, frustrated, drained of hope – are revealing: this misery is not what they signed up for.

Giorgio Mangiamele, a former Roman cop, emigrated to Melbourne less than a year prior to making *The Contract* (1953), a ninety-minute film about four Italian migrants (one played by Mangiamele himself) struggling to find work. This early experiment would solidify the director's themes: isolation and the ostracised.

During those early years, Mangiamele set up a photography studio at his home on Rathdowne Street, becoming the go-to photographer for Italian weddings, communions and other events. He filmed his own projects on Sunday afternoons, his only day off. Formally, most of his films replicated the gritty poetics of neorealism, an aesthetic easily applied to Carlton: all bleak terrace houses, rubble-strewn streets, loathsome little bully boys, and unkempt men with tired faces.

Mangiamele's protagonists were mostly suffering, misunderstood Italian migrants. Neighbours take it upon themselves to fling slurs and poke fun at their eating habits, no matter if they're a young boy on a paper run or a lonesome mechanic, as in the case of the two versions – one released and the other unreleased – of his film *The Stag* (which received an Honourable Mention accolade at the AFI awards in 1963). He never tried to graft a 'happy immigrant', 'persevering through adversity' narrative on his subjects. Even his sole comedy, *Ninety-Nine Percent* (1963), about a widow looking for a wife, involves various cruelties until the protagonist reaches a dead end.

But if his earlier works tapped into the realities of migrants struggling in a society that treated them with disdain and revulsion, *Clay* (1965), his first completed feature film, tended to avoid reality almost completely, in order to construct an insular dream world populated by characters spectral and adrift. The film was shot in Eltham's Montsalvat artists' colony (thanks to his friendship with filmmaker Tim Burstall) and was largely self-financed, after Mangiamele mortgaged his house. *Clay* tells the story of a murderer – who may or may not be called Mick – on the loose, who is taken in by a family and subsequently falls in love with the daughter of the house, an avid sculptor named Margot (the film features a sexy pottery scene that predates *Ghost* by some twenty years). Impermanence suffocates the romance – the jealously of a jilted suitor leads to the pair's demise.

From the film's earliest moments – as Mick's limp, mud-covered body is picked up on the side of the road by Margot and her father – Mangiamele's camera revels in slippery and murky textures. The outside is rendered in a permanent state of gloom: endless fog, grey puddles, glittering rain, unrelenting wind that sends leaves cascading through the air. Faces are often obscured; peering out of foggy windows or covered in thick layers of mud.

The now-79-year-old filmmaker Ettore Siracusa met Mangiamele at a struggling, ramshackle actors' school on Russell Street in the late '50s. The classes were filled with mostly Italian and Greek migrants. Mangiamele taught film classes, while his wife taught movement and dance. Siracusa would become a close collaborator with Mangiamele – first as an actor in his films, then as an assistant director for his later works. He tells me that, while Mangiamele is regarded as creating a unique testimony of migrant lives, the same attention should be given to his lyrical, lush visual sensibility. 'These poetical films are art, not simply social records,' he says.

Clay is certainly a film told through impeccable images, because the dialogue, heavy with symbolism and overwrought to the point of absurdity, sometimes sees the film venture into the arena of clumsy melodrama. But this only heightens the film's unreality, its focus on those stuck and stilted, who routinely want to slip into the solace of dreams. As its title and preoccupation with muddy surfaces spells out, this is a film about the desire to hide and to be made anew, despite a disreputable stain that can never be removed.

Clay copped brutal comments from Australian critics, who couldn't get past the film's hammy dialogue. Even when the film was selected to screen in competition at Cannes Film Festival, only the third Australian film ever to be selected, Mangiamele received no acknowledgement from the Australian government. His trip to France was funded by generosity: an unknown woman who heard about his film dropped off £500 to his photography studio; a discounted boat ticket was provided by a travel company. It was even a saga for Mangiamele to procure an Australian flag, customary for Cannes filmmakers. Despite its attention overseas, *Clay* never received a run in Australian cinemas. He booked out the Palais Theatre in St Kilda for a limited season on his own.

Beyond Reason (1970), Mangiamele's last film made in Australia (soon afterwards, he moved to Papua New Guinea and began making documentaries for the government), was another left turn. The film was about a bunch of psychiatric patients and their doctors stuck in an underground bunker to escape a nuclear bomb, with a dwindling supply of mood-stabilising medication. It is schlocky B-grade fare – dumb nurses, sexually perverse patients, uprisings, and unwavering hysteria – without any of the dreamy compositions conjured up in his previous work.

Siracusa keeps returning to that first, unfinished film. In his video piece *Basement* (2019) the filmmaker splices scenes of *The Contract* with his own shots of Mangiamele's former studio basement, accompanied by abstract microphone recordings that sound as if they are coming from the bottom of a well. The sound is an attempt to reimagine nearly twenty minutes of audio from the original film deleted by the National Film and Sound Archive because it was deemed redundant. In *Hems of Memory* (2008) Siracusa tracked down one of the actresses from *The Contract*, where she is faced with various images of her younger self. He tells me he is currently working on a video project that melds *The Contract* with a live soundtrack, his attempt to build something over the soundless void. 'There's an absence there,' he says, when asked about his fixation with the 1953 film, 'a vacuum.'

1965

In an edition of the Melbourne University Film Society's publication *Annotations on Film* from 1965, the editor, Chris Maudson, boasts of a burgeoning film scene. They had just seen their second Godard, first Demy and two Olmi films at the Melbourne Film Festival, and the society had curated a program full of Renoir, Visconti and Chabrol films. For the first time, there were also films being made within their circle, namely Brian Davies' *Pudding Thieves* (1967) – to be completed in two months – which, apart from Mangiamele's *Clay*, would be the first feature film made in Australia since the start of the '60s. 'Could this be the start of our "Nouvelle Vague?"' asked Maudson. 'Probably not, but it is something to dream about.'

The film wouldn't premiere two months later, but two years later. *Pudding Thieves*, in total, had taken four years to make, a completely self-funded venture that would later be seen to exemplify what is known by several names: 'the Carlton school', 'the Carlton ripple', 'Carlton new wave'. In essence, a small, loose coalition of students, film enthusiasts, writers, theatre kids and ABC staff, who orbited the Melbourne University Film Society – some of whom would go on to make their own films, spurred on by the activity and ideology of the *Cahiers du Cinéma* set (Rohmer, Rivette, Truffaut, Chabrol, Godard).

Jean-Luc Godard's first feature film, *Breathless* (1960), would prove especially incendiary and informative. Its images are eternal, implanted in our brains as totemic of the '60s: Belmondo's Bogart-ian grimace, the furious jump cuts; the improvised urgency that ruptured the classicism of the European film establishment. For those gathered at one of the MUFS' screenings of the film (banned in Australia until the mid-'60s, when it finally became available to borrow at the French Embassy), it also showed them new possibilities, new pathways – what could be done with audacity and style, despite a minimal budget and inexperience. The group's films and film writing did not exactly capture Godard's political savagery, nor his stylish imagery, but they did carry on his insolence, his tendency towards the polemical.

The Melbourne University Film Society's screenings were held two or three times a week at the Union Theatre and other venues near the university (the Carlton Theatre, dubbed the Bughouse, for instance). For those in the inner circle, sometimes in the Carlton share house of Alan Finney (an actor and producer, who would later play a key role in the growth of Hexagon Productions and Village Roadshow). Weekly meetings involved thirty or so committee members, who would select films and create rosters for screenings. 'Nothing was ever delegated to anybody. It was quite democratic. And then you used to put your hand up if you wanted to write about any of the films,' says former MUFS member and previous MIFF director Geoff Gardner.

Conjecture, conversation and gossip swelled in the pages of the society's magazine *Annotations on Film*, and associated publications *Film Journal* and *Melbourne Film Bulletin*. The magazines featured director interviews and cocksure criticism, always with a glamour shot of an actress on the cover (think Karina, Vitti, Bardot, Seberg). Bert Deling – who, in 1963, had run out of money to finish his first film, *Student Action*, but would go on to make two cult films: the freewheeling *Dalmas* (1973) and *Pure Shit* (1975) (more on these later) – derided the Melbourne film scene in cutting fashion. Why, he asked, was Jacques Rivette able to make a great debut film, *Paris Belongs to Us* (1961), on a minuscule budget, but there seemed to be none of that ingenuity in Melbourne? Instead, the film industry was 'a huge, amorphous mass of characterless technicians'.

Pudding Thieves certainly wasn't characterless. Indebted to Godard, it took swipes at Truffaut – specifically the view of friendship in *Jules and Jim* (1962), which Brian Davies found sentimental. Davies was an outlier in this Carlton scene – a university dropout, and a few years older than the rest. Charismatic and brash, he became something of a de facto leader. 'The way he talked about film always seemed to be incredibly smarter than the rest of us. And he wanted to actually do something, whereas the rest of us just sat around dreaming about being film directors,' recalls Geoff Gardner.

'He was the first to start making black-and-white films.

He lived next door and I remember when he shot some of *Pudding Thieves* in our street. It was the first film crew I had ever seen. He was self-funded, probably because he had a job with a big chemicals company. None of us had money,' says filmmaker Margot Nash, who lived in Carlton and was enmeshed in the local theatre scene.

Davies' debut film begins with a woman idling on a film set, barely lit until she poses on a ladder and bright studio lights overwhelm the space. The shot dissolves into a photography darkroom, where the image is being processed, submerged in a container full of water. It's a wink to artifice, how images are illusions, stylised, controlled and duplicated, easily manipulated and made deceitful. The issue of deceit will also surface between the film's two lead characters, Bill and George – two photographers who run a studio together, where they photograph newborns and tacky parties. They also dabble in a far more lucrative side project: pornography. For a film about illicit images, eroticism is never fully expressed (while an attempt to be provocative, the film still bears the traces of chaste provincialism). The only insight into their more secretive work is a truncated scene on set, where the pair try to fool around with two female models, eventually giving up, and the four gather on a bed to share cigarettes.

Complications grow between the pair as rival pornographers get a whiff of their enterprise (in one of the film's best scenes, featuring frantic pacing and a tense sit-down with leather-clad men at the University of Melbourne's Baillieu Library), and when George becomes involved with a woman he meets knocking on his door to warn him of the apocalypse. Morals and loyalties become slippery, splitting the photography pair in two.

Brake Fluid (1970) – Davies' follow-up film – was far more fragmented; a series of scenes involving a pack of young Carlton residents partaking in improvisational theatre, share-house antics, aimless drives and political organising. The scenes are tied together only by the film's two leads – Thomas, a boisterous klutz who is infatuated with the female lead, Julia, but is completely petrified of voicing his desires. Full of panning shots, it is a roving and restless film, with an undercurrent of mordant melancholy. The film won Best Short Film at Sydney Film Festival, much to the dismay of those in favour of Peter Weir's local film *Homesdale* (1971). Davies' response to minor success was to move to Adelaide and give up on filmmaking entirely.

Davies' work was reflective of what would become typical of the films made within this milieu: men suffering through various states of ennui and crisis. They were almost always the Poiccard archetype: jerky, seductive, self-pitying and full of bluster. Their outsized egos got them far, but also got them into trouble. In David Minter's *Hey Al, Baby* (1968), the titular Alan – petulant, entitled – is fawned over by a carousel of women in a ramshackle share house. Nigel Buesst's (a filmmaker not strictly associated with the university scene, but involved in several independent productions) *Bonjour Balwyn* (1971) is about a smarmy louche who starts up his own independent magazine, and continues to push on despite mass debts and threats mounting. Even Peter Carmody's *Nothing Like Experience* (1970), a docufiction chronicling the inaugural Festival of University Arts in 1969, centres around three hopeless male festival-goers – an effusive dork, a cynic who kills the mood, and an overstimulated 'schizoid' – as they attend burlesque shows and Godard seminars, and crawl, semi-nude, through the cellophane-like walls of an art installation.

Many of the films only gesture at politics. Instead of head-on reflections, war and protest are relegated to background noise: the buzz of a radio news report on Vietnam, a television blasting an anti-communist tirade that is swiftly turned off. This is despite a great deal of anti-war activity on campus (Peter Carmody remembers the screen printing of his film poster being bungled multiple times because the student union building was housing a draft evader whom the police were trying to arrest). Like many international films that would reach Australian shores years after they had first premiered, Melbourne political cinema lagged behind Europe in the '60s. As Margot Nash observed, the student uprising and civil unrest of May 1968 in Paris would inspire a further 'surge of resistance to war, to authoritarianism, and then, later, to sexism'.

Despite this political naivety, the films are especially attuned to the tastes and proclivities of Melbourne's bohemia. This is especially true of the films that paid direct homage to their beloved French source material. *Monash 66* (1966), a documentary made by Chris Maudson and Robin Laurie about the transition from high school to university, copied the cinéma-vérité style of Jean Rouch and Edgar Morin's *Chronicle of a Summer* (1961). Peter Elliot's *The Girlfriends* (1967), which followed a pair of female friends unsure of their studies, romantic interests and the ideas around them ('Women prefer their men and art ugly, grotesque!' a young professor avows midway through the short film) ends with a direct nod to Godard's *Band of Outsiders* (1964).

The two friends, plus one of their love interests, a man named Jack (played by Carlton playwright Jack Hibberd), are sprawled out in the living room, lethargic and bored, with conversation turning listless and disjointed (topics include: the faults of Kafka, the allure of Godard's 'weeny little man') until Nancy Sinatra's 'These Boots Are Made For Walkin'' is turned on. Woken from their collective stupor, they clumsily replicate *Band of Outsiders'* famous dance scene – every click, clap and jump.

1969

In 2001, the film director Tim Burstall – known for crafting both vulgar farces and historical dramas – gave an interview to *The Age* where he grimly recalled entering the Australian film industry in the '60s. Practically moribund, there were only sponsored documentaries and advertisements being produced. Every ten years a feature by Australian filmmakers Chips Rafferty or Charles Chauvel might show up. Besides that, everything was as bland as a John Grierson documentary, or, as he said, echoing Patrick White, made in accordance with a 'dreary, dun-coloured realist tradition'.

2000 Weeks (1969), his forgotten debut film, served as a redress to this vision of Australia, specifically Melbourne. In a place so often rendered barren and harsh, devoid of romance, it is an elegant and theatrical portrait of the mundane, which uses European arthouse cinema as its starting point. Beaches, gardens and boats gleam with an inky depth. Cameras peer behind candelabras and cellos. Characters face tombstones, not their lovers. Light swings back and forth like a bulb in an interrogation room. As the film's protagonist says early in the film, it is 'a landscape full of mysteries and silence'. While Mangiamele's *Clay* and *2000 Weeks* are radically different films, both share a desire to create shadowy, sumptuous imagery, tied to their narrative fixation with hallucinations and dreams.

The film revolves around Will, an unhappy journalist juggling an affair, marital woes and an ill father, who is a week away from death. He is also intellectually unfulfilled – working at a newspaper instead of writing what he wants, which is the great Australian novel. Among this consuming angst, the past continues to flood back, leaving Will in a near-constant state of reverie – remembering his childhood full of fantasy and play; his intense love for his wife, which has now dissipated to sexless appreciation; and growing up under the thumb of his domineering, eternally disappointed father, often prone to bouts of rage and dismay.

Reflecting on the film years later, the director would lament that *2000 Weeks* is marred by self-consciousness and inexperience. It is certainly a film trying to prove itself: intellectually, emotionally, artistically. Here was Melbourne's intellectual class, partying in elegant Eltham homes, discussing writing, questioning the obscenity of death, and debating the power struggle between sexes. Its proclamations are a little obvious, clunky: 'See, existentialism is also an antipodean affliction!'

It fares better with its depiction of Australian cultural cringe. This is embodied in the character Noel, Will's childhood friend and an arrogant television producer, who has found success in London. Back in Melbourne on a work trip, he sees everything as crummy and inferior; a cheap palimpsest of British culture. Through his newspaper job, Will lands the possibility of writing for an Australian television drama, which is to be made entirely by an Australian cast and crew – at that point, a total anomaly. But then the UK intervenes: how could this colonial outpost be trusted to make something good?

This was clearly the ambition driving *2000 Weeks* – Burstall wanted to ignite a more interesting independent film culture in the country, while creating a film that would also be taken seriously overseas. 'I think that at the moment we are not a producing culture but are a consuming culture for the most part, that is we consume the products of other people from overseas rather than make them ourselves,' he told the journal *Annotations of Film*, during the production of the film. 'At the same time, I think that the life that's lived here is rich and vivid and as interesting in itself as it would be anywhere else.'

In the mid-'60s, Burstall received a fellowship to study film abroad, and he and his wife, Betty, decamped to America for two years. By then, Burstall was enmeshed with a group of writers and artists (like painter Arthur Boyd), and had set up production company Eltham Films with Patrick Ryan. In America, Tim studied at the Actors Studio under Strasberg, and worked with Martin Ritt on a Hollywood production. Betty spent her days paying pennies to watch 'off-off' Broadway shows in the city. The trip would turn out to be transformative. In the US, Burstall was told that the small film market in Australia should be treated like France, and that he would have more success if he tried to make a personal, arthouse film. He immediately began working on *2000 Weeks*, to be Eltham Films' first feature. Betty, meanwhile, set up La Mama, an experimental not-for-profit theatre company on Faraday Street in Carlton that would for decades serve as the centre for progressive dance and theatre work, which so often intersected with film.

While it received minor praise in Britain and was lauded at the Moscow Film Festival, *2000 Weeks* was derided by Australian critics for its flimsy 'cardboard' characters and indulgence. The film was ridiculed when it made its premiere at Sydney Film Festival, and failed to recover its production costs. Burstall's son, Tom Burstall, says the film was burdened by expectations, and that audiences weren't ready for a window into infidelity and sexually uninhibited relationships. 'It was being delivered to an Australia that was still back in the 1950s,' he says. Affairs were 'unspoken and behind closed doors for most people. In a more broad-minded bohemian world, however, they were discussed.'

In response, it seems, Burstall quashed his more outré ambitions and made a sharp swerve to populist, ocker cinema. *Stork* (1971), his next film, could be read as a rebuttal of sorts to *2000 Weeks*, and to the university students that congregated around Carlton: a comedy poking fun at the political and artistic ambitions of left-wing youth. Funded partly by the money generated from selling his Arthur Boyd paintings, the film was an adaptation of David Williamson's *The Coming of Stork*, which had first premiered at La Mama in 1970.

The film chronicles the exploits of a gangly, 7 foot, wannabe revolutionary called Stork (played by Bruce Spence), who spouts ridiculous, half-baked socialist screeds and is trying to lose his virginity. Fired from his job at General Motors, he overstays his welcome at a friend's share house in Carlton, stuck at an impasse of what to do with himself. He spends his time daydreaming of the various possibilities: pontificating at the Victorian Trades Hall, wooing women while making abstract art out of his own beer-fuelled vomit (affectionally titled 'chunder scapes').

Stork would mark the beginning of mainstream Australian comedies that were to be a boom at the box office; filled with bumbling blokes, sex escapades and crass gags that solidified the mythos of Australian male culture. It is interesting that Burstall, once motivated to assert Australian artistic life in the face of a desolate film culture, would help to uphold a more dopey cultural image. But Stork served as an antidote to this barren film culture. Its success spurred the creation of Hexagon Productions, a joint venture with Village Roadshow. This led to the company becoming one of the major exhibition and distribution companies in Australia. '*2000 Weeks* was a complete box office flop,' says Tom Burstall, 'but it was a failure that informed Tim in a strategy to actually be analytical.'

1973

'After [Godard] made *Breathless*, he said he learned everything he knew about cinema. That's why I like his old stuff, not this new, political crap,' laments John Duigan, playing himself but also the role of a tyrannical, controlling film director in Bert Deling's wild, acid-drenched epic of digression *Dalmas* (1973). By the time a bunch of bohemians had descended on Lake Tyers to drop acid and film what happened, Godard had dismissed his previous work as 'bourgeois' and tried his best to distance himself from the 'auteur' title that dogged him throughout the '60s. In 1968, Godard co-founded the Dziga Vertov Group, dedicated to merciless, hard-to-endure, political video essays, all created as a collective. By 1972, he was an ardent Maoist, crafting collagic agitprop that felt more like sermons than cinema.

Academic and writer Bruce Hodsdon has classified *Dalmas*, as well as Dave Jones's pitch-black satire *Yackety Yack* (1974), as 'the clearest presence of Godard in Australian cinema'. This proclamation is a stretch, but it's true that Deling's film, at its core, shares a similar desire to destabilise the idea of authorship, to shirk the mantle of a single, sole director or auteur.

You wouldn't identify this goal in the first half of *Dalmas*. The film begins rather conventionally. The titular Dalmas is introduced: an ex-cop trying to track down a drug lord in the dope scene. We follow him as he intimidates a heroin-addled cop in a wheelchair, living in a filthy den full of papers and towers of glitching televisions. They project an interview with Timothy Leary's right-hand man, Richard Alpert, who tells stories of Tibetan monks, transcendence and trips (this interview had been conducted by Deling and *Dalmas* cinematographer Sasha Trikojus, originally projected on the walls at avant-garde gallery space Pinacotheca in Richmond. 'It was quite extraordinary because it was the first time many people had seen this community-based video used that way in a gallery space,' says documentary filmmaker John Hughes). We then watch, as Dalmas tracks down the infamous 'Plastic Man', an older anarchist giving away acid to incite social disintegration. 'Your rotten society will crumble away, so watch out motherfuckers!' he screams, delivering a roving sermon in the city streets. Perhaps the last straightforward scene in the film is of a party put on by this balding, effusive ringleader, where a gaggle of stoned revellers bathed in pink light eat bananas with glee and writhe around on the floor together until a police bust ruins all the fun.

From here, the film descends into metatextual disarray. The party-goers are taking refuge in a beachside camping spot, while the mechanisms and challenges of filmmaking enter the frame. But then the plot comes off its hinges completely. Deling appears. The film is too structured, too controlled, take a camera, drop LSD, film whatever you want – he tells the crew congregated in the kitchen. The means of production are seized.

Acid antics come into full view: a group, blindfolded, hold hands and help each other navigate hilly terrain. Men whimper, cry and scream and, in one scene, even wield an axe. There is incessant chatter, conversations of complete narcotic delirium: the kind of ramblings that feel, under the influence, transcendental and meaningful – but when sober, translates to gibberish. However, a few threads of conversation are decipherable: free will and privilege, the desire to live gently, the impossibility of naturalism when a camera is pushed in front of your face. The camera zooms in and out of these groups huddled in pockets of tall grass, while a split screen splinters the audience's focus between figures caught in a trance and glittering ocean vistas.

In *Dalmas*, the boundaries between fiction and documentary, crew and cast, blur until they become indistinguishable. But while the film plays with different forms to present something more multifaceted, more true, *Dalmas* cannot help but come up against cinema's bitter limits, or, as an actor states in the final moments, 'What we're left with is ... a crude representation of what we lived.'

In many ways, *Dalmas* was a warm-up for Deling's more noted drug escapade, *Pure Shit* (1975), or, as it was known under its censored title, *Pure S*. Similarly tapped into the rhythms of being obliterated, the film follows four denim-clad heroin addicts over forty-eight hours, as they try to score a hit. Desperate and resolute, not even the death of a friend, found by the group covered in her own sick, gets in the way of their search. They break into a chemist, partake in an ill-advised, beach-side drug deal, and drive around the scummy parts of the city, scouring the streets for a dope connection. The film's rambling carousel of characters includes a coked-up couple completely paranoid from a bender, and Helen Garner – two years away from publishing *Monkey Grip* – playing an erratic speed-freak, who cannot stop herself from scrubbing her spotless sink. (According to Deling, in a *Crikey* interview from 2009, her excellent performance was thanks to a large dose of amphet-amines, administered by the actor Garry Waddell.)

Pure Shit wasn't as invested in challenging the gulf between depiction and reality as *Dalmas*, but it still toyed with unorth-odox techniques to create a twitchy, more realistic film full of disorder and precarity. Strangely, Deling took his dialogue cues from Howard Hawks' *His Girl Friday* (1940), wanting his cast to speak fast and clipped, with all the gaps in speech to be ignored. What results is a cacophony of cussing, crying and yelling, with characters speaking and arguing on top of one another. The only time there is a moment of silence is halfway into the film, when the foursome finally get to shoot up (thanks to holding up another chemist with a wrench). Some of the film's cast were non-actors, plucked from the Melbourne drug scene, others were actors from the Pram Factory set, who dabbled with hard substances. In an especially debauched example of life imitating art, one cast member allegedly left the set to rob a pharmacy while wearing a Gene Simmons mask. This was the least of the film's problems; the Victorian Vice Squad raided the premiere at Playbox and the Australian Film Commission refused to take the film to Cannes.

Despite *Pure Shit*'s notoriety and cult renown, it's *Dalmas* that truly represents a turning point in underground, independent Australian cinema. By 1968, the political optimism and giddy idealism of the decade had curdled, and more radical militancy was mounting. This inevitably bled into filmmaking. If the radicalism of Australian '60s cinema (spurred by the French New Wave) was defined by crafting not realism, per se, but something that felt truer to life – hand-held camera movements, overlapping voices, and forgoing polish and intricate arrangement for restless energy – then the '70s was about slashing through the images held up as unimpeachable and truthful. This intervention would take several forms: feminist cinema; anti-colonial filmmaking; and the rise of filmmakers' co-ops that would support, screen and disseminate local independent films without the support of established institutions. This also, sometimes, resulted in direct action. When word got out at the Pram Factory theatre that Tim Burstall was at the University of Melbourne, filming a political rally scene for his sex farce *Alvin Purple* (1973) (about an average man inexplicably irresistible to women), a few female performers made a real protest out of the staged one, disrupting the shoot and wielding signs with SMASH SEXIST MOVIES. 'Tim Burstall never spoke to me again,' Robin Laurie, the protest's ringleader, tells me.

Maybe this change is best defined by an experimental short that Margot Nash and Robin Laurie would make together a few years later, *We Aim to Please* (1976). The film was partly inspired by Godard's *2 or 3 Things I Know About Her* (1967), which Nash had first seen in the share house of Alan Finney in the late '60s. The film contains two strains. The first is Godard's essay, where the director whispers over images about capital and consumerism, while the fictional narrative follows twenty-four hours in the life of a mother living on the outskirts of Paris, who turns tricks part-time to maintain her middle-class lifestyle. Besides sex work being a stand-in for a critique of labour (it's one of Godard's favourite, and relied-upon, symbolic ploys), the film is dazzling in its density and its ability to craft digressive, political cinema that isn't dull proselytising. Its rush of images and women full of longing capture the impersonal, cruel crush of modernity.

We Aim to Please, while working in the burgeoning arena of experimental feminist cinema, has a similar chatty, radical quality: aware of, and in conversation with, its audience. Surreal and exuberant, the film is awash with amplified sounds (creaks, slurps, giggles, whispers) and close-up shots of bodies and faces that defy typical modes of framing, and resist sexualisation. Meanwhile, the two directors speak of gaze, spectatorship, and a sexual education that is skewed and oppressive. New ways of seeing, and in turn filmmaking, are needed.

'How beset we were from what we had heard, with what we had been taught,' their two voices intone in unison at the beginning of the film, as they cut between images of an old shabby doll and a bronzed nude statue. 'By whom? BY WHOM? This especially we did not know. But we're finding out fast.'

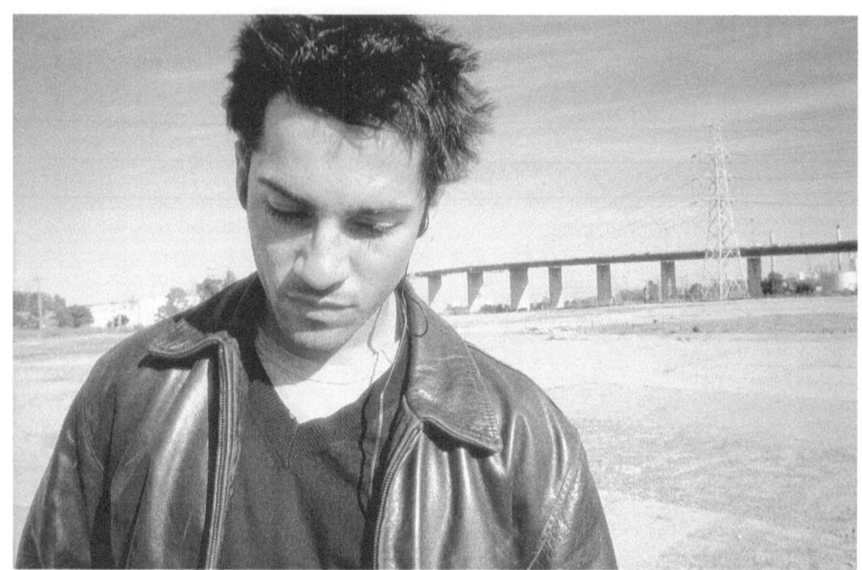

Alex Dimitriades as Ari in *Head On*. Courtesy of Head On Productions Pty Ltd. Photographed by John Tsiavis.

Head On

Shaad D'Souza

There's a meme that emerged a few years ago that revolves around the idea that gay men walk fast: 'They learned to walk to the beat of "Womanizer" by Britney Spears', suggests one variation. In *Head On*, Alex Dimitriades speeds; strutting through Melbourne in a misshapen leather jacket, the stringy wires of his walkman headphones attached to him like life-support cables, he seems seconds away from breaking into a run. As Ari, a nineteen-year-old second-generation Greek man, and a closeted one, he is forever on edge, always surveyed, some invisible threat constantly on his tail; his immigrant parents, the figures of authority for whom he has the most contempt, loom behind every kafenio curtain and landline ring. His racewalker's gait, then, is his method of escape. Or is it? Consider the music Ari is listening to through those tinny earbuds: Lunatic Calm, Paul Mac, Way Out West, Primal Scream. Maybe he's just strutting in time.

Head On (1998), directed by Ana Kokkinos, a second-generation Greek-Australian like Ari, is forever walking this line. Based on Christos Tsiolkas's novel *Loaded*, it's a flick of familial tension, near-constant drugtaking, sketchy sex, police brutality and casual bigotry. What plays like morose, disturbing tragedy on the page is something more complicated when set to a soundtrack of bristling techno, drum'n'bass, reggae, indie rock, and electropop that rarely ever lets up over the film's runtime. Ari is an avowed nihilist, loyal only to the speed he takes (and sometimes sells), the cruising beats he visits at various points throughout the day, and the pummelling, ecstatic dance music that he listens to every waking second. Over the course of *Head On*, Ari is pushed by his family, his friends, and an overwhelmingly rigid Australian culture to demarcate his identity – is he Greek or Australian, gay or straight? – and so he pushes back by being nothing at all, rejecting labels in ways often risky and reckless and finding the most freedom in his spiritual vagrancy. That Ari often finds himself in violent situations throughout *Head On* suggests his unmoored, structureless lifestyle is something of a death wish. But, somehow, his personal mixtape – a never-ending stream of crushed, metallic beats, asphyxiating synth lines and hair-raising drops that is to Ari what Beethoven is to Alex DeLarge – makes it feel like heaven.

Indeed, *Head On* is one of Australia's greatest soundtrack films. Music begins with its very first image, and remains essential well into the credits, when Primal Scream's 'Loaded', a perfect musical distillation of Ari's stand-offish anti-political party-boy ideology, starts playing. Although musical cues are written into *Loaded*, Kokkinos makes significant changes to the music of Ari's life, reframing his favourite songs to reflect the tone and themes of her film, which is profoundly interested in the misshapen and ever-contested identities of second-generation immigrants. Her choices for *Head On* are genius – you get the sense that Kokkinos would make a fabulous DJ, with how deftly she slips one iconic sync into another – and display a surprising, gratifying awareness of pop music's significance to various immigrant classes. Listening to the soundtrack – readily available second-hand on CD, but sadly absent from streaming services – without watching the film almost says as much about a universal migrant experience as does the film itself.

Head On's soundtrack signals its intent, and its misfit migrant perspective. Nearly all the music Ari listens to over the course of the film is some kind of Frankenstein'd mishmash of styles and cultures, some kind of melting-pot music that would never have been created if not for permeable borders and thrifty migrant communities. Early on in the film, we see that Ari is particularly drawn to songs like Lunatic Calm's 'Leave You Far Behind' and Way Out West's 'Ajare', exemplars of big beat – the booming, psychedelic electronic micro-genre that swept through British popular music in the early '90s. Featuring acidic synth lines that reverberate like tesla coils and the kind of boisterous drum-breaks typical of drum'n'bass, big beat sits at the intersection of numerous British migrant sub-genres, including breakbeat and reggae, and is true hybrid music; its origins can be traced to so many different places at once, including Chicago, where DJs were experimenting with new synthesisers, like the Roland TB-303, which would become essential to acid house, and Jamaica, where reggae and raggamuffin music – the building blocks of genres like jungle and drum'n'bass – first originated. Ari races through Melbourne as he listens to big-beat tracks, scoring speed at an austere apartment building and hooking up in the grimy back alley of Footscray Market as the heavenly vocal sample in 'Ajare' begins to crest. Even as he resists identification, transiting through areas that are disreputable and undocumented and hidden from the prying eyes of authority, Ari's choice of soundtrack – a kind of second-generation genre, one sprung from so many different styles and cultures – acts as a beacon of the complex, multifaceted identity he so wishes to shun.

Ari's taste in music, then, while far from fringe, tends to lean towards the skeezy and the weird – hybrid genres perfected and popularised by groups looking, like Ari, for a new lingua franca. In one scene, Ari arrives at a friend's house to find Dannii Minogue – a kind of perfect avatar of White Australia – playing on the stereo; he changes it to Isaac Hayes's theme song for *Shaft*, the 1971 blaxploitation classic whose soundtrack is itself a funk staple. As with big beat, funk is an amalgam of Black musical styles – in this case, jazz, soul and Afro-Cuban music – hybridised to create something liberated in style and liberating for its listener. For Ari, 'Theme from *Shaft*' is the opposite of the kind of lily-white music that his friends Dina and Joe (who earlier in the film is seen blasting The Saints) like to listen to. Their interest in the typically Australian is a perfect match for their assimilationist tendencies; unlike Ari, Dina and Joe are all too happy to get married and settle down, even though they both still seem to be drawn to the sexual experimentation and drug-taking that are key to Ari's lifestyle.

Traditionally 'white' music is rarely heard in *Head On*, and when it is, it's often in service of making characters like Dina and Joe seem straitlaced and disconnected from Ari. Ari flat-out rejects the trappings of Australian pop culture: as he and his friends drive to the Greek club, Ammonia's 'You're Not The Only One Who Feels This Way' begins playing on the stereo, only for Ari to turn it off immediately, despite the protest of his sister, who is on the way to see her white boyfriend. Other kinds of music, though, offer tantalising, occasionally transgressive delight: at his brother Peter's house, Ari dances to 'You Sexy Thing' by the band

Hot Chocolate – a group of Jamaican and Trinidadian immigrants living in Britain – and listens to reggae as he shares a joint with Peter's attractive housemate Sean. Sean is the only character in *Head On* for whom Ari harbours more than fleeting attraction, and he connects with Ari through the kind of coded, knowing banter about music that gay men often share:

> Ari: 'Fuck, everyone owns a Madonna record.'
> Sean: 'Nobody plays her anymore. Like the Stones.'
> Ari: 'I still play the Stones.'
> Sean: 'So do I.'

Ari and Sean's infatuation ends in a moment of violence but, until *Head On*'s final moments, he's one of the few characters Ari doesn't find to be spiritually or emotionally objectionable. Sean is white, but he's worldly: his walls are plastered with flyers for anti-racism rallies; he listens to reggae and appreciates the iconoclastic antics of Madonna and Mick Jagger, white stars who nonetheless align with Ari's fascination with transgressive black musical styles. He understands Ari's codification of certain kinds of musicians, which is a rare occurrence in *Head On*, given that nearly everyone around Ari, even his cross-dressing friend Johnny, seems to be more interested in Australian rock than in the chic, edgy European and American music that Ari likes. Finding kinship through music is one of the few universal tenets of the queer experience, and Ari and Sean's instant spark as they discuss pop records is one of the few times in *Head On* that Ari allows himself any kind of normative gay experience. Ultimately, though, Kokkinos has grander designs than simply using her soundtrack to signal queer affection. (That being said, Ari's obsession with fusion genres does seem to speak to Eve Kosofsky Sedgwick's assertion that queerness is 'the open mesh of possibilities, gaps, overlaps, dissonances and resonances, lapses and excesses of meaning when the constituent elements of anyone's gender, of anyone's sexuality aren't made [or can't be made] to signify monolithically'.) Even when Ari isn't speaking, his choice of music outs him as a proud misfit, a child of immigrants who can choose neither assimilation nor total transgression.

Little about *Head On*'s music feels particularly outdated, despite its reliance on big beat and the hilariously '90s Paul Mac remix of Silverchair's 'Freak'. Unlike many coming-of-age films, *Head On* does not exactly feel like a time capsule – perhaps because, unlike many cities, Melbourne still has a distinctive musical footprint that can be as easily traced now as it was in 1998. Although Tsiolkas divides his book into quadrants – North, South, East and West – *Head On* features no such demarcation. Instead, Kokkinos uses music to sketch out an emotional map of Melbourne – a vision of its peculiar niches and scenes, and so on – rather than a geographically specific one. In the same way that Ari's soundtrack tells us about his mood, the ambient sounds that float through *Head On* say just as much about the environment as the image does.

Kokkinos captures, intensely, the *feel* of transiting through Melbourne. Music is everywhere here, not in a tacky *We're the Music Capital!* kind of way, but just in a way: the city is flat and open, and on any given day you can walk around and hear music spilling from cars and restaurants and buskers on the street. Ari rarely takes off his headphones by choice, but when he does, it's because the caterwaul of a busker playing the violin begins to eat into the refrain of 'Ajare'. At other times, pieces of punk and jangle-pop seem to stand in for suburban ennui: The Saints' 'Know Your Product' welcomes Ari back to the cloistered 'burbs after his excursion through the Footscray Market, and, later, Underground Lovers' 'Las Vegas' plays as he and Johnny talk about their relationships, with Johnny's abusive and homophobic father standing just metres outside the door. 'Las Vegas' is an anomaly on *Head On*'s soundtrack, but it still serves a purpose – like Johnny's plush boudoir inside his harsh family home, 'Las Vegas' is a tumbleweed concealing lovelorn, romantic lyrics – and, in its evocation of Punters Club–era rock, is as essential to Kokkinos's creation of Melbourne as sleek, washed-out techno or Greek rebetiko music.

Indeed, if rock music heralds Ari's entry into the zone of the stiflingly conformist, electronic music announces his arrival into spaces that are queer, lawless and exotic. Ari and Johnny spend much of *Head On* planning to go to 3 Faces, the now-defunct gay mega-club that once stood on Commercial Road, South Yarra. Although the real-life 3 Faces often filled its flyers with exhaustive lists of the kinds of pop hits you could hear at the club – largely Stock, Aitken and Waterman hits, or the latest singles by Kylie and Take That – the 3 Faces of *Head On* is playing frenetic acid techno, and Ari's arrival there is the first time we hear the kind of music *he* likes, and spends much of his time listening to, outside the headphones of his walkman. 3 Faces is a gay club, but you get the sense that Ari's patronage is as much about his connection with the music as with the culture the venue houses. In the same way that he and his friends attend the Greek club to hear rebetiko, Ari attends 3 Faces for the thread of emotional association he gets from being around other people dancing to electronic music.

As is true in real life, the nightlife scene in *Head On*'s Melbourne isn't drawn through geographic lines but musical ones, and although some of the venues in *Head On* are long shuttered, its overall ambiance still tracks today. I can walk 300 metres from my house in Northcote on a Friday night and find raucous crowds revelling in traditional Greek dance at the local Greek restaurant, Ladadika; I can walk another 200 and find punters spilling out of a club that's blasting frenetic, synapse-crushing drum'n'bass music. A little further down the road, I can see a drawling, disaffected rock band perform to drawling, disaffected crowds. (It's not just venues: Floppy-haired, doe-eyed boys like Sean still live in crumbling terraces and still don't have bed-frames; their sparse bedroom walls still feature haphazardly pinned flyers for anti-establishment rallies, and they still argue about whether Madonna is basic or biblical. Melbourne's many kafenios may get facelifts, but the coffee remains the same.)

Of course, *Head On* is never so simplistic as to suggest that Ari's love of *Shaft* and big beat is enough to supersede his very nature. In *Head On*, the body keeps the score: even when Ari is turning his nose up at Greek tradition, he can't help but be drawn in by the sound of rebetiko and the promise of a stage to show off his aptitude for the zeibekiko, the 'eagle dance' that he partakes in many times over the course of the film.

In 1976, Pauline Kael wrote that '*Saturday Night Fever* gets at something deeply romantic: the need to move, to dance, and the need to be who you'd like to be. Nirvana is the dance; when the music stops, you return to being ordinary', and *Head On*, itself an emotional descendant of *Saturday Night Fever*, draws its power from a similar well. Its characters, most notably Ari, fall into naturalistic, almost primal rhythms when they engage in Greek dance – not necessarily the same quick, sleek moves that Travolta might bust out, but ones that show off similar clout. In *Head On*, unlike *Saturday Night Fever*, dance doesn't seem to be an expression of who you might want to be, but of who you *are*: the truth behind all the posturing and renegotiation and refusal.

The first time we see Ari in *Head On*, he's dancing at a wedding. Even as his voiceover expresses deep distaste with the cultural establishment – he practically spits as he mentions the idea of getting married, getting a house, getting a job – Ari's face, the most joyful and carefree we see it through the entire film, gives him away. Throughout *Head On*, traditional dance acts as a coolant for Ari's hot head, a way for him to return to his body when he's on the precipice of blinding rage or discontent.

In an early scene, when Ari is at home with his family, the growing animosity between Ari and his father dissipates when they dance the zeibekiko together: 'You're not a bad dancer', Ari's father admits, literally breaking bread with Ari as he says it. Despite Ari's father's insistence that his children have been 'ruined', dancing reconnects Ari to his father and his family tree – for once, he is a locus of adoration and pride for himself and his family. Contrary to Ari's assertion earlier in the film that you should 'never tell a wog the truth', dancing is a way for Ari's family to speak truths to each other that might be too tense to speak out loud.

At times, dancing connects Ari to his heritage even as he mocks his friends for attempting to capitulate to tradition. When Ari, Joe and Dina attend the Greek club together, Joe rinses Ari for his transgressive, nihilistic lifestyle, only for Ari to mock Joe's engagement – an arrangement that Joe accepted in exchange for a house deposit from his parents. Although Joe is willing to settle down, as his parents wish, his acceptance of tradition is about as falsified as Ari's rejection of it; Joe, Ari says, can't even dance. Joe leaves the club, and Ari moves to the centre of the dancefloor, once again arcing his body into the sublime movements of the zeibekiko.

Although Kokkinos and Dimitriades portray Ari as something of a loose cannon, he is patient and stoic as he dances, graceful and powerful like a bird of prey, slicing through space without ever putting a foot wrong. In these moments, the film is sleek and balletic, its panic-attack jerkiness slipping away in an instant. Kokkinos seems to suggest that the disconnect in Ari's mind – between what he *wants* to do and what he *must* do – is totally illusory: as he dances, Ari is both giving in to tradition and following his own heart, finding some middle point between his two guises that, somehow, embraces both.

It's not just Ari who becomes more embodied through dance: when Johnny arrives at the club dressed as Toula, she begins dancing the tsifteteli, a kind of belly dance performed largely by women. Although she receives jeers from the crowd, it's bolstering for Toula that she can even perform the dance at all: 'They loved me!' she tells Ari. For both Ari and Toula, dancing is a centring, invigorating, fortifying thing: a way of reclaiming one's selfhood even as outside forces attempt to diminish it.

Dancing is at the heart of *Head On*; it might be one of the greatest ever dance films that is not at all about the act itself. In the film's spectacular final sequence, we see Ari on the docks – now another cruising beat – where his parents first arrived from Greece, once again dancing a triumphant zeibekiko. Day has broken once again, after twenty-four hours in which Ari, theoretically, should have been worn down to a husk – he has been brutalised by police, paid out for being not Greek enough, mocked for being too Greek, fetishised, ostracised, tread upon. In Kokkinos's *Head On*, identity is something picked at and scrubbed away every minute of the day. All you can do is look forward, and step to the beat.

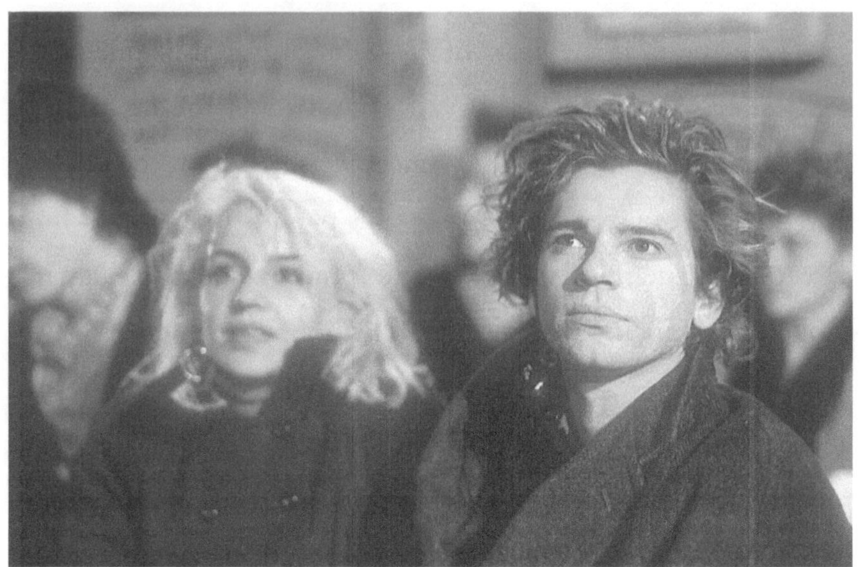

Still from *Dogs in Space* courtesy of Richard Lowenstein.

Dogs in Space

Tim Rogers

I first saw *Dogs in Space* at the Pitt Street Cinema complex in Sydney's CBD on a muggy, cloudy Saturday arvo in 1987. Sartorially, the patrons walking into the Saturday 2.10 p.m. showing looked like they might be going to a Tuesday all-you-can-eat buffet at Sizzler: V-neck jumpers in pastel colours topped stonewash jeans for the fellas, while the ladies had opted for cotton summer dresses with a light cardi in complementary pastel to shield them from the cinema air-conditioning. Date-wear, I guess. And *Dogs* was the date movie of choice. All of this was a long way from the grungy world portrayed in the movie: Berry Street, Richmond in 1978 and Melbourne's 'Little Band' post-punk scene.

My date was my brother Jaimme. He was eighteen and wise in the ways of popular culture, clutching a copy of *NME*, the dispatch for music fiends desiring to follow trends emerging from the UK. I had barely turned seventeen and was lightly clutching the crotch seam of my black stovepipe trousers, torn ignobly in the jump from the Parramatta train to make the session via Central Station. Adding to the frisson of expectation was the paranoiac thought that the type from Jaimme's copy of *NME* was somehow infused with hallucinogens. The smudgy prints on my fingertips submerging into my bloodstream might soon have me in the throes of a lysergic adventure. This was a less comforting entrée to a film than an icy choc-top and a large Coke, but when I heard the opening thrum of lower frequencies as *Dogs* began, the clarion call of 'Hey, Dogface! Show us yer snatch' as Iggy hurled a grunt, the car engines roared and 'Dog Food' burst out of the cinema speakers, I knew I was in safe company. I shed any remaining paranoia along with Dad's corduroy jacket, which I'd pilfered for the arvo. The sweat that poured from me in panic was now a cold slick of pure anticipation. For 103 minutes I descended to the underworld, with more bruises and cuts than I'd have wanted, but no pastel V-neck jumper and no fucking stonewash jeans. Or choc-tops.

The thrill of feeling dunked into a broiling pot of a culture only 880 kilometres away, and voiced in a lexicon and language more familiar than any 'rock'n'roll' movie I'd winced through, had me walking out of the cinema with a loose spine, a loping gait and a nonchalant grin. The pursuit of a life less ordinary did not demand an international flight. Existing in my brother's shadow for the next years, I'd listen to and watch audience members at shows, imagining the lives they must lead in Surry Hills, Chippendale, Newtown, as if they were characters in a movie I'd just seen. One day I'd muster the courage to immerse myself in such an existence.

Some people have been critical of *Dogs* as being inaccurate in its portrayal of the much mythologised and misunderstood 'Little Band' music scene. For these folks, the documentary *We're Living on Dog Food* may prove satisfying. It contains interviews from those directly involved with the scene, telling the story in their own voices. *Dogs* is not a documentary; it is a movie and it has to take liberties with fact. Those liberties infused the film with dizzying pace, even with the slothful movement of many characters. *Dogs* is heady, hectic, and it left an impressionable kid ready to stuff his backpack and move in, despite all the danger and malnutrition.

I've read criticisms that the film is 'too Melbourne' and not representative of the cultural ripples nationwide in other pockets of major cities. So be it. A film doesn't have to be comprehensive, does it? There's nothing quite so picky and bitchy as a music completist. As a seventeen-year-old watching *Dogs* for the first time at a cinema on Sydney's Pitt Street, I found the share houses, backstreets and pubs of Melbourne as foreboding and thrilling as those of any city in the world. Until then, I had been a suburban kid, and this life among the demi-monde in 1970s Melbourne was as evocative as that of LA punks in Alex Cox's *Repo Man*, UK punks in *Sid and Nancy*, or the mods and rockers of Franc Roddam's *Quadrophenia* or Penelope Spheeris' *Suburbia*.

Even at seventeen, I recognised that the motley crew who floated or barged into 18 Berry Street were not monocultural, although all were young and both those who were ripe and those who were sepulchral belonged in the house naturally. It was not as cut and dried as punks v. mainstream. From the first shot of the house after the fantastical opening credits (which immediately establish that *Dogs* has no interest in being a purely realistic film) inhabitants scatter to the parade of VW Bugs haphazardly parked with the care of a toddler's toy set to bustle off to work or study before we are thrown back into the daily existence of those who don't. The film often juxtaposes the squalor and negligence of some with the diligence of others, and while there are often heartbreaking scenes of just how assiduity and filial care can be sucked up and spat out (none more so than Sam's boorish treatment of his mother) the 'straights' are rarely held up for ridicule. There are lives playing out all around the indulgent dervish of (particularly) the musicians, but it is not an Us v. Them proposition. Rather, a question of who will be forced to leave this squalid bubble and join the real world, if still alive. When Barbara from the Socialist Youth Alliance comes knocking to enlist Dogs in Space (the band) to play a rally, her righteousness and passion is thwarted by immediate questions over money for a performance. Rather than leave in disgust, she's drawn into the house further, as if by tentacles, and becomes an inhabitant of the endless kitchen table discussion, a joint in hand and a poster for East Timor flapping loose at the corners behind her shoulder. Within four minutes and ten steps, she's become part of the house flux.

Musicians and artists, huh? I'm guessing I was asked to write about *Dogs* because I'm a musician. I first watched the film as a doe-eyed wannabe and have now watched it as a slow-moving has-been: my feelings about it as a 'music film' have not changed much. The imported songs by Iggy, Eno and Gang of Four are deft and exciting choices as opening salvos, sexual motifs and eulogies, but local performers Primitive Calculators, Marie Hoy, an exhumed Whirlywirld and the recreation of tracks written by The Ears given rattling breath by the Dogs in Space band upturn the tables with rabid energy, whether in rehearsals at Berry Street or the pub scenes. Very little irked us more, as young music nerds, than film scenes where performances were badly synchronised or mimed awkwardly.

In writing this piece, I am indebted to the book *Dogs in Space: A Film Archive* by Ann Standish and Helen Bandis. For anyone interested in filmmaking, particularly the perilous toil of funding a film, it is a compelling, infuriating and very funny read. It includes director Richard Lowenstein's diaries, stills from the shoot, contemporary interviews and telexes between the director and the mysterious 'Deepthroat'-like character of Walter Donohue – and they are a joy for any fan of *Dogs* to immerse themselves in, while the endless slugging match of art v. commerce is depressingly familiar. One of many examples that still makes me giggle and sigh is this diary entry: 'When I mention the film will be the *Easy Rider* of the 1980s, Burrowes seems to think *Easy Rider* is a rock'n'roll magazine ... Due to the conservatism of some of the investors, they suggest the title *Future Tense*. This is about par for the course for them, as it is a nice, meaningless title that isn't going to get anyone's attention.' I strongly recommend this book to any *Dogs* fan.

Lowenstein's diary entries reveal that the production team desperately wanted sound to be recorded in multi-track, allowing live music performances and script to conflate, similar to the way conversations and monologues duck and weave all through *Dogs*. The confluence and chaos of many character voices was new to us back then, having not seen any Altman films apart from *M*A*S*H*. It was a little dizzying at first, but once the verbal and musical collage becomes familiar, it's an audible feast – so hugely quotable that lines still exist in our family badinage. 'How do ya know when you've had a good night? When ya throw yer knickers against the wall and they stick!', 'Chuck's here', 'Ballarat! Ballarat!', 'Hot Brick!', 'Luu-chio! Luu-chio!' 'It's a fucking amazing machine', 'I think we should swallow this in future'. Thirty-plus years after the first time, I'm still catching lines to savour.

I recently watched Lowenstein's adaptation of John Birmingham's novel *He Died with a Felafel in His Hand* for the first time; it's far cleaner and 'proper' in its sound. There's little that's stayed on my tongue. Despite excellent performances by the leads, the drama and humour came anticlimactically. Was it familiarity, I wondered? The share-house experiences were set in a time close to my own share-house experience. Or was it that being an adaptation of a book, the script was more formally tethered?

The haphazard and possibly improvised language of *Dogs* – student politic proselytising, stoned mumbo-jumbo or haphazard housekeeping – is not condescending to its audience in a way many films about life on the margins can be. There's a lot of posturing, lurching and preening, which if I remember correctly is accurate of twenty-somethings, but communication in the household can waver between a kind of tenderness to violence then bemusement or ridiculousness, depending on the circumstances, as a share house inhabited by a group of disparate young people would. There's no shared vocabulary outside common greetings and leavings – Sam grunts and exhales; Luchio pleads desperately for quiet so he can study for exams;

Little Mark and Nick either babble excitedly or drool arrhyth-mically, depending on what drugs have been ingested; Anthony holds court at the kitchen table, gently presenting lysergic logic; while all is seen and barely commented on by The Girl, Berry Street's latest inhabitant – a runaway from what appears to be a privileged family roughing it in the inner city. 'Oh no, not another one,' exhales Anna wearily as she almost trips over the new waif, running to one of the ubiquitous VW Bugs en route to work in an early scene – as if this has been a perennial house of flux.

By the end of the film, we know these rapids are going to be dammed to a trickle as authority, ambition and misfortune come too close and too regularly for the chaos to continue, and the ending is stark. It feels like a curtain flung open by a raging parent – coarse sunlight exposing just how ravaged the house-hold is. Much like in *Withnail and I*, another film we adored around this time, the crepuscular or sepulchral tones surround the chaos and clamour like a warm blanket. The occasional stabs of sunlight or the incarcerated glow of 7-Eleven lighting can make a viewer recoil in horror. Even dust mites look malevolent in the savage morning light.

Lowenstein battled to shoot the film in 35 mm (or Super Techniscope, as he called it) rather than the more fiducially feasible Super 16. Cinematographer Andrew de Groot pro-posed signing over his entire fee to boost the camera equipment budget. As kids we didn't know about their dedication to creating a film of substance and beauty; *Dogs* just looked and sounded exciting, dangerous and, dare I say, grand. Sweeping crane shots through the house or street scenes were enabled by the construction of a custom-built behemoth that, like most things in the production, was only fully functional at the last minute after much pulling of hair. The irony of portraying a scene and a lifestyle not at the zeitgeist of the era but very much on the fringes in such a luscious way is important, I think, to match the delusion or the fantasies of the main players. It also sets *Dogs* apart from films such as *Pure Shit* or *Monkey Grip*, which punch straight to the throat and have no desire to cloche the harsher realities of living on the margins.

The communication between producer Glenys Rowe and Lowenstein as Day One of the shoot looms is gripping. Until the week before shooting, the team had to deal with foxing by INXS management, and persistent worries about funding and casting (in a rare moment of humour, Lowenstein wrote: 'No luck with the Nick character, the pale emaciated, black clothed skeletal type. They don't make 'em like that anymore, or maybe the speed isn't as good as it used to be').

Perhaps all this tension, and the casting of non-professional actors gives *Dogs* an extra energy, an unseen simmering anxiety that strips away the need for more stylised drama or humour? Whatever the reason, it had me rushing back to *Dogs* for another viewing – perhaps the one-hundredth – with a telephone in hand to call my kin. Were there throwaway lines I had missed all those other times?

What I *had* missed was the ambitious streak in the character of Sam. The self-assuredness tucked under the simian sway of his arms. That he's a selfish oaf most times is front and centre, but a little scene where he conspires with bandmates to fire the hapless but noble Tim shows all Sam's louche posturing replaced by a resolve. It isn't dwelled upon – but it's there, sure enough. In cruel exposure is a lingering shot of Tim's face as he realises his fate. A later scene where Anna is smoking in her family home after catching Sam making out with The Girl is devastatingly bleak, the drab suburban surrounds versus her urban chic, but it's introduced, allowed a few breaths then gone. Just enough.

Much was made of the drug taking in *Dogs*. The film's R rating simultaneously disqualified enormous numbers of younger INXS fans from seeing it on release and allowed critics to dismiss anything not sensationalist or salacious about it. Even at sixteen, the public moralising bored me. The perennial schism of truths about drug taking versus the denial that it ever happens. From the excitement of Nick and Lil' Mark finding pure adrenaline and shooting it up to The Girl's mushroom horrors to the stoned politics and remembrances of Anthony (oh to read those rambles in script form!) and yeah, the heroin:

it's as thrilling, dull, wonderful and depressing as drug taking can be.

And now to Michael. It's unavoidable really isn't it? Many regard Michael Hutchence's performance as overcooked or hammy, so it's a delight to hear acquaintances of Sam Sejavka describe it as subtle and underplayed. His commitment to the film and Lowenstein's vision, against every effort to scuttle the film by those he entrusted to look after his career, is evident in his immersion in Sam. To never flash that million-dollar, gusset-rumbling smile of his. To play a character devoid of charm when he was in fact one of the most charming people on the planet is either testament to great direction or his dedication to the role – I'd vote it's both.

Lowenstein and de Groots went on to found production company Ghost Pictures with Lynn-Maree Milburn in 2000 – fifteen years after the filming of *Dogs in Space*, the company name was eerily apt. The ghosts who hover around the film echo the ghostly pallor of the characters who lurch and crawl through 18 Berry Street. As well as sorely missed leading actors, the ghosts include musicians integral to the highly idiosyncratic scene that *Dogs* alludes to, such as John Murphy, who acted in the film as well as providing much to the soundtrack; the late Chris Murphy, manager of INXS and certainly no hero in regard to the production but representative of an establishment who could not see the value of the film before, during or after its creation. Though I've never read the whole script, I can imagine it doesn't leap off the page to someone not enthralled or intrigued with the scene and lifestyle the film represents. And it probably didn't scream 'return on your financial investment'. Much of the dialogue is overlapping non sequitur or soapbox rhetoric (often hilariously so, given the vapid attention of much of the household) with flashes of childlike enthusiasm given to *Countdown* or musical icons such as Bowie, or a foolhardy VW Convoy to a 7-Eleven in Ballarat. Hardly the stuff to lure the uninitiated. Reading the soliloquies and rants of characters such as the Chainsaw Man played by Chris Haywood (the lead in Lowenstein's first feature *Strikebound*), Gary Foley as Barry or Alannah Hill's Girlfriend No. 1 – which could be reproduced on request by the Rogers clan – would make titillating reading for acolytes like us, but were unlikely to win over those looking for a loveable Australian character palatable for a wide audience.

The death of actor Saskia Post in 2020 triggered grief-filled phone conversations between me and my siblings Gabrielle and Jaimme, as if it was a family member who had passed. We referred to her as 'Our Anna'. Though Ms Post lived many lives subsequent to her portrayal of Anna in the film *Dogs in Space*, it was Anna's poise, gliding between scenes like a caryatid among gargoyles and satyrs that fixed her in our imaginations and affections as *the* woman you wanted to be best friends with. The one who would hold your hair back as you spewed, listen to your bilious babble, and tuck you into a bed then resume her conversation with her fascinating friends as if nothing had happened. Anna and the character Tim, played by Cornelius Delaney, aka Nique Needles, add some moral backbone to a largely mercenary crew of characters.

I was stunned to read in *Dogs in Space: A Film Archive* that Lowenstein was disappointed in Saskia's commitment to the role during the first weeks of filming. With the critical nous of a slavish fan, I'd considered the casting and performances in *Dogs* to be floating beyond the reach of critique. Though Lowenstein's opinion of the performance became far more favourable as shooting progressed, any criticism of Post's performance – or, indeed, any performance in the film – will cause my siblings to hiss like feral cats. But critics who dismiss the film, or elements of it, exist now, just as they did on release. They point to its 'incorrect portrayal of a musical scene', its lack of narrative, its portrayal of 'unsympathetic' or 'unlikeable' characters. Hiss and spit. I've watched this film countless times and though the lexicon of 'film' is not natural to me, here is a fan letter.

My siblings and I made a list of the actors and performers we've met and known or worked with associated with *Dogs*: John Murphy, Ollie Olsen, Hugo Race, Hutch, Alannah Hill, Edward Clayton-Jones, Caroline Lee, Emma de Clario, Noah Taylor, producer Glenys Rowe, Tony Cohen. There was that possibly apocryphal story of my sister working theatre with

Sam Sejavka. The Ghost Productions Office is around the corner from where I am writing this in St Kilda and I have Richard's number in my notebook. I was tempted to call or write but I'd only ask about future Ghost productions. My family and I have never asked any of the aforementioned about their experiences on the set, or their subsequent feelings about the film. It's too precious to us. Just as we can be feral and feline against detractors, we feel kinship with those people involved. And miss some dearly.

Vale Saskia Post. You were our coolest best friend.

Notes on Contributors

Shaad D'Souza is a writer from Melbourne. Currently *The Saturday Paper*'s music critic, his essays have appeared in *Pitchfork*, *The Guardian*, *Bon Appetit*, *New York Magazine* and *Frieze*, among others. He has also appeared on *The New York Times*' *Popcast*, *The Guardian*'s *Full Story* podcast, and more.

Osman Faruqi is an award-winning journalist and writer. He has produced and presented investigative documentaries for the ABC, and regularly writes about news, current affairs and culture for leading Australian publications. He was the host of the arts podcast *The Culture*, as well as editor of the *7am* podcast. He is currently the Culture News Editor at *The Sydney Morning Herald* and *The Age*.

Martin Flanagan is the author of twenty books, a play and two movie treatments. He is one of Australia's most respected sports journalists and wrote for *The Age* from 1985 to 2017.

Mish Grigor is a theatre maker, writer and performer. Originally from Western Sydney and now based in Melbourne, her works have been performed at Sydney Opera House, Hong Kong Rep Theatre and once at a church in Ireland. She is artistic director of experimental art organisation *APHIDS*, and is one-third of theatre company *post*.

Rebecca Harkins-Cross is a writer and cultural critic from Naarm/ Melbourne, whose work has been published widely. She is currently based in New York City, where she is a Fulbright Scholar at Columbia University's Writing Program. Her first book, *The Headless Woman*, will be out soon with Fireflies Press.

Tristen Harwood is an Indigenous writer, critic, researcher and educator. He lectures at the Victorian College of the Arts and is a current recipient of the Wheeler Centre's The Next Chapter. Tristen's writing on art, film, fashion and literature is published in *The Saturday Paper*, *Art + Australia*, *Artlink*, *Art Guide*, *ArtReview*, *Overland*, *The New York Times Magazine* and *The Monthly*, among others.

Kate Jinx is a writer, critic and programmer at the Melbourne International Film Festival. She is the director of programming at Sydney's Golden Age Cinema, curator of the Sydney Opera House's inaugural All About Women in Film festival, and co-host of the *See Also* podcast.

Sarah Krasnostein is the multi-award-winning author of *The Trauma Cleaner*, *The Believer* and the Quarterly Essay *Not Waving, Drowning: Mental Illness and Vulnerability in Australia*. She is *The Saturday Paper*'s television critic. Her work appears in a variety of publications in the

US, the UK and Australia. She is a qualified lawyer and holds a doctorate in criminal law.

Judith Lucy is an award-winning stand-up comedian, broadcaster and actress. She is the author of three books: *The Lucy Family Alphabet* (winner of an ABIA for best biography), *Drink, Smoke, Pass Out* and *Turns Out, I'm Fine.*

Kylie Maslen is a writer, critic and author of *Show Me Where It Hurts: Living with Invisible Illness.* Her work has appeared in publications including *The Guardian, Meanjin, InDaily, Crikey* and *Junkee,* and she was the winner of the 2018 *Kill Your Darlings* New Critics Award. She lives on Kaurna Yerta (Adelaide).

Fiona Murphy is an award-winning deaf poet and essayist. Her work has appeared in *The Guardian, The Age, Kill Your Darlings, Overland, The Saturday Paper, Griffith Review* and *The Big Issue,* among many other publications. She was featured in the anthology *Growing Up Disabled in Australia,* and her debut memoir, *The Shape of Sound,* was released by Text Publishing in 2021.

Tim Rogers is the author of *Detours*. Host of radio show *Liquid Lunch*. Singer/songwriter of You Am I and The Hard-Ons. Gives it a go.

John Safran is an award-winning writer and filmmaker. His television work includes *John Safran vs God* and *Music Jamboree.* He is the author of *Depends What You Mean by Extremist* and *Murder in Mississippi,* and his latest book, *Puff Piece,* investigates Big Tobacco and vaping.

Ronnie Scott is a senior lecturer in the BA (Creative Writing) at RMIT University, where he is a researcher on Folio, a new history of Australian comics and graphic storytelling. His debut novel, *The Adversary,* was shortlisted for a Queensland Literary Award and the Australian Literature Society Gold Medal.

Isabella Trimboli is a writer and cultural critic based in Melbourne. Her work has appeared in publications including the New York journal *Metrograph, Sydney Review of Books, The Saturday Paper, The Monthly* and *The Guardian.* She is currently the music editor for *The Big Issue* and the co-founding editor of print music journal *Gusher.*

Christos Tsiolkas is a novelist, playwright, screenwriter and essayist. His novels and short stories have been adapted for stage and for screen. He is the film reviewer for *The Saturday Paper.* His latest novel is *7 1/2.*

Jenny Valentish writes for *The Guardian, The Age* and the ABC. Since the publication of her research-heavy memoir, *Woman of Substances: A Journey into Addiction and Treatment,* in 2017, she has become a consultant and speaker on addiction. Her 2021 non-fiction book, *Everything Harder Than Everyone Else,* examines the fine line between hedonism and endurance.